ALL · IN · ONE

Google Cloud
Certified Professional
Cloud Architect

EXAM GUIDE

ABOUT THE AUTHOR

Iman Ghanizada is a founder, author, and cloud computing authority residing in Los Angeles. At 28, he's an accomplished young technology leader, providing executive vision and strategy around industry-wide security challenges as a Security Solutions Manager at Google Cloud. Previously, he helped Fortune 50 global business executives transform their organizations securely in the cloud at Google Cloud, Capital One, and more. He has 10+ years of experience in the cloud and holds 14 technical certifications, including the Google Cloud Professional Cloud Architect, Professional Security Engineer, CISSP, and several more.

Iman is the founder of TheCertsGuy.com—a blog site intended to provide technologists easy insight into achieving certificates and growing in their careers. He is a proud Hokie, holding a B.S. in Business Information Technology at Virginia Tech.

As a first-generation Afghan-American, Iman seeks to amplify and accelerate the growth of underrepresented communities in their professional lives. He strongly believes that helping others grow and provide for their families is the ultimate form of fulfillment.

He is also an avid gamer and, in his own words, if he were to hit the jackpot and retire, he'd probably start retirement by drinking energy drinks, eating donuts and pizza, and playing all the games he wishes he had time for now.

About the Technical Editor

Richard Foltak is VP, Head of Cloud for Dito (ditoweb.com, a Google Premier Partner). Richard focuses on enriching Dito clients' business value streams in embracing and optimizing leading cloud technologies within their practices. Richard holds a Bachelor of Engineering degree and an MBA, along with numerous industry certifications, including those in Infrastructure Architecture, Data Engineering, Data Analytics, Machine Learning, DevOps, Networking, Cyber Security, IT Governance, and ITIL 4. His professional background includes being chief architect at Deloitte Consulting, distinguished architect at Verizon Data, and senior tech leader at Cisco Systems.

ALL · IN · ONE

Google Cloud Certified Professional Cloud Architect

EXAM GUIDE

Iman Ghanizada

New York   Chicago   San Francisco
Athens   London   Madrid   Mexico City
Milan   New Delhi   Singapore   Sydney   Toronto

1 2 3 4 5 6 7 8 9   LCR   24 23 22 21

Library of Congress Control Number: 2021931080

ISBN   978-1-264-25727-0
MHID   1-264-25727-9

Sponsoring Editor	**Technical Editor**	**Production Supervisor**
Lisa McClain	Richard Foltak	Thomas Somers
Editorial Supervisor	**Copy Editor**	**Composition**
Janet Walden	Lisa Theobald	KnowledgeWorks Global Ltd.
Project Managers	**Proofreader**	**Illustration**
Garima Poddar and Neelu Sahu, KnowledgeWorks Global Ltd.	Lisa McCoy	KnowledgeWorks Global Ltd.
Acquisitions Coordinator	**Indexer**	**Art Director, Cover**
Emily Walters	Claire Splan	Jeff Weeks

To my mom and dad, Nahid and Basir, refugees who escaped a brutal war and sacrificed every ounce of their lives for their children to have a better life than them. No matter the achievement, it pales in comparison to your sacrifices. You are my inspiration for success.

My sister, Marwa, who has been a shining beacon of light and optimism every time I am challenged in life. I love you, and I hope I can give you the world in return.

My brothers, Sajad and Iraj, who are the OG technology nerds and my mentors through life. If it weren't for you hacking those payphones when we were 5 and modding Quake 3 Arena, we wouldn't be here.

My best friend, Sami Ullah, who passed on during college. His infectious positivity inspired me to smile more and look ahead. He dreamed of landing a job at Oracle after college. I wish you were here to see this.

Finally, my Number 0, who has challenged me to grow in every aspect of my life. You mean the world to me.

CONTENTS AT A GLANCE

CONTENTS

ACKNOWLEDGMENTS

Throughout my journey, countless individuals have played significant roles in my life. Nothing is achieved alone, so I'd love to acknowledge a very tiny subset of people who've made their mark on my career, knowing that there are so many more not mentioned.

There were four women who've played significant roles in my career by embracing my potential and letting me shine. Thank you Emily Markmann, Lourdes Caballero, Jessica Rihani, and Ann Wallace.

When I was eager to move to my dream city of Los Angeles, I cold-messaged hundreds of people in LA; Nick Reva was the only one who responded. That call meant a lot to me, and now he's a great friend—thank you Nick.

I will never forget that it was a small introduction by Shawn Horton to Toby Velte that led me to McGraw Hill and this book—thank you Shawn and Toby.

Thank you to the Google team, Rochana Golani, Brian Rice, Jason Martin, Joanie Norwood, Matt Dauphinee, and Michael Zuo, for your support in this effort.

Thank you to the publishing team, Lisa McLain and Emily Walters, for trusting my voice and empowering it through the process.

And thank you Rich Foltak—you've been an incredible colleague, mentor, and friend since we met. Having your expertise and your insight has been incredible through the projects we've worked on together, through every bit of this book, and through our philosophical conversations about life.

To everyone else who has impacted me positively, even in the slightest of ways, you know who you are and I want to thank you.

INTRODUCTION

First and foremost, thank you for purchasing this book. I am truly humbled that you are joining this learning journey by reading this content. Second, you owe yourself thanks for even getting this far in investing in your future. If you're reading this page, you've already set the intention of gaining knowledge in exchange for a better future for yourself and your loved ones. Now you just need to follow through with your decision and spend an hour a day on this investment. Everything you want to achieve in life takes work, and although there are failures along the way, great things never come easy.

Whether you're reading this book because you've been tasked with passing the Google Cloud Professional Cloud Architect certification for your job or for your personal objectives, you should know that having a certification is not the end all, be all. There is a lot more to being a cloud architect than carrying the badge on your belt. But the badge itself can open up so many high-paying doors in a market that is significantly growing for GCP architects. So our focus here is to help you pass the Google Cloud Professional Cloud Architecture exam and also to help you understand Google Cloud architecture from a more pragmatic point of view. This will make more of an impact in your meetings, day-to-day work, and job interviews.

One thing you'll notice about this book is that it doesn't read like a traditional technical certification book. One of the biggest issues I have with certification books is that they prepare you to take an exam, but leave you struggling to identify and articulate concepts in the real world. In this book, you'll find quite a few elements of philosophy, academia, on-the-job scenarios, and humor scattered around. You don't have to take learning so seriously all the time—it can be fun, enjoyable, thought-provoking, and deeply technical all at the same time. You'd much rather be a multifaceted architect—being technical is only one piece of the puzzle. Building relationships and building influence will help you grow in your career, especially as an architect, where you're trusted to design the expensive technology systems that power your organization. Also, know that this book intentionally starts from scratch and iteratively builds on, from basic foundational knowledge of computing concepts to the full-fledged cloud architecture best practices. It picks up heavily when you get to Chapter 6, the networking chapter; that's when the mask comes off and the fun begins!

As technologists, we've innovated at the speed of light, yet the ethical and moral standards of life haven't kept up through our technological advances. Technology runs the world in today's day and age. So you, my friends, hold a lot of power in your fingertips. It takes true representation to solve issues unseen to the common technologist, and that is what makes Google and some of the other leading companies that strive for equality so special. There is a lot of merit involved for everyone who is fighting for equal opportunity. But even if the opportunity is equal, we still need to do a better job of attracting and grooming individuals from all walks of life into tech. Big shout out to every underrepresented and marginalized group that strives for equality and equal representation—women, people of color, LGBTQ+ folks, and beyond. Nobody should ever be discriminated against by the things that are absolute. We need to be aware of the unintended implications our technology might trigger if we're not designing it with everyone in mind.

NOTE Unconscious biases are the automatic, mental shortcuts our minds use to process information and make quick decisions. Your mind filters out these bits of information from your consciousness, so you may not even realize your biases unless you educate yourself and actively work to overcome them. Take a look at all of the research behind Google's philosophy on unbiasing; it's a big element of Google's culture and has been scientifically proven to help facilitate better decision-making: https://rework.withgoogle.com/subjects/unbiasing/.

The Google Cloud Professional Cloud Architect exam is quite a bit more comprehensive than your typical technology certification. Google Cloud has done a phenomenal job of putting together a certification exam that tests more than your ability to decipher vocabulary and includes more than simple multiple choice questions. This exam does not emphasize the day-to-day engineering operations of Google Cloud, which you'd typically see in the Google Cloud Associate Cloud Engineer exam. Rather, it focuses on your understanding of business and technical requirements and your ability to translate that into high-level Google Cloud architecture.

The Google Cloud Professional Cloud Architect enables organizations to leverage Google Cloud products and technologies. The Professional Cloud Architect will have a thorough understanding of cloud architecture and Google Cloud Platform (GCP). This individual can design, develop, and manage robust, secure, scalable, highly available, and dynamic solutions to drive business objectives.

The Google Cloud Certified Professional Cloud Architect exam assesses your ability to

- Design and plan a cloud solution architecture
- Manage and provision the cloud solution infrastructure
- Design for security and compliance
- Analyze and optimize technical and business processes
- Manage implementations of cloud architecture
- Ensure solution and operations reliability

The Google Cloud Platform has hundreds of services, features, and capabilities, but the certification exam focuses on a select amount of those offerings. You likely won't see questions on designing a natural-language processing application. You will spend a lot of time on core infrastructure concepts—identity and access management, computing, storage, networking, and security, with a variety of managed services sprinkled in between all domains.

The exam will often provide scenarios that require you to factor in business requirements and technical requirements to come to a conclusion. Each answer takes time to process, and there is a bit of a methodology involved in assessing the question prior to drawing conclusions; we'll dig into these in the exam tips. It's quite possible that you may encounter more than one answer that is technically correct, but remember that there are both business and technical requirements embedded in each question, and you'll have to delineate between them. For example, a question may present answers that include Dataproc and Dataflow. But the business context in the question may hint that there is a dependency on the Apache Hadoop or Apache Spark ecosystem, so you'd want to assess whether Cloud Dataproc would be a solution. Or the question may say that there is a favorable approach to taking a serverless, cost-effective route for a data processing solution, and you may assess whether Cloud Dataflow will fit into the architecture.

As you dive into this book and the exam, you'll need to shift your mindset into thinking like an architect. As an architect, you'll start thinking ahead of the issue at hand, designing robust solutions that factor in potential future implications, and identifying keywords that outline important requirements for the customer. While taking the exam, you also need to be aware of over-architecting a solution. If you're tasked with building a data processing and storage architecture but the data is not critical whatsoever and the customer emphasizes a cost-effective solution, do you really need to architect a fault-tolerant, highly redundant system architecture with the highest SLA possible? And if the test question is not hinting at cost optimization being a factor—what then? The easiest way to decipher the best answer to a question may be to focus on reading comprehension—gather business requirements, technical requirements, identify detractors (things that don't matter to the solution), and timing considerations and then optimize your solution.

Architecture is so much more important than just knowing what's on the exam. Let's talk about the cloud sales cycle from Google Cloud's perspective and a customer's perspective and where your expertise as a cloud architect fits in. In your typical cloud sales cycle, there is a heavy emphasis on architecture starting at the presales stages. Your organization's account executive (aka sales representative—milk this individual for free donuts and Google shirts if you're allowed to) is typically focused on demonstrating how a customer can dramatically improve their business or introduce new offerings by migrating their technology stack to the Google Cloud Platform. Account executives often have sales engineers (or as Google Cloud calls them, customer engineers) mocking up early architecture designs and proof of concepts to take that business vision one layer deeper and help the customer understand some of the more technical requirements. Attached to the sales team may be an Enterprise Solutions Architect, who is typically very senior and specialized and who engages with the customer's most senior business stakeholder(s) and the most technical stakeholder(s) to gather requirements and flesh out architectures that will give the customer the utmost confidence in their investment. After the sale, and oftentimes for large enterprise deals, there's a Google Cloud Professional Services team staffed with highly talented consultants and engineers that brings these architectures to light and drives full-scale implementations alongside the customer. This team will likely be architecting new designs on the fly when encountering new workloads, new design requests, or unforeseen implications that necessitate changes in architecture.

The architecture at day one is often much more evolved than the presales architecture at day zero, as real-life challenges that are encountered when running a massive cloud transformation can never be predicted ahead of time.

On the customer's side, you can't enter an enormous sales cycle without having staff with enough knowledge of GCP to be able to take their proprietary business context and couple it with a preliminary understanding of how to run those workloads more effectively in GCP. If your business already uses Google Cloud, there will always be a need for a cloud architect to design new solutions based on evolving business needs. In the context of the cloud, it is even more common for your Cloud Engineer to understand how cloud architecture works, which will improve their ability to fulfill their day-to-day job. The Professional Cloud Architect is a certification that brings value to each one of these roles. Our goal is to help you pass the exam and be prepared for the real world by the time you finish this book.

The Google Cloud Platform is not just a big, multimillion-dollar enterprise solution. Tens of thousands of customers are using Google Cloud, ranging from massive enterprises down to startups and individual users. Google Cloud for Startups is an amazing program that often incentivizes startups to use the Google Cloud Platform by offering free mentorship, training, and credits to get tech teams up and running using the same world-class infrastructure that powers Google. There is also typically a referral program in place. So if you have a friend on Google Cloud Platform and you're interested in bringing your startup into their ecosystem, reach out and get a referral! You won't get free pizza delivery, but, hey, there's probably a coupon code for that one anyway.

It's very important that you understand that Google Cloud Professional Cloud Architect expertise continues to evolve much more rapidly than the exam can keep up with. Over the past two years, the cloud has evolved at an exponential pace. We used to think of computing in the sense of virtual machines and PaaS (such as AppEngine). In 2020, we began to see clearly that the future of computing is trending toward more managed services, hybrid/open cloud environments, container-based architectures instead of VM-based, and more.

Does the exam currently have a heavy emphasis on Kubernetes or even mention Anthos? Probably not. Is it possible that the exam could be updated with new content by the time this book gets published? Absolutely. The exam is subject to change at any time without any communication from Google Cloud. So our focus on this book is to equip you with both exam knowledge and overall cloud architecture expertise that is relevant as of today. It's also not a bad idea to parse through the GCP products and services menu to gain a cursory understanding of the portfolio.

Overview of Google Cloud Certifications

As you dive into the Google Cloud ecosystem, you'll be pleased to see that the certification offerings have grown sizably and focus on various areas of technical proficiency of the Google Cloud Platform. Whether this is your first or your last certification, your learning journey continues to evolve. Google will continue to enhance its cloud certifications and offer new certifications to ensure that professionals are meeting a high bar all over the world on their platform.

Certification Path	Certifications
Associate	Associate Cloud Engineer
Professional	Professional Cloud Architect
	Professional Cloud Developer
	Professional Cloud DevOps Engineer
	Professional Data Engineer
	Professional Network Engineer
	Professional Security Engineer
	Professional Collaboration Engineer
	Professional Machine Learning Engineer
Fellow	Hybrid Multi-Cloud Fellow
User	Google Workspace

Table 1   Certifications Offered by Google Cloud as of 2020

There are currently four certificate paths for Google Cloud certifications: an Associate certification, a Professional certification, a User certification, and a new Fellow certification. The Associate certifications are great for individuals who are new to cloud or who are a little more junior and in a more operational role that focuses on deploying, managing, and maintaining projects on Google Cloud. The Professional certifications are typically geared toward individuals who have more industry experience and are already familiar with cloud computing and Google Cloud. This certification path focuses on the professional's ability to assess business and technical challenges, design solutions, develop implementation strategies, and manage the cloud. There is currently only one User certification focused on Google Workspace (formerly G Suite) administration. Lastly, the Fellow certification is designed for elite cloud architects and technical leaders who are experts in designing enterprise solutions.

Table 1 provides a listing of all these exams.

Google Cloud certifications expire after two years. During this two-year period, you'll be a recognized holder of a certification and there is no need to maintain CPEs (Continuing Professional Education requirements) as is the case with many other technical certifications. To maintain your certification credentials in the rapidly growing and evolving Google Cloud Platform, you'll receive a notification 90 days prior to the certification expiration, asking you to recertify. Recertification involves retaking the exam to maintain your accredited state. If you let your certification expire, you'll have to retake it to be officially recognized as an accredited certification holder.

What Does This Exam Guide Cover?

A variety of topics are covered in this book, ranging from those that are extremely relevant, to those that are not extremely relevant, to topics that you'll need to understand to pass the certification. The intent of this exam guide is to help you prepare for the examination and to bolster your ability to do quality work in the real world. Rather than aligning the chapters strictly with the exam outline, we're aligning them with designing, building, and managing a cloud architecture from scratch.

Chapter 1: Introduction to the Professional Cloud Architect Certification   This chapter provides an introduction to what it takes to become a Google Cloud Architect, why it's a hot career path, and some general prerequisite knowledge for this stage of your career. It also dives into the type of questions you'll see on the exam, especially outlining the three case studies that Google Cloud provides online, which you will see on the exam. Then we'll spend time covering some very important test-taking tips that may be your X factor when taking technology certifications. Finally, we'll cover your best strategies for reading through this book and using the supplementary resources in tandem to help you be a better architect.

Chapter 2: Overview of Cloud Computing and Google Cloud   This chapter offers a brief overview of Google Cloud Computing and the competition. Then we'll take a 10,000-foot overview of Google Cloud to cover some of the core Google Cloud concepts. This is a great reference chapter that includes the most common products and services that are included on the examination. You'll learn how to interface with the Google Cloud Platform. Lastly, we'll focus on the business and technical contexts for becoming a cloud architect, which are major focus points on the examination.

Chapter 3: Cloud Identity   This chapter begins with an overview of the first item you'll need to set up when you sign on to the Google Cloud Platform: your Cloud Identity. We'll cover the various ways of authenticating into the cloud, using single sign-on, provisioning users, and auditing.

Chapter 4: Resource Management   This chapter begins with an overview of the Cloud Resource Manager. Then you'll learn about the hierarchy of organizations, folders, projects, and resources. You'll read about the important security and governance feature called Organization Policies that enables you to configure restrictions across your total resource hierarchy. Lastly, we'll discuss a few design considerations and recommendations.

Chapter 5: Cloud Identity and Access Management   In addition to the initial identity you use to set up your Cloud, you'll need to manage user authorization in Google Cloud. This chapter covers that, plus it dives into policies, roles, group management, and service account management.

Chapter 6: Networking   This chapter presents an overview of core networking concepts in Google Cloud, including virtual private clouds (VPCs), regions, zones, and subnets. We'll discuss the various options for connecting to your cloud, how Google Cloud provides load balancing across its platform, and how you can secure and control access to your network.

Chapter 7: Compute and Containers   This chapter covers the various Google Cloud computing offerings, focusing on the Infrastructure as a Service (IaaS) offering, Google Compute Engine (GCE); the Platform as a Service (PaaS) offering, Google App Engine (GAE); the container orchestration offering Google Kubernetes Engine (GKE); the serverless offering, Cloud Functions; and other computing offerings.

Chapter 8: Storage, Databases, and Data Analytics   This chapter covers the various storage offerings available with Google Cloud, with a focus on Google Cloud Storage. It digs into the database offerings of Cloud SQL, Cloud Spanner, Bigtable, Cloud Fire-Store, and Memorystore. Lastly, the chapter covers the data analytics offerings BigQuery, DataProc, Dataflow, and Pub/Sub.

Chapter 9: DevOps   This chapter provides an overview of DevOps in Google Cloud. It also discusses services and offerings such as Cloud Build, the Container Registry, and Cloud Source Repositories. Finally, you'll read about infrastructure as code and why it's critical to modern businesses.

Chapter 10: Cloud Operations   We'll shift into a more operational focus in this chapter, discussing the various logs, how to architect a logging infrastructure, and how to use best practices in managing logs. We'll cover how you can monitor your resources and alert on thresholds for development, operations, and security teams. Lastly, we'll discuss resilience, as well as how you can use metrics to build a highly available, fault-tolerant environment that gives your organization the confidence it needs to grow and scale without interruption.

Chapter 11: Security   We'll cover a deep dive of the shared responsibility model in this chapter with respect to security. Google provides built-in cloud security, and you can design and manage additional security safeguards. We'll cover some general security and compliance concepts, security architecture, and security operations in Google Cloud.

Chapter 12: Billing, Migration, and Support   This chapter provides the fundamentals of managing your billing accounts. As you can imagine, this is simple for a solo entrepreneur, but it can be incredibly complex for a multinational company managing multiple cloud environments. We'll also discuss how you can prepare for a migration and plot your future growth. Lastly, we'll discuss support and why it is a critical aspect for customers on Google Cloud Platform. You'll learn about how you can best engage your support teams, manage escalations, and become a more effective partner with your Google Cloud Support teams.

Objective Map

The objective map included in Appendix A has been constructed to help you cross-reference the official exam objectives from Google with the relevant coverage in the book. The table provides the official exam objectives, exactly as Google presented them at the time of this writing, along with the corresponding chapter number(s) of the book in which each objective is covered.

NOTE   The exam outline can change at any time without notice. For the most accurate exam objectives, take a look at the exam guide: https://cloud.google.com/certification/guides/professional-cloud-architect/.

Online Test Bank

McGraw Hill provides an online test bank to accompany this book. This online content features the TotalTester exam software that enables you to generate a complete practice exam or to generate quizzes by chapter or exam domain. See Appendix B for more information. Between the book and the test bank, you should be in good standing to pass the exam if you're getting through it without too many wrong answers. If you really want to be a rock star on the exam and also be a better Professional Cloud Architect in your day job, you should certainly dive into the supplementary resources, because passing a certification is only one piece of the puzzle.

Supplementary Resources

Many supplemental resources are available to you. I've identified some of the key ones here. We'll dive into these concepts in the book's chapters and discuss how you can use them in tandem with this book to become an expert. As mentioned, the book and the test bank alone should be sufficient to help you pass the exam, but I strongly recommend that you immerse yourself in GCP and dive into the hands-on courses through Coursera and QwikLabs to become an expert. Remember that anyone can pass a certification if they know the answers—the real world consists of a whole new set of challenges.

- **Professional Cloud Architect Certification Exam Guide**   https://cloud .google.com/certification/guides/professional-cloud-architect/
- **Cloud Certification Help**   https://support.google.com/cloud-certification/#0&topic=9433215
- **Professional Cloud Architect sample questions**   https://cloud.google.com/ certification/practice-exam/cloud-architect
- **Google Cloud products and services**   https://cloud.google.com/products
- **Getting Started with Google Cloud documentation**   https://cloud.google .com/docs/
- **Google Cloud Platform free trials**   https://console.cloud.google.com
- **Coursera: Architecting with Google Compute Engine Platform Specialization**   https://www.coursera.org/specializations/gcp-architecture
- **QwikLabs: Cloud Architecture Quest Outline**   https://www.qwiklabs.com/ quests/24

The Power of Social Media

You might know that the most valuable thing I've posted on Twitter was to "invest in Bitcoin" in 2013. Oh how I wish I would've taken my own advice and not day-traded my bitcoins to negative-integer values. That happened twice so far, and I don't even want to tell you that story. Well, I've realized how important one's online presence is, and I'd love to make a case for my readers to get more involved in the community.

In today's day and age, your digital identity helps you get access to better opportunities, build your sphere of influence, learn from others, and network with recruiters and other professionals. As of the day I'm writing this, we're in the midst of the COVID-19 global pandemic, and the value of our digital identities has been proven. We live in a remote world, and if you don't have an online presence, your achievements and your values might go unseen. I'd love to make an emphasis on you, as readers of this book, to build your presence on the Internet so that together we can create a stronger global community of architects.

I also would personally love to spend more time with and engage with my readers online to the best of my abilities. I want to hear about your successes, your failures, your challenges, and your highlights. Tell me if you passed the certification. Share your successes with the world. Tweet me questions, send me posts on LinkedIn and Instagram, or just drop #TheCertsGuy if you need my attention. I would love to share in all the greatness that you're achieving, because the more vocal our community becomes, the more impact we have in the world. So let's connect, and hopefully I can find more ways beyond this book to help my readers get value, whether that be connecting you with recruiters, resharing your posts, or just sharing insights. I can't promise I'll get to every single message, but I will try my best! You can find me on LinkedIn, Twitter, and Instagram.

Lastly, I'm the founder of TheCertsGuy.com—a blog site designed to help you grow your career and pass certifications in 30 days or less! Subscribe to my blog, share posts that can help others, and send me snippets of wisdom to share in each of my blogs. I want the blog to be a representation of all of you! Best of luck, and I'm looking forward to hearing from you!

Introduction to the Professional Cloud Architect Certification

In this chapter, we'll cover

- Career path choices and benefits for becoming a certified Cloud Architect
- The prerequisite knowledge for the exam
- The types of questions you'll see on the exam
- Using test-taking skills to optimize your Professional Cloud Architect exam
- Using a variety of resources in tandem with this book to prepare you for the exam and the job

As we cover the Google Cloud Platform (GCP), you, the gracious consumer of this content, need to put your eyes and attention forward to focus on the next several hundred pages of text.

Technical certification books can be boring at times. I know how it feels. After my first three certifications, I thought I would put the books away—but here I am, 14 certifications later, writing a book, and I don't want to see scathing reviews on Amazon about how you fell asleep reading or how you failed your certification exam! So we're going to do this differently this time around. I'll do my best to keep you engaged and entertained and to make you feel that you're getting the value you need to be a successful GCP Cloud Architect by the end of this book, regardless of whether you take the certification exam or not. I'm going to ensure that you are equipped with the knowledge you need to pass the certification and beyond.

This isn't just about reading a book; it's a journey to a new depth of your career. We're going to get through this journey together, because, although it is quite a challenge, I believe in you!

In this chapter, we'll spend a bit of time covering some topics that are not super-relevant to the exam and some topics that are, but I recommend sticking with it, because there are some very important lessons to learn in this chapter that may give you the edge when it comes test time. Take a deep breath, make sure you've got your snacks and coffee, and pace yourself!

Reasons to Take the Professional Cloud Architect Exam

What the heck is a cloud architect? Why does the cloud need architects? Have you ever asked your friends what they think about cloud architects? Although this book isn't designed to help your friends understand your career aspirations or your job, I always attempt to explain what a cloud architect does in layman's terms to protect my own sanity. After several failed attempts of describing what exactly a cloud architect does to my friends, I realized that the easy way to break this down is to provide a real-world example that my friends can understand: Instagram!

The concept of Instagram is simple in abstract: It's a social network designed to connect millions of users worldwide, which enables individuals to create personal accounts and post photos and videos on their stories; like and comment on posts; add friends; and directly message other users. How does something so simple require hundreds of employees and hundreds of millions of dollars in expenditures to manage?

Let's break this down into a miniature business case study exercise. You'll see a few of these on the test, and we'll spend more time on them throughout the book. As you can imagine, each one of these business features is an entire system architecture on the backend. Creating a personal account and managing the entire user login flow is a system architecture. Directly messaging other users is a system architecture. Serving a live feed to your users is a system architecture. And each of these elements of Instagram requires a cloud architect to understand the business objectives and requirements, to assess the feasibility of various architectures, and to recommend a design solution.

For demonstration purposes, let's look at the Instagram Posts feature. I'm going to make some assumptions here. Instagram's core feature as a business is to enable a user to post a photo or video directly to a personalized feed with a caption, a geolocation, and hashtags and to tag other users in the post. All users worldwide should be able to access this post in near real time, with 99.999 percent availability, and the post should be tamper-proof to maintain its integrity. If the post is archived, it should be invisible to other users.

There are more than 1 billion monthly active users on Instagram posting more than 80 million posts a day, so the solution needs to be cost-effective, because Instagram already manages a storage system of more than 100 petabytes of data. For a rough idea of how much this would cost on Google Cloud Storage, this translates to roughly $31 million per year in at-rest storage fees plus network egress and operations fees. At $0.12 per gigabyte of network egress and $0.05 per 10,000 operations, you could imagine this would raise the cost for Instagram significantly, as the entire business is about users accessing posts globally. As an architect, you need to design a system that can support serving these posts to more than a billion users worldwide in the most cost-effective manner.

As a cloud architect, your goal is to assess a business objective at hand and distil the needs into business requirements and technical requirements. You'll then use those requirements to architect a solution. You won't always get all the requirements laid out so easily, and oftentimes you'll spend hours upon hours diving into meetings with various stakeholders to gather pieces of data that start to formulate the building blocks of the solution. You'll also need to be aware of future technical and strategic implications, ensuring that you're building a solution that won't encounter any major roadblocks.

Imagine, for example, that you're choosing to use a relational database system in the early development of a business with not that many users, and you need to be cost-effective. You'd probably look into using a simple managed relational database such as Cloud SQL, but if you didn't account for the projected growth of the platform, how would you know how long your solution would support the platform and at what capacity? Would you invest the additional money and leverage a tool that is designed for massive-scale database computing, such as Cloud Spanner, from the start? If you decided not do that, how would you know when you'd need to migrate to a more scalable solution and what that migration strategy would entail? How much time would it take? How much would it cost your business? What are potential curveballs and limitations of the current and future design?

Many factors need to be assessed when you're designing solutions, many of which come with time in the field. For that reason, the Cloud Architect exam is typically geared toward industry professionals who have been in the field with a few years of industry experience. While Instagram's open source technology stack is publicly documented and operates on Facebook's cloud, you can be assured that by the end of this book, you'll be able to redesign this infrastructure mentally at a high level on Google Cloud.

TIP Take a look at "Instagram Engineering's 3 rules to a scalable cloud application architecture" blog post at https://medium.com/@DataStax/ instagram-engineerings-3-rules-to-a-scalable-cloud-application- architecture-c44afed31406.

There are plenty of reasons to pursue the cloud architecture path, but let's start with the one reason why we all need careers in the first place: the money! Cloud architecture is a very lucrative career path, as we're still barely 15 years into the development of the cloud overall. There is certainly a big disparity in the supply and demand for certified Cloud Architects and the highly specialized skill set required to do the job. As more companies begin to migrate to the cloud and more cloud-native companies begin to grow beyond their roots, there will be a never-ending demand for the cloud architect. Because of the individual's required years of experience, engineering knowledge, and business and technical depth, you can imagine that this is a very high-paying role as well.

NOTE In the industry, the average Cloud Solutions Architect makes anywhere from $130,000 to $210,000 per year. Factor in stock options, starting bonuses, annual bonuses, and benefits, and you may find yourself deep into $300,000-plus territory. With that type of money, you'll never have to question the value of adding guacamole to your order at Chipotle again.

Even for those not interested in becoming an actual cloud architect, pursuing the certification can benefit folks all across the technical spectrum, including those in technical sales, engineering, management, and leadership roles. Understanding architecture design at a high level helps you become a more effective technical subject matter expert across the board. At the very least, the certification could make you a more effective voice in the room during meetings as you provide input and clarify details that may not be in your expected purview.

Certification can also play a big role in interviews. Let's say you're a hiring manager for a tech company, and you're hiring a cloud engineer who will be tasked with managing the operations of a network. You have two candidates, both cloud engineers, who have a lot of hands-on experience with network engineering. Both candidates may be able to fulfill the job duties, but you're looking to hire the best talent—someone who will be able to grow into a more impactful role within the company. Both candidates understand how to manage networking tasks within the scope of the job duties, but one candidate is a certified Cloud Architect who understands the strategic factors in network design and may be able to take on additional responsibilities. This expertise may give that candidate the edge in the interview, and also when it comes to salary negotiations.

Being an architect can be very fulfilling. While Frank Gehry may be revered for being among the world's most famous architects—designing structures that bring value to the consumers of the world—imagine being the cloud architect who designed the infrastructure that provides computing to the brands that empower the world, such as Facebook, Disney, Activision Blizzard, Mayo Clinic, Spotify, Apple—you name it. Not everyone has the luxury to visit the Guggenheim Museum Bilbao in person, but you better believe that everybody and their mothers have Facebook accounts!

Spotify on Google Cloud

In 2016, Spotify announced that it was going all-in on GCP, with a reported $450 million commitment over three years. As of 2020, Spotify is the world's most popular global audio-streaming subscription, with a user base of more than 299 million users and 138 million paid subscribers across 92 world markets.

Ramon van Alteren, former director of engineering at Spotify, once explained how the company's true intention was to become the best music service in the world, and having data centers did not contribute directly to that mission. Spotify decided to split its migration strategy into two parts, services and data, and moved nearly 1200 microservices and several hundred petabytes of data from on-premises data centers to GCP. The company prepared for two years before the migration, and each part took around a year. Talk about a massive digital transformation!

As a result, according to a 2018 article in *Computerworld*, Spotify's event delivery pipeline went from carrying at peak 800,000 events per second to carrying 3 million events per second. On BigQuery, Spotify was running 10 million queries and scheduled jobs per month, processing 500 petabytes of data. This has given more freedom to developers to build solutions at scale, without sacrificing quality of service.

Prerequisite Knowledge

At this point in your career, if you're pursuing the Professional Cloud Architect certification, you're most likely not a high school senior who just nailed AP History and has a side hobby of learning GCP. This certification is geared toward individuals with multiple years of industry experience. Google Cloud certification does not have hard requirements like Certified Information Systems Security Professional (CISSP) certification does, however, where you have to prove five years of domain-related experience before you can be formally awarded the certification. Anyone can take a Google Cloud certification exam, but Google *recommends* that you have several years of industry experience, with more than a year designing and managing solutions using GCP, before you do so. (See https:// cloud.google.com/certification/cloud-architect for more information about the exam.)

While we're at it, let's discuss some of the prerequisite knowledge that the Professional Cloud Architect should possess. First, let's walk through the job description as defined in the Professional Cloud Architect Certification Exam Guide (at https://cloud.google .com/certification/guides/professional-cloud-architect):

> A Google Cloud Certified Professional Cloud Architect enables organizations to leverage Google Cloud technologies. Through an understanding of cloud architecture and Google technology, this individual designs, develops, and manages robust, secure, scalable, highly available, and dynamic solutions to drive business objectives. The Cloud Architect should be proficient in all aspects of enterprise cloud strategy, solution design, and architectural best practices. The Cloud Architect should also be experienced in software development methodologies and approaches including multitiered distributed applications which span multi-cloud or hybrid environments.

Let's list these out:

- Enterprise cloud strategy
- Solution design
- Architectural best practices
- Software development methodologies and approaches including multitiered distributed applications which span multi-cloud or hybrid environments

As a certified Cloud Architect, you'll most likely be interfacing with senior business and technology leaders. For the C-suite, the key focus is setting the technology strategy, aligning this strategy to the business goals, and leading the charge. You will focus on turning that executive business strategy into tangible solutions by designing a technology architecture that enables the business needs.

Executives don't have enough time to know all the specifics to help in deciding between one cloud program over another, or what technologies to leverage to develop a new core business offering. They need problem-solvers with foresight, who can help distill a business objective into incredibly complex technology, bundle it back up into a clear and concise solution, and present it back to the leadership in laymen's language.

As a cloud architect, you have the ability to speak both languages, the language of the business and the language of the technology, as you'll be interfacing with stakeholders across both worlds.

Beyond the C-suite and leadership, you'll be in the weeds with senior technology leaders and senior engineers. These are the stakeholders who will hold the knowledge of existing systems, team dynamics, and engineering expertise. These are all valid points to consider when you're building a solution with key milestones and timeline considerations.

Suppose, for example, that you've decided to use Kubernetes as your application layer to eliminate the gripes of manual deployment and scaling. The product, however, needs to launch by Q3, and the engineering team does not have any experience in Kubernetes. So how does that affect your solution? Technical stakeholders hold the key to the other half of the requirements, the technical requirements, and you've got to understand how those factor into the situation. A cloud architect must have a strong understanding of software development methodologies, IT/technology systems, and architectural best practices, and the architect must use a methodological approach to designing an architecture. Think about some of the key elements that software architects leverage, such as gathering *functional* requirements and *nonfunctional* requirements:

- **Functional requirements**   The "what"—What is the system supposed to do? For example, my system needs to extract data from this API and load it into a storage bucket.

- **Nonfunctional requirements**   The "How"—How should my system perform? What are the constraints? For example, my system needs to transform the data to a certain format before it's loaded, or it needs to process at least X amount of data objects per second.

A cloud architect would approach designing a solution in a very similar way that a software architect would: Schedule your scoping meetings. Gather your requirements—business requirements and technical requirements. Do some research for more nuanced requirements and understand the constraints of the system. Put together a high-level design diagram. Work through the high-level design and then break it down into deeper design diagrams. Ensure that you're aligned with business and technology stakeholders along the way. Work toward a final draft and get the necessary approvals if you're not the accountable stakeholder.

Then you've got a reference architecture that your development teams can use to begin building. You'll probably want to reuse this pattern for similar use cases and continually refine it. You should also have a solid understanding of Agile best practices and the overall software development life cycle, understanding how code gets built and the various deployment methods (such as blue-green deployments, canary deployments, continuous integration/continuous delivery [CI/CD] deployment).

Aside from all that, by this point in your career you're assumed to have a good understanding of foundational technology and cloud concepts. Here are a bunch of concepts that you're expected to know ahead of this exam. (Don't worry about these acronyms for now; we'll get to that later.) We'll dive into them a little deeper in later chapters:

- Identity and access management concepts such as *LDAP, SSO, RBAC,* and *Active Directory*
- Networking concepts such as *DNS, DHCP, firewalls,* and *CIDR*
- Computing concepts such as *VMs* and *containers*
- Data concepts such as *object storage, block storage,* and *network file systems*
- Engineering concepts such as *DevOps, CI/CD,* and *IaC*
- Security concepts such as *least privileges, segregation of duties,* and *defense in depth*
- General concepts such as *multitiered architectures, service-oriented architecture, microservices, hybrid cloud, multi-cloud,* and so on

---

About the Exam

Length: 2 hours

Registration fee: $200 (plus tax where applicable)

Languages: English, Japanese

Exam format: Multiple-choice and multiple-select, taken remotely or in person at a test center

Exam delivery method:

- Take the online-proctored exam from a remote location; review the online testing requirements.
- Take the onsite-proctored exam at a testing center; locate a test center near you.

Prerequisites: None

Recommended experience: Three-plus years of industry experience including one-plus years designing and managing solutions using GCP

Source: https://cloud.google.com/certification/cloud-architect

---

Let's talk about the exam itself. The exam is typically about 50 multiple-choice questions. You'll be provided with roughly three case studies that will be leveraged for a good amount of your questions. The non–case study multiple-choice questions will test your knowledge of a wide variety of Google Cloud services and may even present you with questions that will test your logical thinking and problem-solving abilities rather than your deep knowledge of certain Cloud products. Fifty questions may not sound like a lot, but don't be fooled: this will take you the full two hours to complete. You won't really see any definition-based questions, but you will get scenarios that will ask what the best solution is. For example, you may see a question that describes a need to implement extraction, transformation, and load (ETL) data warehousing solutions, but the company is very comfortable with its existing Hadoop ecosystem of tools. These are the easy questions, where one keyword may give you the correct answer between two similar services—Cloud Dataproc in this scenario instead of Cloud Dataflow.

 EXAM TIP The content of the exam is always subject to change, without any notice, by Google Cloud. Google Cloud evolves at such a rapid pace that the exam itself has to keep up with the technology. Do not rely solely on the case studies or the common exam questions to pass. Immerse yourself in the world of Google Cloud to be the best exam-taker.

Case Studies

On the Professional Cloud Architect exam, you'll be provided with case studies that will be required for a significant amount of questions. I'll outline a few sample case studies that are provided online. Please note that these are subject to change by Google Cloud at any time without notice. These sample case studies will describe a fictitious business, a solution concept, some background on their existing technical environment, any business and technical requirements, and an executive statement. As you read through these case studies, think about what types of questions you could be asked based on them. Parse for business requirements, technical requirements, keywords, constraints, timelines, and so on. Throughout the book I'll reference key learnings back to these case studies, so put a bookmark on this page or have it handy on your laptop.

Mountkirk Games

https://cloud.google.com/certification/guides/cloud-architect/casestudy-mountkirkgames-rev2

Mountkirk Games makes online, session-based, multiplayer games for mobile platforms. The company builds all of its games using some server-side integration. Historically, it has used cloud providers to lease physical servers.

Due to the unexpected popularity of some of its games, the company has had problems scaling its global audience, application servers, MySQL databases, and analytics tools.

The current model is to write game statistics to files and send them through an ETL tool that loads them into a centralized MySQL database for reporting.

Solution Concept

Mountkirk Games is building a new game, which is expected to be very popular. The company plans to deploy the game's backend on Google Compute Engine to capture streaming metrics, to run intensive analytics, to take advantage of its autoscaling server environment, and to integrate with a managed NoSQL database.

Business Requirements

- Increase to a global footprint
- Improve uptime—downtime means loss of players
- Increase efficiency of the cloud resources we use
- Reduce latency to all customers

Technical Requirements

For the game backend platform:

- Dynamically scale up or down based on game activity
- Connect to a transactional database service to manage user profiles and game state
- Store game activity in a time series database service for future analysis
- As the system scales, ensure that data is not lost due to processing backlogs
- Run hardened Linux distribution

For the game analytics platform:

- Dynamically scale up or down based on game activity
- Process incoming data on the fly directly from the game servers
- Process data that arrives late because of slow mobile networks
- Allow queries to access at least 10TB of historical data
- Process files that are regularly uploaded by users' mobile devices

Executive Statement

Our last successful game did not scale well with our previous cloud provider, resulting in lower user adoption and affecting the game's reputation. Our investors want more key performance indicators (KPIs) to evaluate the speed and stability of the game, as well as other metrics that provide deeper insight into usage patterns so we can adapt the game to target users. Additionally, our current technology stack cannot provide the scale we need, so we want to replace MySQL and move to an environment that provides autoscaling and low-latency load balancing and frees us up from managing physical servers.

Dress4Win

https://cloud.google.com/certification/guides/cloud-architect/casestudy-dress4win-rev2

Dress4Win is a web-based company that helps its users organize and manage their personal wardrobes using a web app and mobile application. The company also cultivates an active social network that connects its users with designers and retailers. The company monetizes its services through advertising, e-commerce, referrals, and a "freemium" app model. The application has grown from a few servers in the founder's garage to several hundred servers and appliances in a colocated data center. However, the capacity of the infrastructure is now insufficient for the application's rapid growth. Because of this growth and the company's desire to innovate faster, Dress4Win is committing to a full migration to a public cloud.

Solution Concept

For the first phase of its migration to the cloud, Dress4Win is moving its development and test environments. It is also building a disaster recovery site, because its current infrastructure is at a single location. The company is not sure which components of its architecture can be migrated as is and which components need to be changed before migrating them.

Existing Technical Environment

The Dress4Win application is served out of a single data center location. All servers run Ubuntu LTS v16.04.

- **Databases**   MySQL: one server for user data, inventory, and static data
  - MySQL 5.7
  - 8 core CPUs
  - 128GB of RAM
  - 2× 5TB HDD (RAID 1)
- **Compute**   Forty web application servers providing microservices-based APIs and static content
  - Tomcat – Java
  - Nginx
  - 4 core CPUs
  - 32GB of RAM

  Twenty Apache Hadoop/Spark servers:
  - Data analysis
  - Real-time trending calculations
  - 8 core CPUs
  - 128GB of RAM
  - 4× 5TB HDD (RAID 1)

  Three RabbitMQ servers for messaging, social notifications, and events:
  - 8 core CPUs
  - 32GB of RAM

Miscellaneous servers:

- Jenkins, monitoring, bastion hosts, security scanners
- 8 core CPUs
- 32GB of RAM

Storage appliances:

- iSCSI for VM hosts
- Fibre Channel SAN: MySQL databases (1PB total storage; 400TB available)
- NAS: image storage, logs, backups (100TB total storage; 35TB available)

Business Requirements

- Build a reliable and reproducible environment with scaled parity of production
- Improve security by defining and adhering to a set of security and identity and access management (IAM) best practices for the cloud
- Improve business agility and speed of innovation through rapid provisioning of new resources
- Analyze and optimize architecture for performance in the cloud

Technical Requirements

- Easily create nonproduction environments in the cloud
- Implement an automation framework for provisioning resources in cloud
- Implement a continuous deployment process for deploying applications to the on-premises data center or cloud
- Support failover of the production environment to the cloud during an emergency
- Encrypt data on the wire and at rest
- Support multiple private connections between the production data center and cloud environment

Executive Statement

Our investors are concerned about our ability to scale and contain costs with our current infrastructure. They are also concerned that a competitor could use a public cloud platform to offset their up-front investment and free them to focus on developing better features. Our traffic patterns are highest in the mornings and weekend evenings; during other times, 80 percent of our capacity is sitting idle. Our capital expenditure is now exceeding our quarterly projections. Migrating to the cloud will likely cause an initial increase in spending, but we expect to fully transition before our next hardware refresh cycle. Our total cost of ownership (TCO) analysis over the next five years for a public cloud strategy achieves a cost reduction of between 30 percent and 50 percent over our current model.

TerramEarth

https://cloud.google.com/certification/guides/cloud-architect/casestudy
-terramearth-rev2

TerramEarth manufactures heavy equipment for the mining and agricultural industries. About 80 percent of its business comes from mining and 20 percent is from agriculture. With more than 500 dealers and service centers in 100 countries, TerramEarth's mission is to build products that make its customers more productive.

Solution Concept

There are 20 million TerramEarth vehicles in operation that collect 120 fields of data per second. Data is stored locally on the vehicle and can be accessed for analysis when a vehicle is serviced. The data is downloaded via a maintenance port. This same port can be used to adjust operational parameters, enabling the vehicles to be upgraded in the field with new computing modules.

Approximately 200,000 vehicles are connected to a cellular network, enabling TerramEarth to collect data directly. At a rate of 120 fields of data per second, with 22 hours of operation per day, TerramEarth collects a total of about 9TB per day from these connected vehicles.

Existing Technical Environment

TerramEarth's existing architecture is composed of Linux- and Windows-based systems that reside in a single U.S. West Coast–based data center. These systems gzip CSV files from the field, upload via FTP, and place the data in a data warehouse. Because this process takes time, aggregated reports are based on data that is three weeks old. With this data, TerramEarth has been able to stock replacement parts preemptively and reduce unplanned downtime of its vehicles by 60 percent. However, because the data is stale, some customers are without their vehicles for up to four weeks while they wait for replacement parts.

Business Requirements

- Decrease unplanned vehicle downtime to less than one week
- Support the dealer network with more data on how their customers use their equipment to better position new products and services
- Have the ability to partner with different companies—especially with seed and fertilizer suppliers in the fast-growing agricultural business—to create compelling joint offerings for their customers

Technical Requirements

- Expand beyond a single data center to decrease latency to the American Midwest and East Coast
- Create a backup strategy

- Increase security of data transfer from equipment to the data center
- Improve data in the data warehouse
- Use customer and equipment data to anticipate customer needs

Application 1: Data Ingest

A custom Python application reads uploaded data files from a single server and writes to the data warehouse.

- **Compute**   Windows Server 2008 R2
  - 16 CPUs
  - 128GB of RAM
  - 10TB local HDD storage

Application 2: Reporting

Business analysts use an off-the-shelf application to run a daily report to see what equipment needs repair. Only two analysts of a team of ten (five West Coast, five East Coast) can connect to the reporting application at a time.

- **Compute**   Off-the-shelf application; license tied to number of physical CPUs
  - Windows Server 2008 R2
  - 16 CPUs
  - 32GB of RAM
  - 500GB HDD
- **Data warehouse**   Single PostgreSQL server
  - Red Hat Linux
  - 64 CPUs
  - 128GB of RAM
  - 4× 6TB HDD in RAID 0

Executive Statement

Our competitive advantage has always been in our manufacturing process, with our ability to build better vehicles for lower cost than our competitors. However, new products with different approaches are constantly being developed, and I'm concerned that we lack the skills to undergo the next wave of transformations in our industry. My goals are to build our skills while addressing immediate market needs through incremental innovations.

General Tips on Taking Technical Certification Exams

Google Cloud certifications are very challenging certifications to earn. A key difference between Google Cloud certifications and other common technical certifications are that Google Cloud certifications test both your understanding of technology principles as well as your hands-on experience in an evolving cloud ecosystem. Other certifications, such as the CISSP, are a bit easier, because they remain technology-agnostic and test your core understanding of principles and concepts—so the content doesn't change too often. That being said, one incredibly important and often overlooked skill is your test-taking habits. Proper studying and test-taking habits could be what puts you over the edge for a passing score. Let's dive into these.

- *Sleep is your superpower!* Sleep plays the most important role in memory retention when you're learning something new. Get good-quality sleep after studying, and get a great night's rest before you take your exam.

- *Pace yourself.* It sounds easier running through as much content as fast as possible, but your goal is to pass the exam and develop expertise in cloud architecture. Get some rest and don't burn yourself out!

- *Use the supplementary resources in tandem to the book.* I'll discuss these in the next section. Reading a book is going to give you only so much context; doing exercises and immersing yourself in Google Cloud will make you an expert.

- *Eat a clean diet and drink lots of water.* Plenty of research has shown the effects of sugar, dehydration, and a poor overall diet on your body. Your body needs nutrition to be its best, so treat yourself like a Ferrari, not like a jalopy!

- *Take a break during the exam and get your blood flowing.* Do some jumping jacks, pushups, or take a brisk walk to the restroom. It's so easy to doze off during this exam because it is so technical and mentally draining, so a little micro exercise will get your mind and cognition stimulated.

- *When an exam question takes you longer than 30 to 45 seconds to solve, flag it and skip it.* It's easy to get through all the questions you know the answers to immediately and then go back to the flagged questions at the end. That way, you aren't rushing through any potential easy questions if you're running low on time by working through everything in one sprint.

- *Identify the keywords provided to you in each exam question.* Certain words can change the entire context of the question or the order of the answer; list them out while you're looking for an answer. For example, if you're asked, "What is the most cost-effective strategy for storing objects in a data store that need to be accessed only once a month?" *Cost-effective, object storage, accessed once a month*— these are all keywords or key phrases. In this case, storing the data in Google Cloud Storage on a nearline storage class would be the right answer.

If you use these tips and techniques during your journey, it's almost guaranteed that you'll pass the exam. The pushups alone might've saved me from failing a few certifications in the past—ha!

How to Use the Supplementary Resources

Google Cloud has gained a lot of popularity over the years and has seen a tremendous amount of growth in the enterprise. Alongside this, there have been strong investments from both the Google Cloud learning team as well as the community on developing supplementary resources for professionals who want to become an expert in the Google Cloud ecosystem. For your exam, it is highly suggested that you take on some of the supplementary resources listed next so that you can not only talk the talk but walk the walk and actually perform many of the activities that a cloud architect is required to do. Don't overwhelm yourself with trying to use every resource possible; find what works for you and your time. Here's the scoop.

Professional Cloud Architect Certification Exam Guide   Use this as a guiding rubric for the content you should be studying. I've outlined this in the book, but because the Cloud continues to evolve, it'll be good to check in and make sure there are no changes. **https://cloud.google.com/certification/guides/professional-cloud-architect/**

Certification Frequently Asked Questions   Self explanatory—review these at some point in time. **https://cloud.google.com/certification/faqs/#0**

Google Cloud Professional Cloud Architect Practice Exam   This practice exam gives you 25 official practice questions from Google Cloud that will give you a precise idea of the types of questions you'll see on the exam. **https://cloud.google.com/certification/practice-exam/cloud-architect**

Google Cloud Products   The products page provides an immense amount of knowledge of the ever-changing landscape of Google Cloud offerings. This is a great place to start to get an overview on many of the key products discussed in this book. I recommend that you review each product covered in this book, and anything else you're interested in. **https://cloud.google.com/products**

Get Started with Google Cloud   The documentation page is the "Google it" answer to everything. Everything you want to know about Google Cloud is here. This site will become your best friend beyond this exam when you're working on Google Cloud in your day job. About 90 percent of the answers people are looking for around technologies and best practices are located here! **https://cloud.google.com/docs/**

Google Cloud Console   What could be more helpful than getting your hands dirty in the Google Cloud Console and causing mayhem in your cloud environment as you're learning new things? It can't hurt! Dive into the services and look through some of the informational tabs as you're learning. **https://console.cloud.google.com**

Coursera: "Architecting with Google Cloud Platform Specialization"   Coursera is Google Cloud's premier partner in providing comprehensive interactive coursework on GCP. This specific course is designed for the Cloud Architect exam and will give you all the conceptual and hands-on skills (via QwikLabs) to be successful in a cloud architect role. **https://www.coursera.org/specializations/gcp-architecture**

QwikLabs Cloud Architecture Quest   This "quest" is a set of curated labs designed to give you hands-on practice with the topics covered in the exam. It provides a simulated lab environment, so there is no need to set up your own GCP environment. **https://www.qwiklabs.com/quests/24**

A Cloud Guru Google Cloud Certified Professional Cloud Architect Course   A Cloud Guru provides a phenomenal video-based series for the Cloud Architect certification. **https://acloud.guru/learn/gcp-certified-professional-cloud-architect**

Blog Posts   Many blog posts are incredibly helpful and give you retrospective feedback from people's experiences taking the certification exam. Just Google these! **https://jayendrapatil.com/google-cloud-professional-cloud-architect-certification-learning-path/https://medium.com/@jk.jaiswal/how-i-passed-gcp-professional-cloud-architect-exam-during-this-summer-c90234c9f752**

Google Cloud Platform YouTube Channel   Fantastic content can be found on specific Google Cloud technologies and solutions, what they are, and how to use them in a very in-depth manner that goes into much more detail than most training courses. **https://www.youtube.com/googlecloudplatform**

Chapter Review

Whew! You've just begun your journey toward becoming a Google Cloud Architect, and you have a lot of content to digest. You're doing great if you've made it here without feeling overwhelmed. Give yourself positive reaffirmation on your progress, stay focused, and take a break. Let's discuss what we covered in this chapter.

In this chapter, we started off covering some of the benefits of becoming a cloud architect: it's a very lucrative space to be in but also a very fulfilling role. Consider the cloud architect who designed the unemployment application processing platform for the State of New York during the COVID-19 pandemic, for example. This person helped millions of Americans get access to income that may have saved their families from disaster—talk about fulfilling.

We also discussed the prerequisite knowledge in becoming a certified Cloud Architect. The Cloud Architect exam is not designed for a beginner who is new to Google Cloud; it's recommended that you have a few years of experience under your belt and have a good understanding of business challenges along with the technical prerequisite knowledge. Enterprise cloud strategy, solution design, architectural best practices, and common software development methodologies are important things to understand for the exam.

We dove into the exam specifics. You'll get 50 questions that vary in complexity, but all require careful analysis to distill the keywords and determine solutions. Most questions are based on a few case studies that will be provided during your exam. We'll look into these case studies throughout the book. We also dove into some tips and tricks on taking technical certification exams to help give you a nudge to pass your certification. Lastly, we dove into the supplementary resources that you can utilize in tandem with this book. It's very important that you do use some of those resources to help you become a better architect and better prepare you for the exam. Your journey has just begun, and don't worry, because you'll be very confident going into the exam if you follow the best practices outlined in this chapter!

Questions

1. What best describes the role of a Google Cloud Architect?

   A. An individual within an organization who architects

   B. An engineer who is interested in designing robust solutions in an enterprise

   C. A technical subject matter expert who understands business and technical requirements and is able to translate those requirements into technical designs

   D. An individual who can design, develop, and manage robust, secure, scalable, highly available, and dynamic solutions to drive business objectives

2. Which one of these objectives is *not* covered on the Professional Cloud Architect exam?

   A. Manage and provision the cloud solution infrastructure.

   B. Ensure hybrid cloud solutions are integrated into cloud architecture.

   C. Analyze and optimize technical and business processes.

   D. Manage implementations of cloud architecture.

3. All of the following requirements are technical requirements *except*

   A. Dynamically scale up and down based on user activity.

   B. Connect to a transactional database service to manage user profiles and game state.

   C. Reduce latency to all customers.

   D. Run a hardened Linux distribution.

4. All of the following requirements are business requirements *except*

   A. Improve security by defining and adhering to a set of security and identity and access management (IAM) best practices for cloud.

   B. Build a reliable and reproducible environment with scaled parity of production.

   C. Analyze and optimize architecture for performance in the cloud.

   D. Implement an automation framework for provisioning resources in the cloud.

5. You are consulting on a project with Mountkirk Games for its migration to Google Cloud Platform. Mountkirk Games would like to migrate its virtual machine infrastructure onto Google Cloud and dynamically scale its infrastructure. What solution would you advise them to leverage?

   A. Google Compute Engine with managed instance groups

   B. Google App Engine

   C. Google Kubernetes Engine with horizontal pod autoscaling

   D. Google Cloud Functions

6. What is a blue-green deployment method?

   A. An application release model whereby users from a previous version are gradually transferred over to a nearly identical release in a production environment to reduce risk and minimize downtime

   B. An application release model in which you roll out releases to a subset of users to test your changes and then roll them out to the rest of the users

   C. An application release model whereby users are granted access based on how long they've been using the application

   D. An application deployment in which instances are slowly replaced with newer ones and health checks are performed to validate that they meet the requirements

7. What is the difference between functional requirements and nonfunctional requirements?

   A. A functional requirement is a business requirement that describes what a system is supposed to be doing, and a nonfunctional requirement is a business requirement that describes how a system is expected to perform.

   B. A functional requirement is a technical requirement that describes what a system is supposed to be doing, and a nonfunctional requirement is a technical requirement that describes how a system is expected to perform.

   C. A functional requirement is a business requirement that describes how a system is expected to perform, and a nonfunctional requirement is a business requirement that describes what a system is supposed to be doing.

   D. A functional requirement is a technical requirement that describes how a system is expected to perform, and a nonfunctional requirement is a technical requirement that describes what a system is supposed to be doing.

8. Which one of the following answers is an example of a functional requirement?

   A. Application X needs to pull data from the third-party API, transform the data, and load it into a PostgreSQL database that will be surfaced back to end users through a frontend application.

   B. Application X needs to process 10,000 requests per second as it is performing its ETL.

    C. Application X needs to provide less than 1ms latency to all end users who are requesting the data.

    D. Application X should achieve the four nines of availability to ensure user satisfaction.

  9. Which one of the following answers is an example of a nonfunctional requirement?

    A. Application X needs to pull data from the third-party API, transform the data, and load it into a PostgreSQL database that will be surfaced back to end users through a frontend application.

    B. Application X will send users an e-mail after they sign up to confirm their enrollment.

    C. Application X will enable users to open an account that links their information to a unique identifier used to process transactions after they sign up.

    D. Application X will have less than four hours of downtime per year.

 10. Which one of these is *not* a recommended tip for taking your certification exam?

    A. Eat a healthy diet and sleep well throughout your studying sessions.

    B. Cram out all of the pages in this book as fast as possible so you can take the exam sooner.

    C. Use the process of elimination while taking the exam, looking for distractors and minimizing the possible answers before choosing the right one.

    D. Use supplementary resources in addition to reading this book to prepare for the exam.

Answers

  1. D. Although all answers are technically correct, the question is looking for the *best* description of the role of a Google Cloud Architect, which is an individual who can design, develop, and manage robust, secure, scalable, highly available, and dynamic solutions to drive business objectives.

  2. B. Although hybrid cloud solutions are a big aspect of cloud architecture and you may be asked about them on the exam, this is not an exam objective.

  3. C. Reducing latency to all customers is a business objective, not a technical requirement, because it states what the business has defined to improve user experience, not the technology stack.

  4. D. Although this answer may end up supporting the business in very beneficial ways, an automation framework is a technical requirement that enables the technology teams to have a smoother and more effective deployment across their applications.

  5. A. Google Compute Engine is a Google Cloud infrastructure component that enables you to migrate or build large-scale virtual machine environments and manage instance group autoscaling by increasing or decreasing the virtual machines on demand.

6. **A.** While B and D describe valid deployment models (they describe canary deployment and a rolling deployment), blue-green deployment methods have two nearly identical production environments.

7. **B.** Functional requirements and nonfunctional requirements are both technical requirements. Functional requirements define the "what," while nonfunctional requirements define the "how" of a system.

8. **A.** Application X needs to pull data from the third-party API, transform the data, and load it into a PostgreSQL database that will be surfaced back to end users through a frontend application. This is an example of a functional requirement. All other answers describe performance, reliability, and scalability requirements.

9. **D.** Application X will have less than four hours of downtime per year. This is an example of a nonfunctional requirement. All other answers describe "what" a system is supposed to do, while uptime/downtime is a performance indicator.

10. **B.** Take your time; you shouldn't go through the book as quickly as possible so you can take the exam sooner. You'll pass the exam in due time! Just follow the recommendations and you'll be a certified Cloud Architect in no time.

Overview of Cloud Computing and Google Cloud

In this chapter, we'll cover
- Cloud computing basics
- How Google Cloud differs from other cloud platforms
- The various Google Cloud products and services of relevance to the cloud architect
- The various ways you can access and manage your cloud
- The business and technical context of cloud architecture

The development of the Internet has been one of the most transformational events in the history of human civilization, especially with regard to social evolution. In more than two million years, there has never been a point at which we humans have been able to communicate globally and in real time to share knowledge and data that can be digested by virtually anyone who wants to consume it. The Internet has eliminated nearly all communication barriers and has "open-sourced" the availability of knowledge.

We are no longer forced to rely solely on potentially biased sources of information to gain knowledge. Before the Internet, education, media, and everyday speech were very much predisposed to bias because of the extremely limited access to and availability of sources of information that could provide accurate knowledge and help build perspective. Before the Internet, if you were a curious "free thinker" with access to books, funding, and time, you could dive into as many opportunities as possible to become an expert. But that was not so easy for the average person. Although biases still exist on the Internet, nowadays you can do a quick Google search and find hundreds of perspectives that can help you formulate a more rational understanding of virtually any topic.

The Internet has also provided a blank canvas of infinite possibilities, enabling humans to conduct transactions, connect and develop relationships, and solve problems, all without being physically present. And the engineers of the world continue to build new possibilities. Although the Internet has given humans the ability to analyze data at scale, as the scale has continued to grow, we've encountered many performance bottlenecks along the way that hindered our ability to progress at the pace we wanted. Today, cloud computing provides massive-scale computing resources to nearly everyone, enabling petabytes of data to be analyzed and surfaced back to the end user in microseconds.

Cloud computing enables innovation and on-demand growth that is unconstrained by the resource bottlenecks of traditional data centers that powered the world since the inception of the Internet. But the cloud has also presented many new conflicts for the world. With massive-scale computing, we've been able to develop algorithms that provide us with new ethical challenges. We've trusted corporate entities with enormous troves of our personal data, which they correlate with petabyte-sized databases to build digital profiles of our individual identities and activities. We now have machine-learning algorithms that can mimic our voices, simply by listening to us speak a single sentence. Deepfake algorithms can record and render our faces into artificial scenes that look entirely real. Hackers can analyze data at light speeds to identify vulnerable users, and then use these massive computing resources to attack one user or millions of users in an instant. How can we maintain the security, privacy, neutrality, and transparency of data stored on the Internet considering all of the constantly emerging technologies that represent only the tip of the iceberg of possibility?

Although these philosophical meanderings are not part of the Professional Cloud Architect exam, as certified Cloud Architects, we should understand the philosophical impacts of this technology, especially with regard to how we can build ethically and protect ourselves and the world against unethical activities. It's important that we're purposeful in the way we develop solutions and that we understand how our work can ensure a safer future for our children. We must build solutions that are representative of goodness and morality across all walks of life.

As I'm writing this book, we are undergoing a significant historical event in American society with regard to the acknowledgment of the inequalities faced by African Americans and people of color. The serious consequences of the situation are widespread; we're also experiencing inequalities created by technology with regard to the enormous amounts of data collected about individuals. Consider facial recognition technologies, for example. Amazon recently announced a yearlong moratorium on police use of its facial recognition tool (Amazon Rekognition) because the tool has been unable to properly identify African Americans. The Rekognition API has wrongfully tagged innocent African Americans as criminals because of a lack of proper police training on the algorithm and because of many other built-in blind spots inadvertently included by developers when they built the tool. In addition, IBM announced it would no longer offer, develop, or research facial recognition technology for many of the same reasons.

Despite these issues, it's immature to assume that because these big-tech companies are not investing in facial recognition software, it doesn't exist anywhere outside that space. In fact, the open source community has already provided many free and open solutions that do the same thing. No matter how much we may think that the progression of technology is in the hands of big tech, it turns out that it's not necessarily so; it's actually in the hands of the many technologists who are advancing this profession at work or in their off hours. Technology will move at the pace it's going to move at, unhindered by world governments. Our job is to ensure that we minimize the side effects and promote goodness.

Facial recognition tools are also used for good ends, such as to identify and rescue human-trafficking victims, to secure access to our homes, and to simplify our lives. But we need to be constantly aware of all of the implications of using this technology to ensure that we have developed rationality ourselves and to ensure that our diverse set of voices is heard beyond the technical solutions we develop.

It's important that you think about the philosophy of your work and take pride in shaping the future of the world—and that you use that power for good. Share your ideas with your peers, ask for help and guidance, and ask others to assess your blind spots. In the last 30 years, we've seen technology change the fabric of society at an exponential speed. Think about how you want the next 30 years to look for yourself and for society and how that reflects in the work you do to give back to the world.

Overview of Cloud Computing

Cloud computing is the on-demand availability of computing services over the Internet that offers faster innovation, flexible resources, and economies of scale. This includes providing servers, storage, databases, networking, software, analytics, and business intelligence to businesses and consumers alike, without requiring these users to maintain any physical infrastructure. In the traditional world, where we used to think of three-tier architectures, cloud computing has eliminated all traditional computing paradigms and brought forward the notion of service-based architectures in the cloud, where the myriad computing activities performed are broken down into the most miniscule services and are decoupled from the former monolithic computing model. With microservices architecture, deployment gets simplified as the functionality is separated into smaller units. There is more freedom to use various languages and frameworks in development, there are fewer dependencies between teams, and it's easier to design for reliability. Google has been doing microservices-based architecture prior to the advent of the cloud, notably with Borg, the company's internal corporate cluster manager that led to the creation of Docker and Kubernetes.

In the cloud, customers and cloud service providers operate using fundamentally different responsibility models. In traditional computing environments, a business typically would own the entirety of a data center environment and all of the labor associated with it, or it would be contracting with managed data center companies and purchasing equipment to be stored in the contractor's environment, paying them to perform physical management and some level of logical management. Figure 2-1 shows the Google Cloud shared services model.

In this shared responsibility model, the cloud offers a few new concepts, namely, *Infrastructure as a Service* (IaaS), *Platform as a Service* (PaaS), *Software as a Service* (SaaS), and as a bonus, serverless, or *Function as a Service* (FaaS), a term used these days to describe fully serverless environments.

IaaS provides the most flexible cloud computing model and enables you to retain the most control over your infrastructure. Google Compute Engine is an example. With an IaaS solution, you can deploy virtual machine environments onto servers, giving you full ownership of the infrastructure end-to-end, without having to manage the physical

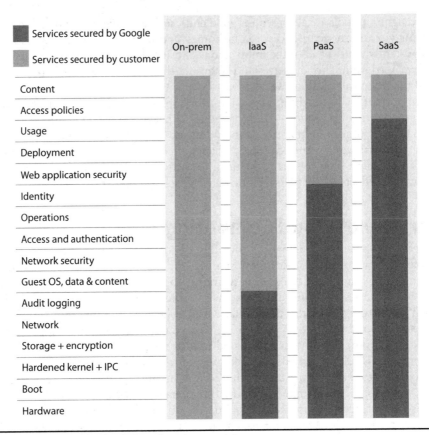

Figure 2-1 The Google Cloud shared services model

servers yourself. IaaS does have limitations as well; for example, you need more overhead to manage your resources, since you retain a lot of control. That inherently means you have a lot more responsibility for the security of your environments.

The PaaS model offers a simple, cost-effective solution to developing and deploying applications on a scalable and highly available platform. PaaS typically offers development teams a lot more speed for application deployment, and because it typically ramps up and down based on usage, a PaaS solution can be more cost-effective. Google App Engine is an example; however, while developer expertise has evolved, App Engine is no longer the default model, and the current trend for consuming cloud computing by application developers is to use Google Kubernetes Engine (GKE), which falls somewhere in the middle between PaaS and IaaS. Some of the limitations of PaaS concern data security, since the cloud service provider controls the underlying infrastructure; vendor lock-in (although this is not an issue with GKE); operational limitations; and a lack of full developer flexibility.

The SaaS model is the most familiar to everyone, in which an application is delivered over the Internet through a web browser, without the need to download or install anything on the client side. SaaS solutions are advantageous for software that is designed to perform a general set of tasks and to disallow a developer end user to customize or modify the application. Examples of SaaS are Salesforce, Intuit QuickBooks, and Google Workspace. There are several limitations to SaaS: these solutions are designed to solve only certain use cases and are not designed as solutions that enable developers the freedom to build. Google Drive, for example, is a SaaS solution designed purely for file storage on the Internet. End users don't have much control here beyond the service catalog of options Google Drive provides. Major implications of SaaS are vendor lock-in, lack of interoperability, lack of control and customization, and concerns about data security.

With a move to the cloud, businesses are typically concerned about the following:

- Reducing capital expenditures and turning them into operational expenditures
- Scaling resource expenses to actual end-user demand rather than initial projected demand, significantly reducing program risk
- Eliminating or transitioning much of the overhead of IT resources and letting companies focus on building great products and experiences for their customers
- Accelerating the pace of innovation to achieve a competitive edge or unlocking new business opportunities

If you're not dabbling in the cloud by 2020, that's pretty much a negative. Companies that have full, on-premises environments are looked down upon as not being "technically savvy" (minus companies such as Facebook, which has its own "cloud"). Most talented engineers want to focus on solving complex business problems and don't want to worry about the mundane and often painful tasks required to build and operate infrastructure. As such, the best talent these days doesn't want to work at traditional enterprises.

Lastly, you'll need to know the ins and outs of the following key cloud concepts for the exam:

- A *public cloud* offers cloud services to the public; think of the big providers such as Google Cloud, Amazon Web Services (AWS), Microsoft Azure, and Alibaba Cloud.
- A *private cloud* is developed in-house, specific to a business. Think of the Facebook Cloud, which Facebook had built for its own use. Or think of an on-premises cloud, where all servers, storage, and networks are dedicated to the company and hosted in a dedicated data center.
- A *hybrid cloud* uses a mixture of a public cloud and a private cloud to create a more diverse environment. Customers with highly sensitive data, such as financial services or healthcare, like to have their own environments under their full control, where they can store their most highly sensitive workloads and data. Or maybe the customer hasn't gotten around to migrating fully to a public cloud because of a lack of commitment, features, time, and so on.

- A *multi-cloud* is similar to a hybrid cloud, in that multiple clouds are at play, but typically in a multi-cloud environment, a business will be using multiple *public* clouds. Many top companies today use this model, such as Snapchat, which uses both Google Cloud and AWS for its workloads.

- A *community cloud* (which is not covered in the exam) is a collaborative effort in which infrastructure is shared between several organizations from a specific community with common concerns. It may be managed internally or by a third party, and can be hosted internally or externally.

Google Cloud vs. Other Clouds

Although several other cloud service providers focus on the whole spectrum of offerings, from IaaS to highly specialized PaaS or SaaS offerings, the key players in this space globally are Amazon Web Services (AWS), Google Cloud, Alibaba Cloud, and Microsoft Azure.

In 2018, Alphabet (Google's holding company) disclosed the revenues of Google Cloud at $1 billion per quarter. In its Q1 2020 earnings call, Google Cloud reported that it generated $2.78 billion in revenue—that's 52 percent higher than one year prior and almost triple its growth since 2018. Although AWS is dominating the market at $10 billion per quarter and Microsoft Azure is inherently present across enterprises because of Microsoft's global dominance in computing, Google Cloud is continuing to grow at a rapid pace as an alternative cloud service provider with several advantages. A major trend today within many companies is to employ a multi-cloud strategy. Given the tenant isolation design advantage of designing public cloud solutions from traditional on-premises architectures, different workloads can and should be enabled to run on the most suitable public cloud platform to achieve the desired business outcome. Google Cloud Platform is gaining traction into every major enterprise globally, signing big names like Equifax, Home Depot, McKesson, Disney, Snap, Salesforce, PayPal, and HSBC. What is it about Google Cloud that is becoming so appealing to these massive enterprises?

Although Amazon built the AWS platform from scratch, Google had already designed a massive global computing platform and networking backbone that served all of its employees and users worldwide. In a way, Google used its existing internal infrastructure to develop a new layer of abstraction to externalize it to customers worldwide—the Google Cloud Platform (GCP). Four key core competencies and a set of principles based on system design provide the framework for GCP's design.

Security First

Security and data protection is at the core of Google and its products. As a customer of the Google Cloud, you own your data and control how it is used. GCP also has strong internal controls and auditing features that protect customers against insider access to their data. It offers continuous security monitoring and several security features as part of its shared responsibility model, providing its customers confidence that their businesses are safe from malicious activities. Lastly, one of the major benefits of using GCP is that it is built from Google's already existing private global backbone, so Google is able to encrypt data at rest and in transit by default. Google controls the majority of the service delivery, and thus the user experience, all from within its own infrastructure.

Open Cloud

It's become increasingly evident throughout the evolution of the cloud that customers don't want to lock themselves into one cloud provider; instead, they often use the strengths of various cloud providers for different aspects of their business and for business continuity. Google offers an open cloud that enables customers to leverage multiple different clouds and follow a common development and operations approach to deliver their applications. Customers can innovate, build, and scale rapidly while minimizing the constraints of a single technology. Google strongly emphasizes this approach because of its pioneering efforts in building and cultivating the open source community, which is a key element of its corporate philosophy.

 NOTE   Check out Google's corporate philosophy to read the "Ten things we know to be true," which have held true since the company's beginning: https://www.google.com/about/philosophy.html.

Analytics and Artificial Intelligence

Analytics and artificial intelligence (AI) remain two of Google's strong points as a company that is heavily data driven. GCP offers fully managed, serverless analytics products and services that eliminate the constraints of scale, performance, and cost. GCP empowers customers to leverage real-time insights, enabling them to improve their decision-making and accelerate innovation—all without having to manage any infrastructure. Google has historically been on the forefront of researching and improving AI, offering innovations such as MapReduce, Dremel, Apache Beam, and TensorFlow, which both customers and Google can use to power its products with more AI capabilities. Simply stated, Google provides superior analytics and AI products as part of the great selling points for customers migrating to GCP.

Global Data Centers and Network

As mentioned, Google Cloud was built on the same infrastructure that Google uses to serve more than 100,000 employees and billions of consumers worldwide. This massive private network consists of more than 24 regions, 73 zones, and 144 network edge locations and is available in more than 200 countries and territories. This is arguably the largest and most advanced software-defined network, delivering the highest level of performance and availability in a secure and sustainable way. This global backbone has been tested and vetted with billions of users worldwide, using all of Google's products and internal technology. Building a cloud on top of this backbone only makes sense, especially when reliability is increasingly one of the more important performance indicators for successful businesses. Talk to someone on the presales side at Google Cloud, and they will talk your ears off about the Google network.

Principles of System Design

Google Cloud follows a very strict framework that enables them to build robust, secure, and scalable systems. Four principles provide guidance on designing systems for internal users and customers, as outlined next.

Operational Excellence

Operational excellence is the principle of building a foundation that successfully enables reliability across your infrastructure by efficiently running, managing, and monitoring systems that deliver business value. Three key strategies drive this principle:

- *Automating build, test, and deployment by using continuous integration and continuous deployment pipelines.* This enables customers to programmatically do rapid deployment and iterations based on a continuous feedback loop.

- *Monitoring business objective metrics by defining, measuring, and alerting on key metrics.* Data needs to be measured and output to your business leaders to give insight into where they have the competitive edge and where they can further optimize or reassess.

- *Conducting disaster recovery testing proactively and periodically.* Disaster can strike a company in so many different ways, often causing financial and reputational business harm. This is overlooked too many times by customers until disaster strikes and ends up costing them exponentially more than it would cost had they been prepared.

Security, Privacy, and Compliance

It is critical for any customer doing business in the cloud to ensure their intellectual property is protected and their customers are safe from malicious activity. This is a core principle of Google's system design. Four key strategies drive this principle:

- *Implementing least privileges with identity and authorization controls.* Centralizing your identity management system and designing your access management structure in a way that allows users to do only what they're intended to do, while ensuring *nonrepudiation* (a user cannot deny their activity) and audit logs that are available to be consumed by automated and manual detection mechanisms.

- *Building a layered security approach.* Also known as defense-in-depth, this involves the implementation of a variety of security controls at each level of the infrastructure and applications designed on top of the infrastructure. The idea is to assume that any security control can be breached, and when it is breached, several other layers of defense are available to protect intellectual property.

- *Automating deployment of sensitive tasks.* Humans continue to be the weakest link in performance and security of administrative tasks. By automating the deployment of these tasks, you can eliminate the dependency on humans.

- *Implementing security monitoring.* Part of a strong security model is to prevent, detect, and respond to malicious activity. By implementing automated tools to monitor your infrastructure, you can gather data to continue protecting your weak points and prevent malicious activity from occurring in your environment and harming your business.

Reliability

Google sees reliability as the most important feature of any application. Without reliability, users begin to churn (stop using the product). Google suggests 15 strategies to achieve reliability; here are three key ones:

- *Reliability is defined by the user.* Many data points can encompass all sorts of important factors in your workload, but truly measuring using key performance indicators (KPIs) requires an understanding of user actions, and the metrics define the success of those actions for reliability.
- *Use sufficient reliability.* There's no need to overinvest in reliability if you're meeting user satisfaction. Figure out what sort of availability keeps your users happy and retained, and ensure that you continually assess reliability as your infrastructure grows.
- *Create redundancy.* Always assume that if you depend on a single point to provide a function, that point can and will fail someday. When building your infrastructure and applications, always try to leverage resource redundancy across resources that can fail independently.

Performance and Cost Optimization

Managing the performance of your applications and the associated costs is a balancing act, as highly performant environments often end up costing more to maintain. Understanding where you've met your minimum performance requirements and where you need to optimize cost is an important principle for system design. These three strategies are relevant here:

- *Evaluate performance requirements.* Determine the minimum performance you need from your applications.
- *Use scalable design patterns.* Leverage automatically scaling products and services where applicable to minimize cost to what is necessary.
- *Identify and implement cost-saving approaches.* Understand the priority of each of your services with respect to its application to your business objectives. Use these priorities to optimize for service availability and cost.

A 10,000-Foot Overview of GCP

We're going to dive into a bit of an overview of GCP to help you understand the overall elements of the cloud, including several of the products and services you'll need to know about for the exam. It's a lot of content, so don't worry about memorizing everything right now; we'll be diving into these concepts and services to a greater depth throughout the book. It'll be good to get some initial exposure, so that the next time you read about these ideas in the book, you'll be able to memorize their salient points.

You can always refer back to this discussion if you need to do some quick memorization exercises when preparing for your exam. You'll notice that I've mentioned AWS comparisons where I could—if you are familiar with AWS, this may be beneficial for you. If you are not familiar with AWS, you're getting free multi-cloud knowledge. You can leave a tip at the door! It's important that a Google Cloud Architect understand multi-cloud deployments, so there's no reason to avoid discussing other major clouds in this book.

NOTE I need to shout out to Ryan Kroonenberg from A Cloud Guru for introducing me to this 10,000-foot overview concept; it's brilliant!

Lastly, there are hundreds and hundreds of concepts, products, and services in GCP—we'll cover those that you're most likely going to be tested on in the exam. As a Google Cloud Architect, you should go beyond the scope of this discussion in your job and familiarize yourself with the entire GCP portfolio.

EXAM TIP When you're done with this book, come back here and review this entire section to ensure that you know the function of each and every product outlined here. Remember that the exam will ask you for keywords that may differentiate similar solutions. For example, think about the various database types and get to know the differences between them as well as when to use each technology.

Compute Solutions

GCP includes various computing- and application-level offerings.

Google Compute Engine

Google Compute Engine (GCE) is an IaaS solution that enables users to launch virtual machines (VMs) on demand. With GCE, users manage the entire underlying infrastructure associated with the VM instances, including the machine types. VMs can be launched on predefined or custom machine sizes. GCE supports live migration, OS patch management, preemptible VMs (PVMs), and more. It is similar to Amazon Elastic Compute Cloud (EC2).

Preemptible Virtual Machine

Preemptible virtual machines (PVMs) are low-cost, short-term instances that are intended to run batch jobs and fault-tolerant workloads on Compute Engine. They offer significant cost savings, typically up to 80 percent, while still offering the same performance and capabilities of regular VMs. It is similar to Amazon EC2 Spot Instances.

Google App Engine

Google App Engine (GAE) is a PaaS solution that offers a fully managed, serverless application platform for building and deploying applications, without users having to manage the underlying infrastructure. With no server management and no configuration deployments, developers can focus on building applications. GAE supports popular development languages such as Go, Ruby, PHP, Java, Node.js, Python, C#, and .NET Framework, and you can bring your own language runtimes and frameworks. It is similar to AWS Elastic Beanstalk.

Google Kubernetes Engine

Google Kubernetes Engine (GKE) is a PaaS solution that offers a secure managed Kubernetes (K8s) service. GKE offers enterprise-ready containerized solutions with prebuilt deployment templates, enabling customers to ensure portability, with simplified licensing and consolidated billing. GKE is the direction that most modern enterprises and cloud-natives are heading, and although you may not encounter much about it on the exam, it's very important for the modern Google Cloud Architect to learn. It is similar to Amazon Elastic Kubernetes Service (EKS).

Cloud Run

Cloud Run is a PaaS solution that offers a fully managed compute platform for deploying and scaling containerized applications. Cloud Run eliminates infrastructure management and is able to scale up and down on demand, charging only for the exact resources used. It supports any language, library, or binary and is built upon the open standard Knative. It is similar to AWS Fargate.

Cloud Functions

Cloud Functions is a FaaS offering and is an event-driven, serverless computing platform. With Cloud Functions, you can run your code locally or in the cloud without having to provision any servers. It scales up or down on demand, so it is cost-effective, and you pay only for what you use. Developers can write code, and Google Cloud does the rest. It is similar to AWS Lambda.

 EXAM TIP Take a look at the actual Google Cloud products website and skim through it, check out some blog posts of people who've recently passed the exam, and gather as much data as you can. The exam is notorious for asking questions that are related to the certification subject matter but are not specific to GCP.

Storage Solutions

Various storage offerings are available on GCP.

Google Cloud Storage

Google Cloud Storage (GCS) is a globally unified, scalable, and highly durable object storage offering. It offers object life cycle management to move your data automatically to lower-cost storage classes based on criteria you define to optimize your cost. GCS is often used for content delivery, data lakes, and backup. It offers varying service level agreement (SLA) availability levels depending on the storage class, ranging from 99.0 to 99.95 percent. It is similar to Amazon Simple Storage Service (S3).

Cloud Filestore

Cloud Filestore provides high-performance, managed file storage for applications that require a file system. Like the Network File System (NFS) protocol, Filestore offers the ability to stand up a network-attached storage on your GCE or GKE instances. Filestore is highly consistent, fast, fully managed, and scalable using Elastifile to grow or shrink your clusters. Filestore offers a 99.9 percent SLA availability level. It is similar to Amazon Elastic File System (EFS).

Persistent Disk

Persistent Disk (PD) provides high-performance, durable block storage for solid-state drive (SSD) and hard disk drive (HDD) devices, which can be attached to GCE or GKE instances. Storage volumes can be resized and backed up and support simultaneous reads. It is similar to Amazon Elastic Block Store (EBS).

Local SSD

Local solid-state drives (SSDs) are high-performance, ephemeral block storage disks that are physically attached to the servers that host your VM instances. They offer superior performance, high input/output operations per second (IOPS), and ultra–low latency compared to other block storage options. They are typically used for temporary storage use cases such as caching or scratch processing space—think of workloads such as high-performance computing (HPC), media rendering, and data analytics. It is similar to Amazon EC2 SSD-based instance store volumes.

Database Solutions

Various database offerings are provided on GCP.

Cloud Bigtable

Cloud Bigtable is a fully managed and scalable NoSQL database for large analytical and operational workloads. It's able to handle millions of requests per second at a consistent sub-10ms latency. Bigtable is ideal for things like personalization engines, advertising technology (ad-tech), digital media, and Internet of Things (IoT), and it connects easily to other database services such as BigQuery and the Apache ecosystem. Bigtable offers a 99.99 percent SLA availability level. It is similar to Amazon DynamoDB.

Cloud SQL

Cloud SQL is a fully managed relational database for MySQL, PostgreSQL, and SQL Server, offering a simple integration from just about any application such as GCE, GKE, or GAE. You can use BigQuery to directly query your Cloud SQL databases. CloudSQL offers a 99.95 percent SLA availability level. It is similar to the Amazon Relational Database Service (RDS).

Cloud Spanner

Cloud Spanner is a fully managed, scalable, relational database for regionally and globally distributed application data. It offers the benefits of a relational database structure while scaling horizontally like a nonrelational database, allowing for strong consistency across rows, regions, and contents with a 99.999 percent SLA availability level. Cloud Spanner solved a major issue with traditional databases by eliminating the trade-off between scale and consistency with its horizontally scaling, low latency, and highly consistent characteristics. Cloud Spanner is similar to Amazon Aurora, but Aurora's biggest benefit is performance over RDS and MySQL/PostgreSQL compatibility. Cloud Spanner promises a high-performance, globally distributed RDBMS, which is not MySQL/PostgreSQL compatible.

Cloud Firestore

Cloud Firestore is a fully managed, fast, serverless, cloud-native NoSQL document database that is designed for mobile, web, and IoT applications at global scale. Firestore is the next generation of Datastore, which was the original highly scalable NoSQL database for mobile and web-based applications. Firestore offers a 99.999 percent SLA availability level. It is similar to Amazon DynamoDB. The key differentiator between Firestore and Bigtable is that Firestore is designed for mobile applications and Bigtable is designed for analytical workloads.

Memorystore

Memorystore is a scalable, secure, and highly available in-memory service for Redis and Memcached. It enables you to build application caches that provide sub-millisecond data access, and it's entirely compatible with open source Redis and Memcached. Memorystore provides a 99.9 percent SLA availability level. It is similar to Amazon ElastiCache.

Data Analytics

Various data analytics offerings are available on GCP.

BigQuery

BigQuery is a highly scalable, cost-effective serverless solution for data warehousing in the cloud. It enables you to analyze petabyte-scale data with zero operational overhead. BigQuery is one of Google Cloud's top products and is based on the Dremel query engine that Google developed. It has a 99.9 percent SLA availability level. There are no direct comparisons with AWS products, because BigQuery is an industry leader and is in a class of its own.

Dataproc

Dataproc is a fully managed data and analytics processing solution based on open source tools. You can build fully managed Apache Spark, Apache Hadoop, Presto, and other open source clusters. A very cost-effective solution, Dataproc is pay as you go and offers per-second pricing. It is similar to Amazon Elastic MapReduce and AWS Batch.

Dataflow

Dataflow is a serverless, cost-effective, unified stream and batch data processing service that is fully managed and supports the Apache Beam SDK and runs on a system of workers and jobs. If you see a question about Apache Beam on the exam, look for an answer that refers to Dataflow. It is similar to AWS Batch and Amazon Kinesis.

Pub/Sub

Pub/Sub is a global messaging and event ingestion solution that provides you a simple and reliable staging location for your event-based data before it gets processed, stored, and analyzed. Pub/Sub offers at-least-once delivery, exactly once processing, no provisioning, and is global by default. Pub/Sub offers a 99.95 percent SLA availability level. It is similar to Amazon Simple Queue Service (SQS), Amazon Simple Notification Service (SNS), and Amazon Kinesis.

Cloud Composer

Cloud Composer is a fully managed workflow orchestration service built on Apache Airflow that simplifies orchestration and empowers you to author, schedule, and monitor pipelines across clouds and on-premises environments. It is similar to AWS Data Pipeline and AWS Glue.

Networking Solutions

Various networking offerings are available on GCP.

Global Resources

Global resources can be accessed in any zone within the same project. These resources include such things as images, snapshots, Virtual Private Cloud (VPC) networks, firewalls, and their associated routes.

Region

Regions are independent geographic areas that contain multiple zones (or data centers). Regional resources offer redundancy by being deployed across multiple zones within a region. Some services, such as Datastore, BigQuery, Bigtable, and Cloud Storage, are distributed within and across regions—known as multiregional deployments.

Zone

Zones are deployment areas for resources within a region. One zone is typically a data center within a region and should be considered as a single failure domain. In fault-tolerant application deployments, the best practice is to deploy applications across multiple zones within a region, and ideally to deploy across multiple regions. If a zone becomes unavailable, all of the zonal resources will be unavailable until the services are restored.

Virtual Private Cloud

A virtual private cloud (VPC) is a virtual network that provides connectivity for resources within a project. Projects can contain multiple VPC networks, and by default new projects start with a default auto-mode VPC network that also includes one subnet in each region. Custom-mode VPC networks start with no subnet. VPC networks are global resources and are not associated with any particular region or zone.

Subnet

Subnets, or subnetworks, are logical partitions within a VPC network with one primary IP range and zero or more secondary IP ranges. Subnets are regional resources, and each subnet defines a range of IP addresses. You can create more than one subnet per region. When an auto-mode VPC network is created, one subnet from each region is automatically created within it using predefined IP ranges. When a custom-mode VPC network is created, no subnets are automatically created, giving you complete control over the subnets and IP ranges. Custom-mode VPC networks are better suited for enterprises and production environments.

Shared VPC

A Shared VPC network enables an organization to connect resources from multiple projects to the same VPC. This enables project resources to communicate securely using internal IP addressing from that network. In the Shared VPC model, you designate one project as a host project and attach one or more services projects to it. A shared VPC is referred to as "XPN" in the console and CLI.

Cloud DNS

Cloud DNS offers a reliable, resilient, low-latency authoritative Domain Name System (DNS) service that guarantees 100-percent availability. It provides automatic scaling, enabling users to create and update millions of DNS records. Cloud DNS is a simple and very cost-effective solution to individuals who host their own DNS servers or leverage other third-party DNS providers. It is similar to Amazon Route 53.

VPC Flow Logs

VPC Flow Logs are used for network monitoring, forensics, security analysis, and cost optimization. These logs provide a sample of network flows sent and received by VM instances or GKE nodes within a network. VPC Flow Logs can be very expensive to use, so it is not recommended to leave them on indefinitely.

Firewall

When deploying a VPC, you can use firewall rules to allow or deny connections to and from your application instances based on the rules you deploy. Each firewall rule can apply to ingress or egress connections, but not both. Rules are enforced at the instance level, but the configuration is associated with the VPC network—so you cannot share firewall rules among VPC networks, including peered networks. VPC firewall rules are stateful. Once a session has been established, firewall rules allow bidirectional traffic. It is similar to security groups in AWS.

Cloud Content Delivery Network

Cloud Content Delivery Network (CDN) is a fast, reliable web and video content delivery network with global scale and reach. It provides edge caches, known as points of presence (PoPs), that are peered with nearly every major Internet service provider (ISP) worldwide, and it uses the Anycast architecture to provide a single global IP address for global distribution. CDN leverages Google's proprietary fiber-optic backbone to carry network traffic globally.

Cloud Load Balancing

Google Cloud Load Balancer (GCLB) offers a fully distributed, high-performance, scalable load balancing service across GCP, with a variety of load balancer options. With GCLB, you get a single Anycast IP that fronts all your backend instances across the globe, including multiregion failover. In addition, software-defined load balancing services enable you to apply load balancing to your HTTP(S), TCP/SSL, and UDP traffic. You can also terminate your SSL traffic with an SSL proxy and HTTPS load balancing. Internal load balancing enables you to build highly available internal services for your internal instances without requiring any load balancers to be exposed to the Internet.

Cloud NAT

Cloud NAT is GCP's managed network address translation service that enables users to provision application instances without public IPs and to access the Internet for updates, patching, configuration management, and more. It does not allow outside resources to access any of the private instances behind the NAT gateway. Cloud NAT works with both GCE and GKE and offers regional high availability. It is similar to a NAT Gateway on AWS.

Cloud VPN

Cloud VPN enables users to connect their on-premises environment or other public cloud networks to their VPC networks securely over an encrypted IPSec virtual private network (VPN) tunnel for data bandwidth needs up to 3.0 Gbps. This is useful for low-volume data connections. It offers an incredible 99.99 percent availability. One of the newer features supported by Cloud VPN is the support of multiple tunnels; you can use this functionality to augment data bandwidth beyond 3.0 Gbps. It is similar to AWS Client VPN.

Cloud Interconnect

Cloud Interconnect offers an enterprise-grade connection to your VPC networks via either a Dedicated Interconnect or a Partner Interconnect. Using a Dedicated Interconnect, you can deploy a connection directly to a Google edge network, choosing between a 10-Gbps or 100-Gbps pipe. Using a Partner Interconnect, you can deploy a connection to Google through a supported third-party service provider, choosing between a 50-Mbps or 10-Gbps pipe. SLAs vary with regard to the type of connection you select. It is similar to AWS Direct Connect.

Peering

With peering, you can establish a direct connection between your network and Google while cutting egress fees, if you meet the requirements to connect directly with Direct Peering or through a partner with Carrier Peering. The recommended methods for accessing Google Cloud are through a Dedicated Interconnect or Partner Interconnect.

VPC Network Peering

VPC Network Peering enables internal IP address connectivity across two VPC networks, including VPC networks that do not belong to the same project or the same organization. VPC Network Peering enables two VPC networks to communicate internally on Google's software-defined network, and it does not traverse the public Internet. This is advantageous to using external IP addresses or VPNs to connect because it improves network latency and provides network security, as traffic does not get exposed to the Internet. It also minimizes costs; there are no egress costs because traffic communicates using internal IPs.

Private Google Access Options

There are four main access options for privately accessing Google Cloud: Private Google Access, Private Google Access for on-premises hosts, Private Services Access, and Serverless VPC Access. Each access option enables virtual machine instances that have internal IP addresses to access certain APIs and services. This is helpful for scenarios in which you don't want to assign an external IP address for your VM instances to connect to APIs or services outside of your internal network.

Operations Solutions

Various operations offerings are available on GCP.

Cloud Logging

Cloud Logging, previously known as Stackdriver Logging, is a real-time log management and analysis tool that enables you to store, search, analyze, monitor, and alert on log data and events. It allows for ingestion of any custom log data from any source and is a fully managed service. Integration into Cloud Monitoring enables you to define alerts based on certain metrics you select. It is similar to Amazon CloudWatch logs.

Cloud Monitoring

Cloud Monitoring is a full-stack, fully managed monitoring solution that gives you visibility into the performance, uptime, and overall health of your applications. It integrates with AWS out of the box, and it enables you to define custom metrics for key alerts your business is looking to monitor for. It is similar to Amazon CloudWatch monitoring.

Cloud Trace

Cloud Trace is a distributed tracing service that you can use to collect latency from your applications and track how requests propagate through your application. It can provide in-depth latency reports to surface performance issues, and it works across VMs, containers, or GAE projects. It is similar to AWS X-Ray.

Developer Tools

Various developer tools are available to us on GCP.

Cloud SDK

The Cloud SDK is a set of command-line tools and libraries that enable you to interact with Google Cloud products and services directly from the command line. The SDK supports popular languages such as Java, Python, NodeJS, Ruby, Go, .NET Framework, and PHP. The **gcloud** command-line tool is used for interacting with your cloud environment, along with other product-specific command-line tools such as **gsutil** for Cloud Storage, **bq** for BigQuery, and **kubectl** for GKE.

Cloud Source Repositories

Cloud Source Repositories is a private Git repository service that you can use to design, develop, and securely manage your code. It enables you to extend your Git workflow by connecting to other tools such as publish/subscribe (pub/sub) messaging, Cloud Monitoring, Cloud Logging, and more. You can mirror code from GitHub or BitBucket to get powerful code search, browsing, and diagnostic capabilities. You can also use regular expressions to refine your search across the directories.

Container Registry

Container Registry is a private Docker repository that enables you to store, manage, and secure your Docker container images. You can also perform vulnerability analysis and manage access control to the container images. With Container Registry, you can integrate your continuous integration/continuous delivery (CI/CD) pipelines to design fully automated Docker pipelines. It is similar to JFrog Artifactory or Amazon Elastic Container Registry (ECR).

Hybrid Cloud and Multi-Cloud Solutions

Several hybrid cloud and multi-cloud offerings are available on GCP.

Anthos

Anthos is a fairly new offering from Google Cloud. It is Google Cloud's solution to the increasing need for hybrid and multi-cloud PaaS requirements and for preventing vendor lock-in. With Anthos, you can run, manage, and govern applications in a hybrid or multi-cloud environment. Anthos GKE enables you to run enterprise-grade container orchestration and management in cloud and on-premises environments.

With Anthos Config Management, you can govern configuration policies across your environments. Anthos Service Mesh (powered by Istio) is a service mesh architecture that eliminates a lot of networking and traffic routing concerns by leveraging mutual Transport Layer Security (mTLS) to secure your service-to-service or end user–to–service communications, so that your developers can focus on building applications. It also lets you easily make role-based access controls and fine-grained access controls. Anthos Security is a tool that enables you to define and enforce security controls across your environments.

Migration Solutions

Various migration offerings are available on GCP.

Storage Transfer Service

Using Storage Transfer Service, you can complete large-scale online data transfers to your Cloud Storage buckets. Use Google's high-bandwidth network pipes to leverage ultra-high-speed connections to transfer petabyte-scale data—if you have a strong network yourself. For massive scale data transfers, it is advised that you use a transfer appliance. It is similar to AWS DataSync.

Transfer Appliance

Transfer Appliance is a physical device that Google provides in increments of either 100TB or 480TB models that enable you to accelerate the speed at which you transfer data to Google Cloud. It is similar to AWS Snowball.

Security and Identity Solutions

Various security offerings are available on GCP.

Cloud Asset Inventory

Cloud Asset Inventory is a metadata inventory service that enables you to view, monitor, and analyze all of your GCP resources and policies. You can export your entire inventory, analyze changes, build real-time notification when assets are changed, and sift through your resources and identity and access management (IAM) policies. It gives you a deep and detailed view of all the resource metadata and is similar to AWS Config.

Security Command Center

Security Command Center is a security management and data risk platform that provides a straightforward view of your cloud security vulnerabilities, threats, and compliance issues. Security Command Center includes an underlying suite of tools that provide all the logic for its capabilities, some of which come only with the paid premium version. Security Health Analytics does scanning for security misconfigurations and compliance violations. Event Threat Detection does log-based threat detection using Google's threat intelligence engine. Web Security Scanner identifies common web-based vulnerabilities on public-facing endpoints. All detections are surfaced as "Findings" into the Security Command Center dashboard, and all the findings can be exported into a customer's security information and event management (SIEM) platform.

Cloud Audit Logs

Cloud Audit Logs give you visibility into all user activity in your Google Cloud. It provides a full view of all administrative activities, access to data, and a hardened, always-on trail that cannot be disabled. Audit trails are immutable and reside in highly protected storage. You can leverage these logs for incident management and to track user activity for your security operations teams. This is similar to AWS CloudTrail.

VPC Service Controls

VPC Service Controls enable you to define a security perimeter for constraining your managed GCP services such as Cloud Storage, BigQuery, and Bigtable to your VPC network, so that you can ensure that malicious users cannot exfiltrate data in the event of a misconfigured access control or configuration.

Access Transparency

Access Transparency logs are near-real-time logs that show you when a Google administrator accesses your data. Though Cloud Audit Logs provide visibility into the actions of the privileged users in your environment, sometimes Google administrators may need to access your environment (for example, to respond to an outage, or when you opened up a support ticket that required data access). These events are logged as Access Transparency logs.

Cloud Data Loss Prevention

Cloud Data Loss Prevention (DLP) is a fully managed service that minimizes the risk of data exfiltration by enabling you to discover, classify, and protect your sensitive data. With Cloud DLP, you can use de-identification methods with streaming and stored data, and you can also continuously scan for environments where data does not meet your classification requirements.

Cloud Key Management Service

With Cloud Key Management Service (KMS), you can manage your cryptographic keys on Google Cloud. KMS offers the ability to generate and manage the key encryption keys (KEKs) that protect sensitive data by using customer-managed encryption keys (CMEKs). KMS also supports customer-supplied encryption keys, although that service has not seen much development and may be replaced by External Key Manager (EKM), a service that will enable you to store your own supplied encryption keys at a third-party colocation. KMS has integration with Cloud HSM, enabling you the ability to create a key protected by a Federal Information Processing Standards (FIPS) 140-2 Level 3 device.

Cloud HSM

Cloud HSM is a managed, cloud-hosted hardware security module (HSM) that enables you to protect your cryptographic keys in a FIPS 140-2 Level 3–certified HSM. This is critical for financial services customers who need to meet compliance requirements, for example. HSM easily integrates with Cloud KMS, and you pay for what you use.

Interacting with the GCP

You can interact with the GCP in several ways: via the Google Cloud Console, via the command-line interface (CLI), and via client libraries. As a cloud architect, you should have hands-on experience interacting with the platform through all three mechanisms.

Google Cloud Console

You can use a web-based GUI to manage your projects and resources. Within the Cloud Console, you can also access the Cloud Shell, which enables you to manage Google Cloud projects and perform more complex development tasks. You can SSH into your instances directly though the browser. With both a native iOS and Android application, you can perform some functionality on the go.

Command-Line Interface

For users who prefer to work in a terminal environment, the Google Cloud SDK provides the **gcloud** command-line tool that gives you access to a more familiar interface for engineers. You can use **gcloud** for both your development workflow and your GCP resources.

Other important tools to know for the exam (and that we'll cover later in the book) are the **bq**, **gsutil**, and **kubectl** command-line tools. You may see a few questions on the exam regarding syntax of these tools, so it's a great idea to review the reference links included in the "Additional References" section later in this chapter. Here is a quick reference guide:

- **gcloud** is the primary command-line tool to create and manage resources:

  ```
  gcloud GROUP | COMMAND
  ```

- **bq** is the BigQuery command-line tool. You probably won't see questions about this on the exam, but remember that **bq** = BigQuery.

  ```
  bq --global_flag argument bq_command --command-specific_flag argument
  ```

- **cbt** is the Cloud Bigtable command-line tool. You probably won't see questions about this on the exam, but remember that **cbt** = Cloud Bigtable.

  ```
  cbt [-<option> <option-argument>] <command> <required-argument>
  [optional-argument]
  ```

- **gsutil** is the Google Cloud Storage command-line tool:

  ```
  gsutil [command] [OPTIONS] [BUCKET_NAME]/[OBJECT_NAME]
  ```

- **kubectl** is the Kubernetes command-line tool:

  ```
  kubectl [command] [TYPE] [NAME] [flags]
  ```

EXAM TIP You may see a question about how to use the command line to make a change to a GCS bucket. If you have four answers, two of which start with **bq** and two of which start with **gs**, you can immediately eliminate two of those answers from the question, as **bq** would not be the correct syntax to use here.

Exercise 2-1: CLI Example

In this exercise we're going to use the **gcloud** command-line tool to perform pub/sub messaging operations. We'll create a topic, subscribe to the topic, publish a message, and receive the message.

NOTE Before you begin, take a look at the "gcloud pubsub" section in the gcloud reference guide at https://cloud.google.com/sdk/gcloud/reference/pubsub.

Syntax:

```
gcloud pubsub GROUP [GCLOUD_WIDE_FLAG ...]
```

1. Initialize the Cloud SDK:

```
gcloud init
```

2. Create a topic:

```
gcloud pubsub topics create my-topic
```

3. Subscribe to the topic:

```
gcloud pubsub subscriptions create --topic my-topic my-sub
```

4. Publish a message to the topic:

```
gcloud pubsub topics publish my-topic --message "hello"
```

5. Receive the message:

```
gcloud pubsub subscriptions pull --auto-ack my-sub
```

Client Libraries

With client libraries you can call Google Cloud APIs by exposing application APIs and administrative APIs. You can also use the Google API client library to access APIs for products such as Google Maps, Google Drive, and YouTube. Application APIs provide access to services. They're optimized to support languages such as Node.js and Python. Use administrative APIs to manage your resources.

Business and Technical Context for the Google Cloud Architect

A vitally important skill for a cloud architect, beyond being a senior engineer, is the ability to understand business objectives and translate those into requirements and design cues. Remember that a cloud architect is the most trusted advisor to an organization's business and technical leaders. You should be an excellent collaborator on both sides of the organization and should be able to convert the organization's needs into tangible solutions. It's not the technology that pays your salary, after all; the business does that. And without a business, there is no technology.

EXAM TIP The biggest element of the Google Cloud Professional Cloud Architect exam is your ability to understand and look for business goals and technical requirements. You'll be presented with scenario-based questions as well as questions based on case studies. As you're reading through the questions, carefully look for keywords that describe elements of the solution. Once you start to parse through a question and gather all of the keywords, make mental bullet-point notes (as I don't believe you're given paper and pencil for this exam) of all these words and phrases, because they'll help you sift through the answers presented.

Assessing Business Requirements

Business requirements are typically broader objectives that are necessary for a business to achieve an operational goal. These may include requirements about reducing expenditures, improving the organization's security, improving data reliability, reducing downtime, minimizing disruptions to services or the impacts of an incident, and so on. Think about how you can capture all of these important business elements when you're assessing a problem or in the room with a stakeholder. A more seasoned cloud architect will know how to probe for important requirements in discovery from stakeholders, rather than waiting on stakeholders to define them. Oftentimes, the stakeholders don't have their requirements entirely fleshed out.

Reducing Expenditures

One of the biggest value points in moving to the cloud is the ability to convert your capital expenditures into operational expenditures. In traditional computing, the business's capital expenditures (CapEx) relate to the money spent up-front on buying servers and equipment, which you'd hope to use for years and years to come. Depreciation, maintenance, and the rapid pace of technology often render hardware obsolete, and this makes traditional capital expenditures a tough challenge in the on-premises environment. With the shift to the cloud, businesses are able to convert their capital expenditures into operational expenditures (OpEx) by paying for services as they're consumed and only for what they consume. Although that can make the cost of your technology cheaper, it doesn't mean companies should stop optimizing their OpEx. It's very important that a business experiences financial gain by investing in the cloud, which is known as the return on investment (ROI). Typically, as companies are looking to move to the cloud, the chief financial officer (CFO) is looking to understand what will be the total cost of ownership (TCO), or the total cost of all the direct and indirect technologies.

 EXAM TIP You'll see several questions on the exam that mention the words "most cost-effective" or something similar. This is an example of a key phrase that will help you identify a potential solution.

There are many ways to save money in the cloud. Some engineering teams may be accustomed to setting up an entire VM infrastructure just to perform some services that could easily be done through a managed service. Imagine, for example, that you have to trigger a batch job based on an event that gets published in pub/sub, where you may have considered setting up a VM to trigger this job. You have to pay for all the costs of your VM infrastructure, and you have to pay for all the labor-hours of your resources who are maintaining this VM environment. You have a lot more security overhead to manage, and your VMs don't automatically know to spin up and spin down when a job has been triggered. In such a scenario, you could substitute an entire VM-based architecture for a managed service (Cloud Functions) or even for a preemptible VM. Preemptible VMs may be a great option to save money in this case, because they're designed for short-lived batch jobs or fault-tolerant workloads and are up to 80 percent cheaper than normal VMs.

EXAM TIP When you see questions on your exam that mention "cost-efficiency," think about managed services, serverless services, and things like preemptible VMs.

SLIs, SLOs, SLAs... So What?!

It's very important that you understand the level of service that you offer your users. It's almost impossible to manage a service well if you don't know what is important for that service and how to measure its behavior. To that end, it's important that you understand service level indicators (SLIs), service level objectives (SLOs), and service level agreements (SLAs). You may not see a question on the exam that asks you to define SLIs and SLOs, but you may be presented with a data point or a requirement indicating that the business is looking to maintain or achieve a higher SLA with a new architecture. SLA seems to be a broad term that the industry uses to represent a variety of meanings, so let's break down these three terms here.

A *service level indicator* is a quantitative measure of a chosen characteristic of the level of service that is provided from a product or service. If the characteristic is availability, the SLI could be a percentage of time, often expressed in the number of "nines" (for example, 99.99 percent is "four nines"). Remember that SLA does not mean service level availability—it means service level agreement, even though the availability is oftentimes expressed in the agreement. The actual number itself, or the range of numbers, is the *service level objective*. If we're expecting 99.999 percent availability for a system, "five nines" is our objective and the availability is our measure. What's left if we don't meet these requirements is described in our *service level agreement*. The SLA is a contract that describes the expectations and consequences of meeting or missing an SLO. For example, if Google Cloud Storage doesn't meet its availability targets of 99.95 percent (for the storage class—there are other SLOs for other storage classes), customers are eligible to receive financial credits of a percentage of the monthly bill for the service.

In short, the SLI is the indicator, the measure itself—availability, error rate, and so on. The SLO is the objective, the numerical value that describes the expectation of the measure—99.99 percent availability, 2 to 5 percent error rate, and so on. And the SLA is the agreement, the contracted expectations of using the product or service and what happens if the objectives aren't met. Remember how important reliability is to a successful product and business, and think about how you can use these acronyms effectively in your business meetings.

Assessing Technical Requirements

Technical requirements are based on the functional and nonfunctional requirements of a system that were defined in Chapter 1. As a refresher, functional requirements are the "what"—what is the system supposed to do? For example, the system needs to extract data from this API and load it into a storage bucket, or the system needs to process orders in this format. Nonfunctional requirements are the "how"—how should my system perform? How do we deal with the constraints? For example, the system needs to process at least X amount of data objects per second. It's not so important that you understand the difference between functional and nonfunctional requirements on the exam because you're just parsing for technical requirements, but this is helpful in your day-to-day work as a cloud architect.

Exam Strategies

On the exam, you'll be tested on technical requirements after being presented with questions that are based on case studies or scenario-based questions. I've got some strategies you can use, so let's start by looking at the technical requirements from the Mountkirk Games case study, as presented in the "Case Studies" section of Chapter 1.

Case Study–Based Questions   If you refer back to the solution concept on the full case study, you know that the plan is to deploy a new game on Compute Engine and also to leverage a managed NoSQL database. Dynamically scaling the game up or down provides both cost savings and scalability. Scaling up enables the game to support new users as needed without engineering bottlenecks. Scaling down enables the system to save on expensive and unnecessary resource costs. Although many other services dynamically scale up and down, including managed services that cost less than GCE, the case study stated in the solutions concept that the company has decided to build this on Compute Engine. For the sake of this exam, you won't have to sway the exam writers in another direction for the answers. There are much better solutions in the real world than using GCE here, but we'll save that one for another time. In this case, using managed instance groups (MIGs) on GCE would be useful, because MIGs provide autoscaling that automatically adds or deletes instances based on load.

For the second requirement, Mountkirk Games is looking to connect to a transactional database to manage user profiles and game state. The company also wants to integrate with a managed NoSQL database. Firestore (or Cloud Datastore if the exam uses the old terminology) would be a great solution here, because it's a highly scalable NoSQL database built for global applications.

For the third requirement, Mountkirk Games wants to store game activity in a time-series database for future analysis. Immediately Bigtable comes to mind, because Bigtable is a time-series database, but ultra-low latency is not important here because the company wants to store the game activity "for future analysis." BigQuery is another time-series database, and Mountkirk Games wants to query 10TB of historical data on its analytics platform. Tricky, right? You can't get an answer just by reading one line. You know that the company wants to store the data for future analysis in one requirement, and it wants to query 10TB of historical data in another requirement. For that reason, BigQuery is the right answer here.

If you read one keyword and think you can come to a conclusion, hold your horses—and keep reading for additional data points. You might have a feasible solution, and then come across another requirement that completely changes that answer, and that initial solution you thought of may be one of the answers they trick you with on the exam! So be careful as you work through your questions.

(continued)

Scenario-Based Questions   Consider the following test scenario:

> CatSnap, a popular cat videos application, wants to build a solution that enables its extended workforce—contractors and temporary staff—to access an environment in which they can upload and download marketing materials for the marketing team.

How do you turn this into a solution? A lot more information is needed here. Luckily, on the exam, you'll get all of the information you need (though in real life, you'll have to probe a little deeper).

Here's an example of a scenario-based question:

> CatSnap, a popular cat videos application, needs to store 50TB of data in an environment where it can share it with extended staff that does not have CatSnap credentials, so that these staff members can upload and download marketing materials that they will be editing. The data needs to have non-repudiation of who accessed it for auditing and monitoring, and data that is older than six months needs to be moved to an archive, where it'll be accessed at most once a year. What is the most secure, cost-effective, and fastest way to do this?
>
> **A.** Provision a private GCS bucket, apply object life cycle policies to move it to coldline after six months, onboard the extended workforce with a CatSnap identity account, and enable bucket logging for the security team to review.
>
> **B.** Provision a private GCS bucket, apply object life cycle policies to move it to archive after six months, onboard the extended workforce with a CatSnap identity account, and enable bucket logging for the security team to review.
>
> **C.** Provision a private GCS bucket, apply object life cycle policies to move it to coldline after six months, enable data owners to create signed URLs that will be provided to the extended workforce as needed, and enable bucket logging for the security team to review.
>
> **D.** Provision a private GCS bucket, apply object life cycle policies to move it to archive after six months, enable data owners to create signed URLs that will be provided to the extended workforce as needed, and enable bucket logging for the security team to review.

So here's what you'd want to parse from this question:

- 50TB of object storage
- Shared user environment
- Untrusted users without credentials

- Upload and download permissions
- Nonrepudiation of each audit log entry
- After six months, move to a new storage class
- Archive is accessed once a year
- Most secure
- Cost-effective
- Fastest

You may have an answer already, but if you look at the four potential answers provided, you can identify another pattern and gather another data point:

- Provisioning a private GCS bucket is a given across all answers.
- Applying object life cycle policies is next, but what's the difference between coldline and archive storage classes? Well, if you knew that the data is accessed once a year and they're looking for the most cost-effective solution, it sounds like archive is the answer here. Coldline would still work, though, because you can access it once a year or more as well, but the key words here are "most... cost-effective."
- Ah, here's an interesting one—do we onboard and provision users with CatSnap identities, or do we use signed URLs? It says the fastest way, so granting signed URLs is the fastest way here. But wait, there's also a requirement of nonrepudiation of all user accesses, so can I have nonrepudiation if my users are using signed URLs? That requirement is an example of a distractor: "fastest" doesn't matter here, because the fastest solution does not satisfy all requirements.
- Bucket logging is enabled across all four answers.

As you start to dissect each exam question, you'll need to have this mind-set: What are patterns I can identify? Where can I find more requirements or keywords in my questions and in the answers provided? How can I eliminate multiple questions at once? While all four of the answers are technically correct, at the end of the day, if you parse through this question properly, the answer should be B, because you cannot use signed URLs as a means to prove nonrepudiation of all the users who could be accessing your data.

Chapter Review

This long chapter provided an overview of a wide variety of complex concepts, including the basics of cloud computing. When you're done reading this book, come back to this chapter and review it to ensure that you know this information. The rest of the book will be more focused on one cloud concept at a time.

This chapter discussed a philosophical overview of your profession and why it's so important for you to think outside of the box of your job. You're on the path to becoming (or already are) someone who designs systems that can fundamentally change society. Beyond your job, think about the moral and ethical duty you have to ensure that the work you do serves a positive purpose to society and to ensure that your voice is always heard as a rational voice in a room with stakeholders who may be a bit one-sided.

We also covered a quick overview of cloud computing, much of which you already know, and discussed some of the key differences between Google Cloud and the other public clouds. Remember that security, open cloud, analytics and AI, and Google's massive global private network are some of the key differentiators between Google, AWS, and Azure. Think about how you structure your conversations with your stakeholders when it comes to deciding where to develop your workloads if you work in a multi-cloud environment. For the exam, you most likely won't see any questions around this topic.

We took a 10,000-foot overview of the Google Cloud Platform products and services that are most likely to be the focus of your exam, as well as the ways you can manage your cloud. It's important that you understand all the Google technologies identified in this chapter, though this discussion is not inclusive of all that could be on your exam (in other words, additional things may show up on your exam).

Lastly, we discussed the mind-set you'll need when attending meetings or taking the exam and parsing for business and technical requirements. Work on some practice questions and try to understand how certain words may trigger an entirely different meaning for your solution. Unfortunately, the exam can be more difficult for non-English speakers or non-Japanese speakers, because the exam is offered in only those two languages as of this writing. But don't fret, because you're doing great, and you're going to know a lot about Google Cloud Platform by the end of this book.

Additional References

If you'd like more information about the topics discussed in this chapter, check out these sources:

- **Google Cloud Architecture Framework**   https://cloud.google.com/architecture/framework
- **Google Cloud Adoption Framework**   https://cloud.google.com/adoption-framework
- **Kubernetes CLI**   https://kubernetes.io/docs/reference/kubectl/overview/#syntax
- **gsutil Tool**   https://cloud.google.com/storage/docs/gsutil
- **bq CLI**   https://cloud.google.com/bigquery/docs/bq-command-line-tool
- **gcloud CLI**   https://cloud.google.com/sdk/gcloud/reference
- **Jayendra Patil's PCA Blog Post**   https://jayendrapatil.com/google-cloud-professional-cloud-architect-certification-learning-path/

Questions

1. You are looking to buy a new computer for personal use. You want a powerful enough computer to surf websites and run (mostly gaming) applications. But you realize that you are short on cash. What computer should you buy?

   A. MacBook Pro

   B. Chromebook

   C. Windows 10 desktop

   D. Windows 10 laptop

2. Your company has made plans to roll out OpenShift, a Kubernetes platform solution offered by IBM Red Hat, across all its on-premises and public cloud environments. Given that you are the lead architect responsible for your company's GCP deployments, what type of shared responsibility model will this deployment entail for you?

   A. On-premises

   B. IaaS

   C. PaaS

   D. SaaS

3. VPC networks are:

   A. Global

   B. Regional

   C. Zonal

   D. Local

4. Subnets are:

   A. Global

   B. Regional

   C. Zonal

   D. Local

5. You need to attach high-performance storage with very high IOPS and low latency to your VM instance. Which technology should you use?

   A. Google Cloud Storage

   B. Local SSD

   C. Cloud FileStore

   D. Persistent SSD disk

6. Google's operational excellence principle demands the building of a foundation to enable reliability successfully across your infrastructure by efficiently running, managing, and monitoring systems that deliver business value. Which of the following is not a key strategy that drives this principle?

   A. End-to-end automation

   B. Monitoring business objectives

   C. Performance and cost optimization

   D. Disaster recovery

7. Which of the following service level measures are considered a legally enforceable contract between the service provider and the service consumer?

   A. SLA

   B. SLE

   C. SLO

   D. SLI

8. Your development team is building a new business-critical application using virtual machines to be deployed in a dedicated production project. As part of this effort, the team is looking to implement a dedicated application testing environment within a development project. The tests generally take less than an hour to complete. They need to keep the testing machine costs low, but consistent with their production environment. Which type of virtual machine optimization strategy would you use for their testing project environment?

   A. Use sole-tenant nodes.

   B. Automate the VM life cycle.

   C. Use preemptible VMs.

   D. Use purchase commitments.

9. Which Google Cloud Platform database offering is best suited for integration with client-side mobile and web applications, gaming leaderboards, and user presence at global scale?

   A. BigQuery

   B. Cloud Memorystore

   C. Cloud Bigtable

   D. Cloud Firestore

10. You decide to use GCP to host a simple website using Drupal Content Management from Google Cloud Platform Marketplace to run a Google Compute Engine VM instance. You have global ambitions but a limited budget. What feature would you enable to provide a better experience to your global audience?

   A. Cloud Interconnect

   B. Cloud DNS

   C. Cloud CDN

   D. Cloud Load Balancer

Answers

1. **C.** This question is about parsing requirements. First, the requirement of surfing websites can be accommodated by all the computers listed. Second, running locally installed applications, including games, eliminates Chromebook from the picture and even the MacBook. Third, you have a requirement for the most performance with the least cost. Lastly, while both the Windows desktop and laptop seem to be strong answers, the prerequisite knowledge of the gaming PC space will help you answer this question effectively, making the Windows desktop the best answer, because these computers typically offer the most bang for the buck. You'll see questions on the exam that are very tricky, just like this one.

2. **B.** The key to remember here is that for a service provided (GCP in this case) to take responsibility for its PaaS, it must offer the service as a managed service. GCP offers its own Kubernetes platform called GKE. But OpenShift is not a Google-offered PaaS solution. As such, Google will not take responsibility for the backend operations and design of your OpenShift environments. You will need to manage all the VMs that OpenShift will provision as part of its GCP deployment. So this is an IaaS deployment from a shared responsibility model perspective.

3. **A.** VPC networks are global in GCP. Most questions on the exam are multilayered. So you will generally not get a straight question like this. Knowing this element will help you answer multilayered questions more effectively.

4. **B.** Subnets are regional within GCP. That means that you can create instances within your subnet across multiple zones. Keep that in mind when building highly available solutions. Many other cloud service providers support only zonal subnets.

5. **B.** From a storage perspective, you can attach each of the provided answers to your VMs. Google Cloud Storage can be mounted to a VM. But this is not the highest performer. The highest performance possible is achieved when the storage is included with the CPU and not attached via the network. The only answer that satisfies that criteria is Local SSD. Its read and write IOPS are almost ten times higher than persistent network attached storage options.

6. C. Operational excellence does not include performance and cost optimization; that is a different system design principle.

7. A. A service level agreement (SLA) is an enforceable legal contract between a service provider and a service customer. A service level indicator (SLI) is a measure of the service level provided by a service provider to a customer. SLIs form the basis of service level objectives (SLOs), which in turn form the basis of SLAs. In this way, SLAs define the level of service expected by a customer from a supplier, laying out the metrics by which that service is measured and the remedies or penalties, if any, should the agreed-upon service levels not be achieved.

8. B. This is typically the type of question you might see on the exam. You're provided a set of requirements that can often be met by a number of approaches. Between B and C, there are many cost savings. In fact, I would try to use automated preemptible VMs to get the most bang for my dollars. Preemptible machines give you up to 80 percent off and would satisfy the ability to use the same type of machines as the production systems (as do purchase commitments). Furthermore, with a one-hour timetable to run your tests, preemptible VMs are ideal. Even if you get preempted, you can try again later. If you automate your VM life cycle, you immediately get about a 96 percent savings. That means you run the machine for only 1 hour of 24 hours a day. The ideal answer in real life could be to use both preemptible instances and VM life cycle management as part of an automated CICD build and test process. But that is not how the question presented things. So the biggest contributor to cost savings would be automation of the VM life cycle.

9. D. You can argue that certain database technologies are cross-purpose and could be deployed in other situations. You would be right. But, again, the key to passing the test is to provide the best answer based on the key information presented. Firestore would be the best database to integrate with mobile and web apps.

10. C. The only answer that helps with the content distribution is Cloud CDN (Content Delivery Network). Although DNS may be in use, it won't make an impact on the global audience, which this question is asking for. Furthermore, since this is a simple VM, adding a load balancer to the architecture does not buy you anything. To leverage a load balancer, you would want multiple VMs within multiple regions, which is clearly not the case in this question.

Cloud Identity

In this chapter, we'll cover

- Setting up Cloud Identity
- Compliance requirements for the exam
- Key security principles of access management
- Setting up Cloud Identity in your Google Cloud environment
- Authenticating into your Google Cloud environment
- Provisioning and auditing users

In earlier chapters, I promised that I'd provide information to help you be successful as a cloud architect—beyond what you need to know for the exam. In this chapter, we'll step into building a Google Cloud environment, and that starts with you signing up for your first administrative account on the Google Cloud Platform (GCP). To do this, you'll need to head to cloud.google.com and look for the Get Started or sign-up button.

Setting Up a Cloud Identity and Admin Account

After you've scrolled through the various pages of sales pitches telling you why you should try out the GCP, you can begin the process of setting up a Cloud Identity and signing up for an administrator account. You'll be required to agree to a few click-through agreements.

Click-through agreements are legally enforceable online contracts that indicate user consent; you've likely encountered many of these, because every time you sign up for a new service or a privacy policy is updated, you have to agree to abide by or acknowledge certain requirements in click-through agreements. Whether or not you decide to read the many pages of click-through agreements, you should understand their importance and your organization's stance on your entering into a contract in this way. Some companies, such as highly regulated companies, will require that legal counsel review any contracts, including click-through agreements, before you agree to them. In addition, a ton of legal and contracting work goes into a sales deal before a customer can launch the GCP environment.

Compliance Requirement Scenarios and the Exam

You'll see scenario-based questions about compliance requirements on the exam. Here's an example of a scenario where understanding agreements is important in your role as a cloud architect: A question may describe a scenario in which you're an enterprise architect for a healthcare company, and you are required to abide by the European Union General Data Protection Regulation (EU GDPR). The GDPR dictates how data must be protected and how data privacy must be ensured. One of its requirements states that personal data within the European Union cannot leave the European Union.

In the scenario, you're required to use a tool to perform message queueing and delivery, but you'll also be required to ensure that data can persist in its region no matter what, even if there is a service outage (to meet GDPR requirements). The question then asks you to choose between the Apache Kafka or Pub/Sub messaging systems. What architecture do you design?

For this question, you'll need to know that Pub/Sub is a global service, and its contract agreements state that, because of its global availability, if a region goes down, Pub/Sub will route data through other regions to maintain its high availability. This conflicts with your GDPR compliance requirements, so you may want to choose Kafka in this case, which offers you more control over the architecture versus a managed service. (Note that I threw a curveball here, because Pub/Sub now supports controlling where your message data is stored.)

 EXAM TIP You will see questions about general compliance requirements, so it's a good idea to brush up on the top compliance frameworks in the industry, such as the European Union General Data Protection Regulation (EU GDPR) and others.

Cloud Identity is an Identity as a Service (IDaaS) solution that provides a unified identity, access, application, and endpoint management platform. It offers a variety of avenues to enable various users consuming GCP to connect and access resources. When you sign up for GCP, you'll create an administrator account that will have access and ownership of your Cloud Identity, and you'll have to set up a billing account. For a single user or small company, this is pretty straightforward. For an enterprise, the process can get pretty complex. You can create multiple billing accounts, depending on the size of your organization. For a huge, multinational company, with dozens of subsidiaries under its umbrella, for example, it would not make sense for one administrator to be responsible for paying all the bills for all the subsidiaries. Your organization's Cloud Billing account pays for Google Cloud projects and Google Maps Platform projects, and it can be linked to one or more projects.

During the Cloud Identity setup process, you'll be asked to add your domain, verify your domain with Domain Name System (DNS) records, and then create your Cloud

Identity users. Typically, a text (TXT) record will be automatically generated in your DNS records to verify your domain, but you may sometimes have to do this manually. You may be working at an enterprise that is spinning out new organizations, for example, or that has not yet adopted GCP, so you'll need to enter a vast amount of information.

EXAM TIP The Google certification exams are typically not updated every time a new feature is released, because cloud computing evolves so quickly. Be aware that you may see questions on an exam that may no longer be entirely accurate because of the rapid feature releases of the cloud products. The likelihood of seeing an exam question about a deprecated or changed feature is pretty slim, however. But you'll need to choose the right answer no matter what.

Security Principles in the Cloud

With the advent of cloud computing comes a new paradigm for how enterprises build and manage their technology stack. In the pre-cloud, traditional computing world, we thought about computing as a multitiered, or n-tiered, architecture, where the frontend served content, the middle tier handled application logic, and the backend was typically reserved for the database or data stores.

In the traditional monolithic application model, identity and access management (IAM) was typically brokered within the application. If a malicious user gained access to an application, he would have full access to everything within the monolith. With the rise of service-to-service communications is a reinvigorated emphasis on following the principles of least privilege and separation of duties, as applications are broken down into *microservices*. While this may increase the complexity of the enterprise architecture in some ways, it minimizes the threat surface, because authorization is required to grant access to services. Because these services are divided into smaller, loosely coupled chunks of work, or microservices, they hold fewer responsibilities. The same security principles apply in the cloud and are, at the core, the most important security controls for preventing malicious activity. As you design solutions for the cloud, think about how a hostile actor may gain access to a service, and think about how you could minimize the impact if a service were compromised.

The AAA Security Model

Authentication, authorization, and accounting (AAA) security is one of the core principles of security in the cloud:

- **Authentication**   The act of proving your identity; this is often referred to as identity assertion.

- **Authorization**   A set of privileges (known as permissions in GCP) that grants a user access to certain resources. I refer to this as "access management" in this book.

- **Accounting**   A process (typically referred to as *auditing* in GCP) that ensures that a digital log accounts for every user's access and that these logs are immutable, or unable to be tampered with. These GCP resource access logs are typically stored in Cloud Audit Logs at the platform level, but applications also have their own form of audit trails that could be stored in system logs, application logs, and more.

Let's look at an example of how AAA works. Suppose, for example, that you walk into your office wearing your employee ID badge that your company gave you. You walk to the kitchen, only to find that the snack cabinet is empty, but you know that the management team has secret snack room. You use your badge to try to get in to grab a snack, but you can't, because you're not authorized to enter the room because you're not part of the management team, darn it. Unfortunately, the security team now knows that your badge was used to attempt to open a door you weren't authorized to use.

Later, after you've had one too many drinks at a happy hour after work, you're still wearing your badge, and you're bragging about the unreleased Banana Phone X under your desk to your teammates. John the Ripper, a cyber criminal, overhears your conversation and realizes how much money he could make if he could get his hands on the unreleased Banana Phone X. He slips your badge into his pocket with a simple sleight of hand and walks out of the bar. He now holds your ID badge, and all the privileges associated with it, and plans to go to your office, find your desk, and steal the Banana Phone X to resell it on the black market. But when John the Ripper tries to badge in, he is prompted to authenticate his identity with a fingerprint scan. Now he's out of luck. He has encountered *multifactor authentication* (MFA), which is known as 2-Step Verification (2SV) in GCP. In this type of authentication, the factors could be a combination of two of more of the following: something you know (such as a password or PIN), something you have (such as your badge), or something you are (such as your fingerprint). MFA security increases the confidence that a user is who he says he is.

In this case, when John the Ripper unsuccessfully attempts to access your office, the badge reader logs that attempt (accounting). When you report to your security team that your badge was stolen, and they look through their audit logs at the login attempts, they see an unsuccessful attempt with your badge on Tuesday at 7:43 A.M. So they look through the video footage and put together a story to report to law enforcement. This is the concept of *nonrepudiation,* which assures that someone cannot deny something. With the video recording of his face and the audit log of his access attempt, John the Ripper cannot deny that he attempted to enter the building with a stolen badge.

Now imagine you're a multinational and multiorganizational company with offices all over the world with varying levels of requirements of who can access what, when, and how. How exactly do you ensure you've implemented a unified and secure authentication and access management system across the globe? Now consider designing a robust, centrally enforceable, secure, and unified identity and access management system for all of the digital assets your enterprise has that probably go ten layers deeper than the physical access they need to manage. This is the most important security aspect of the cloud and at the core of the defense-in-depth security model that we'll discuss in depth later.

Least Privilege and Separation of Duties

Least privilege and separation (or segregation) of duties are two of the building blocks of security for computing systems (it also applies to physical security) focused on access management. The principle of *least privilege* states that we should provision an individual user or a system account with the least amount of privileges needed to perform their job functions so that we minimize the threat surface. *Separation of duties* is the idea that you should separate all of the duties needed to perform a critical business function across multiple users so that in the event one user is compromised, a whole system or process is not compromised.

These principles are why *role-based access control* (RBAC) has become the standard for IAM over the last 15 years or so. In the RBAC model, you define roles for your organization and your users, whether they are individuals, groups, or service accounts, and for each of these roles, you define the least amount of permissions necessary to enable the user to do their job.

NOTE Attribute-based access control (ABAC) is becoming more prevalent in the cloud, offering users the ability to allow or deny authorization to a resource based on certain conditions—such as blocking a user from accessing an application outside of work hours, or blocking access from a user in another country. You won't see this on the exam, but leveraging ABAC will continue improving the layers of defense for your enterprise and should be considered for your most critical applications.

There are many examples of incidents happening in the world because of improper security access management principles. Every so often, they are significant enough to make the news. As a cloud architect, it's important that you are also a security professional. Your role is to design an architecture that is safe from harm. Far too often, cloud architects are focused on performance, functionality, and reliability, while overlooking security.

Defense-in-depth requires security controls that work together to amplify protective measures to prevent unauthorized access to resources. Unfortunately, security measures are only as good as the weakest link. As companies look to leverage infrastructure as code (IaC) tools such as Terraform, Ansible, and others, they often need to grant powerful roles to the virtual machines (VMs) running those orchestration engines. Then the playbooks/modules are able to provision and configure anything and everything on the cloud that those roles allow. That may seem great from a high-velocity IaC business-value perspective, but that VM is the weakest link. Think about that for a second. If someone can gain access to the operating system (OS) on that VM, they can do almost anything on any cloud resource within its purview. The ability to access the shell of the OS gives them all they need to command the cloud resources because of the software development kit (SDK) software installed on the machine. As a result, all of the cloud service provider's protections have been downgraded to the quality of the OS's protective controls. That's not a good design choice.

There are many better ways to secure such an environment, from changing the OS access approach, to avoiding super admin–like roles, to not making the VM accessible indirectly from the Internet. Implementing all of these factors in your design is a lot easier said than done, however. It's not often that cloud architects are taught to think like an attacker, but as you read through this book and/or design architecture, you should try to think from a hacker's point of view. The ultimate goal of designing secure systems is to assume that things can and will go wrong and then manage your risk accordingly. Although plenty of risk management books and certifications go into the formulas for effective risk management, I focus on the overall concept of minimizing risk for the intents and purposes of this book.

NOTE Here are a couple of terms you should know about in your day-to-day work, though you're unlikely to see any questions about these in your exam: *Entitlements* refers to the process of granting users privileges and the scope of the privileges that are granted. *Privilege creep* occurs when a user accumulates too many privileges over time, which violates the principle of least privilege. Privilege creep can result from a user's various promotions, job transitions, or requests for one-time access privileges that are not removed.

Cloud Identity Overview

As mentioned, Cloud Identity is an IDaaS solution that provides a unified identity, access, application, and endpoint management platform. Cloud Identity is an identity provider (IdP) that leverages the same identities used to power Google Workspace, and it integrates with various third-party applications. Cloud Identity supports Security Assertion Markup Language (SAML) and Lightweight Directory Access Protocol (LDAP) applications. SAML provides an open standard for exchanging authentication and authorization data between parties, commonly between an identity provider (Cloud Identity) and a service provider (third-party application). LDAP is an open cross-platform protocol that is commonly used for directory services authentication, such as Active Directory.

Cloud Identity includes two editions: a Free tier and Premium tier. In the Free tier, you can perform user security management via 2SV, perform basic mobile device management, leverage Google Cloud Directory Sync, and gather audit logs from the admin console. In the Premium tier, you get access to advanced mobile device management, secure LDAP, Google Security Center, BigQuery log exports, and a 99.9-percent service level agreement (SLA). Many companies already have third-party tooling that performs a lot of the Premium tier's functionality, so they may elect to leverage the Free tier.

Managing Users in Cloud Identity

As a cloud architect, it's important that you understand the following with regard to Cloud Identity:

- How to create or import user accounts into your Cloud Identity directory
- How to manage your user life cycle, including when users are onboarded, when they switch to new roles, and when they leave the organization

- How to leverage 2SV mechanisms to give you more confidence in nonrepudiation of your user identities

- Whether you'll use single sign-on (SSO) and whether Cloud Identity or a third party will provide your identity

Creating Users and Groups

Users and groups are created in Cloud Identity, which is managed from the admin .google.com page rather than the GCP console. The users and groups that you create receive *Google identities* that can be consumed by Cloud IAM for role/permission management from the GCP console. You can create identities in many ways: by bulk uploading them, importing them, or manually creating them. Think of Cloud Identity as one layer of abstraction higher than Cloud IAM.

You first create users and groups that authenticate to the cloud in the admin page (admin.google.com) via whatever mechanism you choose. Then, when you launch the GCP console to access Cloud IAM, you can manage authorizations for these users and groups, assigning them roles that manage permissions to cloud resources. Cloud Identity roles are focused solely on managing authentication and information of users/groups in the admin page. GCP roles are provisioned and managed via the GCP console and enable access to cloud resources.

NOTE Cloud Identity is focused on user and group authentication and is administered via the admin console (admin.google.com). Cloud IAM is focused on user and group authorization, managing GCP roles that provide permissions to cloud resources via the GCP console (console.google.cloud.com).

Provisioning Users with GCDS

It's recommended to use Google Cloud Directory Sync (GCDS) to provision users. This integrates with LDAP and requires minimal effort. Users can also be provisioned via bulk uploads, by manually creating them in Cloud Identity, by using Okta or another third-party tool, or by programming them in the Directory API within the Admin SDK. GCDS provides a one-way directory sync from Microsoft Active Directory or your LDAP server to synchronize your users, groups, organizational units (OUs), aliases, profiles, and shared contacts to match the information in your LDAP server. In addition, the LDAP server is never updated or altered. You can use custom mapping rules, and GCDS offers a simple user interface that enables you to simulate your configuration before you run it.

TIP Many users have Google accounts that have access to consumer products such as YouTube, Google AdWords, and so on. However, it's not recommended that these accounts be used in GCP. Users should be provisioned separately with a Cloud Identity–managed account.

Super Administrator and Organization Administrator Roles

In Google Cloud, the super administrator role can be a super admin in Cloud Identity, and the super admin is granted the GCP organization admin role by default. Super admin users manage the user and group account life cycle as well as the security settings of the organization from the Admin console. Super admins have full visibility of Cloud Identity and the GCP environments, and in a multiorganization setup, the super admin has full visibility of all the organization's GCP environments. Organization admins have the ability to define IAM policies, grant other users IAM roles, determine the structure of the resource hierarchy, and delegate key cloud responsibilities to other users via roles. Organization admins cannot perform other actions, such as creating folders, unless they grant themselves the appropriate role.

 CAUTION   Super admins are users in Cloud Identity who are managed via the Admin console, and they are granted the organization admin role in the environments that are created under that domain. They are *not* the same as organization admins that are created solely in GCP, although they get that organization admin role by default.

Hardware Security Keys   It's very important that you secure your super admin accounts, usually with hardware security keys. Super admin users will always bypass SSO and can authenticate with Google. They have the most powerful permissions that don't typically need to be leveraged daily, so it is important that you limit these users to three or four accounts and provide rigorous protection and monitoring to prevent malicious activity. You should also do the following:

- Keep a backup security key in case your super admin user loses a security key.
- Have proper recovery options in place and protect backup e-mails with 2SV.
- Ensure that there is more than one super admin user to avoid a single point of failure, but don't provision too many.
- Separate duties by delegating the roles of the super admins and the organization admins.

How Users Authenticate to GCP

There are three primary ways for users to authenticate into Google Cloud:

- Via Google authentication without SSO
- Via SSO by using Google authentication and Cloud Identity as the IdP
- Via SSO by using an external IdP such as Okta, ADFS, or Ping Identity

The first option is most uncommon; most organizations prefer to leverage SSO for security and governance purposes. For organizations that strictly use GCP, the second option is more common as it doesn't require any other vendors and has minimal overhead. Most enterprises use the third option, which offers the simplest onboarding and the most interoperability between cloud providers and on-premises environments. Enterprises often split several corporate applications between environments that have existing IdM solutions in place. This simplifies onboarding the same users into Google Cloud. Many third-party solutions such as Okta, Ping Identity, and ADFS already apply several security controls to users holistically across their enterprise.

2-Step Verification

It's very important that you use 2SV—what Google Cloud calls multifactor authentication, across your enterprise. For privileged users, this should be mandatory, and you'll have to perform a risk assessment for unprivileged users to determine the value of 2SV.

You can implement 2SV in several ways:

- **SMS/voice** This has its challenges, because it's not a secure method of implementing 2SV. This method was actually removed from the National Institute of Standards and Technology (NIST) recommendation for MFA best practices because experienced hackers can exploit your phone number through various ways. It's still better than nothing.

- **Backup codes, authenticator app, or push notifications** These solutions could be phished, but it's significantly more secure than SMS.

- **Hardware security keys** Security keys are the most secure mechanism, although not all IdPs support security keys.

The mechanism by which hardware tokens are compliant is known as the FIDO U2F (Fast Identity Online Universal 2nd Factor) protocol that was defined by the FIDO Alliance. The alliance was founded by PayPal and other industry leaders to eliminate the world's reliance on passwords and to promote strong authentication mechanisms. The FIDO Alliance has more than 260 members as of this writing, including Google, and its protocol is widely leveraged across most hardware tokens. Essentially, FIDO U2F is an open-authentication standard for a second factor of authentication that offers strong defense against phishing, session-hijacking, man-in-the-middle, and malware attacks. It does this by binding your physical hardware key to the IdP. So even if you tried logging in to a malicious website that looked exactly like your Google authentication page, it would not work, because the malicious website does not have your cryptographic binding to your physical hardware key. FIDO U2F–compliant tokens can be leveraged in Google Cloud. Google offers their own version of FIDO U2F–compliant hardware tokens, known as Titan Security Keys. Titan Security Keys are a FIDO U2F–compliant hardware token that is built with a secure element, the Titan chip, which verifies the integrity of the keys at the hardware level to make sure they are not tampered with. These are phishing-resistant keys and can also be leveraged across many services, including Facebook, Twitter, and more. Any FIDO U2F–compliant hardware key offers the highest level of security for 2SV.

Security Auditing

There are various ways to ensure that you're adhering to the AAA security model best practices in Google Cloud, and security teams often leverage multiple elements of an audit trail to ensure they're in the know.

In the Admin tab, you can review user settings and monitor user password strength. You can generate audit reports that provide some visibility into user logins and other audit logs across your services. You can set up custom alerts to be alerted about any suspicious user activity.

Use the Security Center (included in the Premium tier) to perform more advanced security threat detection. Your Cloud Identity Admin logs should be routed to your security operations team. We'll dive into security auditing in more depth in Chapter 11. Auditing is a very important aspect of building a secure Cloud.

Chapter Review

In this chapter we discussed the first building block of GCP, Cloud Identity, and began discussing how understanding agreements is an important element of enterprise architecture. You'll have to abide by many types of agreements in Google Cloud Platform. You should understand the language of these agreements so that you can properly select services and features to leverage for your enterprise and align with your enterprise cloud strategy and your compliance requirements. The service level agreement, in particular, could make or break your decision to use a product or not, depending on the objectives for your business use case.

We then went into the key security principles of identity and access management with the AAA security model and the principles of least privileges and separation of duties. Identity and access management is one of the most important security controls in any environment, especially with the rise of service-to-service or microservices communication. It's important that you are aware of the roles your users need to complete their work to avoid delays in users' speed of innovation.

In the AAA security model, it's important that you understand that authentication, authorization, and accounting (or auditing) are three entirely different concepts that also go hand-in-hand. Authentication means validating that a user is supposed to have access to the environment. Authorization is what type of access level(s) that user is supposed to have. Accounting (or auditing) is ensuring that adequate logs are capturing every user action to enable monitoring for malicious activity. These logs are typically stored in GCP audit logs and can be surfaced to users in various ways. The principle of least privilege focuses on ensuring that users, whether they are individuals or programmatic accounts, are granted only the minimum required privileges to do their job and no more. Privilege creep occurs when users accumulate a lot of privileges by job rotations, promotions, changes, and the security team does not properly deprovision their previous entitlements.

The principle of separation of duties is focused on splitting the tasks to complete a critical business job between multiple individuals, so that one individual does not have all the keys to the kingdom. The role-based access control model restricts system access to authorized users, and authorized users have to be entitled to a role, where that role defines all of the permissions that they have.

Cloud Identity is different from Cloud IAM. Cloud Identity is a unified identity, access, application, and endpoint management platform that enables you to add and manage all the users who should be able to authenticate into GCP. Cloud IAM is focused on managing access to the users within GCP. Cloud Identity is managed via the Admin console at admin.google.com, whereas Cloud IAM is managed via the GCP console. There are access control mechanisms in Cloud Identity because it's important that you understand the role of a super admin and how best to secure the super admin account. It's very important that the super admin account is not used on a day-to-day basis, and it requires the utmost control and monitoring to prevent that account from being compromised. Multifactor authentication, or 2-Step Verification (2SV), and leveraging hardware-based security keys make up the best dual-factor mechanism to protect those super admin users. You can use any FIDO U2F–compliant security key in GCP. Titan Security Keys are Google's answer to hardware-based security keys, and they are FIDO U2F compliant.

Users and groups are first created in Cloud Identity, where they are given Google Identities. These Google Identities are then able to be authorized to access projects and resources in GCP via Cloud IAM. It should be mandatory that 2SV be enabled for all privileged users, and it is highly recommended that all users of GCP be forced to use 2SV. There are three main ways to authenticate to GCP: You can manually create users without SSO directly in GCP. You can leverage Cloud Identity as your identity provider (IdP), where your IdP is the entity that creates, maintains, and manages your identity information and provides authentication to your environment(s). Lastly, you can leverage a third-party IdP, such as Okta or PingID, which is common for enterprises that already leverage third-party tools to unify access across all of the users in their company. In a multi-cloud world, most companies typically leverage a third-party IdP. Users are recommended to be provisioned via Google Cloud Directory Sync (GCDS) because it provides a one-way directory sync from Active Directory or your local LDAP server. Most user data is synchronized into GCP, and it is a very simple process to perform.

Think about the complexities of designing this initial building block of GCP in your role as a cloud architect. On paper, it's easy to think about the best solution to everything. In practice, many considerations may factor into other solutions that appear to be more optimal. Managing 30 users is easy, but authenticating and managing 30,000 users is a whole new ballgame. Keep up your great work and knock out some labs on Coursera or Qwiklabs when you get some spare time!

Additional References

If you'd like more information about the topics discussed in this chapter, check out these sources:

- **Cloud Identity product overview**   https://cloud.google.com/identity
- **Security Authentication vs Authorization: What You Need to Know**   https://towardsdatascience.com/security-authentication-vs-authorization-what-you-need-to-know-b8ed7e0eae74
- **Single Sign-On Best Practices for Google Cloud**   https://www.youtube.com/watch?time_continue=20&v=9-GMVX_OOG0&feature=emb_title

Questions

1. Your development team at Acme Corporation needs to create a highly privileged role for users who work with customer data. Where would they create this role?

   A. Cloud Identity

   B. Admin.google.com

   C. Okta

   D. Cloud IAM

2. In the AAA security model, the three A's represent which of the following?

   A. Access, authorization, and auditing

   B. Authorization, access, and auditing

   C. Authorization, authentication, and access

   D. Authentication, authorization, and accounting

3. The principle of least privilege is focused on:

   A. Ensuring that you give users the least amount of privileges possible

   B. Separating the amount of responsibilities that each of your applications has into logical chunks

   C. Ensuring that roles are defined for your company's access model

   D. Minimizing the amount of privileges that a single user has to the bare minimum needed to perform their job duties

4. The principle of separation of duties is focused on:

   A. Minimizing the amount of privileges that a single user has to the bare minimum needed to perform their job duties

   B. Ensuring that you give users the least amount of privileges possible

C. Spreading out the duties required to complete a business-critical task across multiple users to minimize the amount of risk in the event a single user is compromised

D. Hiring many people in various roles to separate the duties of a security operations team

5. You're the lead cloud architect at Acme Corporation, and your company has just acquired KittyPoo, a leading cat litter scooping service that crowdsources its scoopers like Uber does its drivers. KittyPoo has a total of 5300 developers working across multiple geographic areas. You're expected to set up a meeting with the lead architects to come up with a solution for integrating and onboarding all of these developers into Google Cloud. What is *not* an important decision point you need to get to in order to select and implement a solution?

A. How your organization model will be structured for sandbox, dev, staging, and production project environments

B. What DevOps practices will be followed by developers and what project environments developers will be given access to and roles for to accommodate least privilege

C. How developers' identities will be synchronized into Google IAM from their current Identity solution

D. What GCP resources and services will be whitelisted for developers to use

6. You learn that KittyPoo has loosely given its developers access to developer and production environments, reasoning that it was tough managing all of their permissions and developers could just use a password to log into their environment. What is your immediate next step to prevent compromise, knowing that the integration may take some time to formalize and implement?

A. Have KittyPoo enforce 2SV across the enterprise.

B. Have KittyPoo right-size all of its user permissions so that a compromised user cannot do too much damage.

C. Identify KittyPoo's most critical systems and locate who has privileged access to those systems. Enforce 2SV on those users and remove users who don't need access.

D. Onboard KittyPoo into your environment immediately.

7. What is a click-through agreement?

A. A nonbinding agreement that provides a guideline on using a certain product or service

B. An agreement you must click through and skip to the end to get to the actual tool

C. A legally binding agreement that is surfaced through a digital prompt, where an end user will have the ability to accept or decline a digitally mediated policy

D. A nonbinding agreement that is surfaced through a digital prompt, where an end user will have the ability to accept or decline a digitally mediated policy

8. Your development team is building a new business-critical application using virtual machines to be deployed in a dedicated production project. As part of this effort, the team is looking to implement a dedicated application testing environment within a development project. After a centrally managed infrastructure team creates the new development project, development team members realize that they cannot access the new environment. What is likely the issue?

A. In Cloud Identity, the super administrator has forgotten to onboard the development team's identity into Google Cloud.

B. In the admin.google.com page, the development team is missing the proper access requirements to be able to work in this environment.

C. The development team is missing the privileges needed in the GCP console and should reach out to the centrally managed project owners to provision their access.

D. The development team should not be working in this environment if they don't have access. There's probably a reason why they don't have access in the first place.

9. Your 230-person company has multiple cloud providers and several business applications across the clouds. It has become difficult to manage all of the permissions and identities across all of these applications. The company is looking at a solution that will help alleviate some of the governance and operational challenges of managing user identities. What would you suggest your company do?

A. Look into a third-party identity provider (IdP) such as Okta or PingID as a solution to building a unified single sign-on system.

B. Leverage Cloud Identity as your IdP, and for any applications that are incompatible, manually manage those users.

C. Don't use single sign-on. When a single user account is compromised, an attacker can gain access to the entire technology stack.

D. Leverage GCDS and synchronize your directory with Google Cloud.

10. What is the best second factor for ensuring the utmost security of user authentication?

A. SMS

B. Phone call with voice recognition

C. E-mail

D. Titan Security Key

Answers

1. D. Cloud IAM is where you build roles within GCP to manage user access. This question specifically asked about a role that will be managing customer data, which is within GCP. Had the question said your user needs to be highly privileged and manage the user directory synchronization or authentication, then you would have chosen Cloud Identity.

2. D. The three A's represent authentication, authorization, and accounting. Authorization is synonymous with access management, so the answers that include authorization and access are incorrect. Authentication and authorization are both separate concepts that are part of the AAA security model, with accounting (or auditing) being the last element.

3. D. D is the best answer listed. The goal of least privilege is to ensure that your users are privileged or entitled to doing only what their job duties entail, and nothing more.

4. C. When it comes to minimizing risk, think about the implications if one user performed all the duties that could be accomplished by multiple users in a critical business application. The goal is to minimize the amount of damage in the event one user is compromised. You've probably experienced this at retail stores when another manager needs to approve a return, or at the bank when the manager needs to validate a withdrawal. The same concept applies to technology.

5. D. Whitelisting resources and services as a policy enforcement practice is not generally necessary and can often lead to wasted effort. Most environments should be provisioned using infrastructure as code practices, which improve architectural security inherently. If developers properly set up a framework for IaC deployments, they generally should not need access to production systems (beyond read access, if that), while CI/CD tools generally take care of application deployments into production systems. In all cases, integration of identity verification with an Identity solution must be done. Proper identification of developer access rights to specific projects must be designed early and communicated.

6. C. The question asks for the immediate next step, so there is a sense of urgency here. Although several answers may be valid here, the most effective solution in the least amount of time is to identify the critical assets and require those privileged users to leverage 2SV. Enforcing 2SV across your enterprise will require a bit more planning and communication.

7. C. Click-through agreements are legally binding. Every time you click "Accept" on the several thousand of agreements that you've accepted since the beginning of the Internet, you legally agreed to a company's terms and conditions.

8. **C.** This is related to access of resources, which are within GCP, and for that reason you'll need to look to Cloud IAM to identify whether users were granted the proper access to do their job.

9. **A.** Most companies using multiple clouds with several business applications they'd like to unify under a single IdP would look to third-party companies such as Okta or PingID for a unified solution. Cloud Identity can serve this purpose as well, but we're looking for the best, most industry-relatable answer.

10. **D.** Titan Security Keys are FIDO U2F–compliant hardware security keys that are vetted by more than 230 companies as part of the FIDO Alliance. All the other options are phishable options.

Resource Management

In this chapter, we'll cover

- What resources are included in Google Cloud Platform
- How to design an effective organization hierarchy
- Organization policies and how to leverage them as a control to keep your business secure
- Some design considerations when you're building a new GCP environment

Most of us have heard the nonstop complaints about how the company's technology stack was so poorly set up that it's almost impossible to get your act together. You're working on a project to solve multifactor authentication for your enterprise, but it really doesn't matter so much, because your developers are all over-permissioned. The environments are not set up to segregate duties properly and prevent "stupid." It's hard to lose sight of all the mistakes that exist in your enterprise, because, well, your company has been around for ages and carries a lot of technical debt. This is not the fault of architects in the late 1990s and early 2000s, however, because they had to work within the constraints of available technologies, and the offerings we have today were unfathomable then. Now we seem to be at a level of maturity where we can not only understand the tools at our disposal, but, given the history of mistakes we've made in the computing space over the last 20-plus years, it's a little easier for us to predict what the future might look like.

Think about it: back in the 20th century, we thought that by the year 2000, we'd have flying cars and androids intermingling in society. As time has gone by, our predictions of future capabilities have started to become a bit more realistic. I firmly believe that we're still at an early stage of computing, and all of it is going to change exponentially with the growth of the cloud. By now, we can reasonably think about future-proofing our businesses in a much more logical way. By "future-proofing," I don't mean designing a point-in-time environment that's going to last for a few years in the future; I'm referring to designing an environment that is able to be easily modified and adapted to any major paradigm shifts as technologies continue to be released and the dynamics of cloud computing evolve. Case in point: In the early 2010s, Google Cloud pushed App Engine as the savior of technological society—an idea that was completely revolutionary at the time. But now we're at a point where having a container-based application stack is the most modular and best solution. If someone told you that you could redo everything, how would you re-architect your technology stack? This is your opportunity.

NOTE BMW is known for designing their cars to be of the times, both operationally and cosmetically. For at least seven years and midway through the seven years they do a major iteration of the current models. They called this the BMW Life Cycle Impulse. If you think about it in software terms, it's almost like an *x.x.x* versioning system such that the first *x* is the seven-year model version of the car, the second *x* is the Life Cycle Impulse or major iteration, and the third *x* is any minor iterations or enhancements that they performed during its life cycle that required you to take your car back for service. This sounds like BMW was ahead of the curve, but when you consider Tesla by comparison, you realize that Tesla's model years don't really matter: the company creates its vehicles on a continuous deployment and feedback loop life cycle, whereby improvements, feature enhancements, and fixes are all updated in Tesla vehicles as software releases. You know that your Tesla is being continuously improved. Talk about industry-changing innovation!

As a certified Google Cloud Architect, when you're thinking about how you want to design your organization's infrastructure, you must think about how the design can continue to grow and evolve in the future so that you're designing an organizational hierarchy that enables your company to adapt to rapid change. Turning your infrastructure into code modules massively enables this. But the way your environments are all provisioned also plays a big role in the culture of your enterprise. Your goal is to release your developers from their limitations in the cloud and enable them to think and build freely and innovate in the most unique ways, while also protecting the security and safety of your cloud environment. If you're designing your organization hierarchy now, it is an exciting time for your company.

Cloud Resource Manager Overview

Google Cloud Resource Manager is a mechanism that provides resource containers such as organizations, folders, and projects and enables you to group and hierarchically organize GCP resources into those containers. With the Cloud Resource Manager API, you are also able to programmatically manage these resource containers. Having the ability to manage all of your projects centrally is an important function for the administrators of the cloud. With the Cloud Resource Manager, you can create an organization that contains all of your projects and resources within those projects. You can also create folders to group your projects according to teams, business units, environment, products, and so on. IAM policies can also be applied at the organization and folder levels. If you think about this structure, you'll realize that it enables you to set access control policies (ACLs) at various levels that will propagate to all of the child resources below. Lastly, the Cloud Resource Manager gives you the ability to programmatically manage all of this, including all of the change history, so that you can identify recently deleted projects and changes and, if necessary, undo those changes.

Organization Hierarchy

How you design and set up your organization hierarchy is quite an important aspect of a well-architected cloud environment. As companies begin to move to the cloud, some of the technical debt that was accumulated from the various changes and growth stages in on-premises technology during the past 30 years may look like a California wildfire zone: California being dry is only one reason why these massive wildfires continue to happen. When trees and brush dry out and die due to lack of water, they remain in forests, where they slowly decompose, creating fuel for future fires. Natural wildfires are apparently good for the environment, because they return trapped nutrients back to the soil and remove disease-ridden plants from an ecosystem. But you can read more about that in a science book. The moral of our cloud story is this: although it might be okay for dead trees to remain in a forest to fuel future fires and nurture the earth, we want to avoid fires in our cloud environments. If you think of technical debts as dead trees in your cloud forest, you realize that at some point, these debts may be responsible for turning a small event into a major incident. The word *fire* is something that all technologists hope never to hear in the workplace.

Imagine how many remnants of an application or design may remain in your on-premises environment because people thought that the infrastructure was needed elsewhere, they didn't know where it belonged, or they were just afraid to delete it because it could accidentally take down the entire business. Staying organized enables security and governance teams to have full visibility over what's going on in their enterprise so that they are able to manage change, decommission and remove unnecessary bits of technology, prevent internal users from making mistakes, and prevent malicious or incompetent users from doing bad things. That's one compelling aspect of staying organized. Another one is that with the move to the cloud, companies must adopt a culture of rapid innovation and growth. Can you imagine being tasked with redesigning your living room if your roommates were hoarding junk? That's not an environment that promotes innovation and growth. Like the Marie Kondo philosophy that promotes organizing your environment to improve your well-being and mental performance, your goal for developers is to eliminate all potential distractions so they can think clearly, try bold ideas, and rapidly deploy changes while minimizing the risks to reliability and security. That being said, let's talk about the organization hierarchy in GCP.

 EXAM TIP Remember the two major elements of the resource hierarchy in GCP: it provides a hierarchy of ownership that binds your resource life cycle to its immediate parent in the resource hierarchy, and it provides points to attach and inherit access control and organization policies.

Organization, Folders, Projects, and Resources

Let's talk about what this resource hierarchy looks like. You need to know the capabilities of each level of the hierarchy, the typical uses for each level, and the importance of your naming conventions. Companies use a variety of design patterns for their organizational hierarchies.

Resources

Resources are the lowest level of components that make up GCP services. Think about a virtual machine (VM), a GCS bucket, a container, and even pub/sub (publish/subscribe) topics: these are all resources. Resources can be parented only by projects, not by other resources, and each resource has only one parent. That way, when you apply any policies to a parent, it is inherited by all the child resources. So when viewing billing or usage data, for example, you can dive into the lowest common denominator, your resources, to discover what costs the most or what is driving up your metrics.

Projects

Resources roll up into *projects*, which are the first grouping mechanism for the resource hierarchy. Projects can contain multiple resources. As mentioned, ACLs, VMs, APIs, and other cloud resources can all be grouped into projects. Projects are not tied to one another, and it's important to group related resources into your projects, both from a functional and access control standpoint. Projects provide a point to attach ACLs, and you can have as many projects as you want without any associated costs. Each project's logical grouping is completely independent of other projects.

You are required to use projects on GCP. It provides the foundation to create, enable, and use all GCP services, manage APIs, do billing, and manage permissions. There are a few key components of a project:

- Two identifiers:
  - A project ID, which is a unique ID for your project
  - A project number, which is a read-only number that gets automatically assigned upon project creation
- One mutable display name
- The life cycle state of the project (ACTIVE or DELETE_REQUESTED)
- Any labels that are attached to it
- The time of its creation

It's also important that you know how the structure of these resources looks behind the GUI. Take a look at the following code snippet for the structure of a project:

```
{
  "name": "myproject",
  "projectId": "my-project-123",
  "labels":
  {
    "my-label": "prod"
  },
  "projectNumber": "464036093014",
  "lifecycleState": "ACTIVE",
  "createTime": "2016-01-07T21:59:43.314Z"
}
```

Every time you interact with a resource, you'll need to identify the project info for every single request you make. You can use either the projectId or the projectNumber field. By default, the creator of the project is granted the owner role for any newly created projects.

EXAM TIP It's important that you know the difference between a mutable and immutable object. *Mutable objects* can be changed after they've been created. *Immutable objects* cannot be changed after they've been created. An example of a mutable object is the project resource; you can change it as you please after it's created. An example of an immutable object is a file that is uploaded to Google Cloud Storage; once you upload the file, it cannot be changed throughout its storage lifetime.

Folders

Projects roll up into *folders*, which are additional logical containers that are intended to group similar projects. You want to group similar projects inside your folders so that you can apply a level of consistency to the policies you attach to your folders. While it's easy to think about what makes the most logical sense based on the way your business is organized, it's best for you to think about designing your GCP organization hierarchy in a manner that is aligned with how you want to separate your access patterns or how you apply your policies. Suppose you have a bunch of VMs that run a highly sensitive workload, grouped into a project, which is then grouped into a single folder that propagates the ACLs to all developers. Since that folder contains all development projects, you're not following the principles of separation of duties and least privilege. You can have up to ten levels of folders, so it's common that companies would typically start with one or two and work their way up to as many as they need. Think about how you'd like to organize your folders—by business units, applications, environments, or products. Sometimes even creating a separate folder for your control plane can be a pattern as well.

You need to have appropriate permissions to view any folder resources. Folders act as a policy inheritance point for identity and access management (IAM) and organization policies. So if you grant an IAM role to a folder, it'll be automatically inherited by sub-folders and all projects underneath it.

Take a look at this code snippet example to see what the structure of a folder looks like:

```
{
  "name" : "folders/my-folder",
  "parent" : "organizations/my-organization",
  "displayName" : "Engineering",
  "lifecycleState" : "ACTIVE",
  "createTime": "2016-01-07T21:59:43.314Z"
}
```

Organization

Folders roll up to an *organization*, which is the root node and top-level element of this whole hierarchy. All resources that belong to an organization are grouped under the organization node, enabling companies to have central visibility and control over all the resources that apply to the organization. An organization can represent a company, and any IAM policy that applies to that organization will propagate throughout the entire hierarchy beneath it. When your first user with a Google Workspace or Cloud Identity account creates a project, an organization is automatically provisioned alongside it.

Here is a code snippet that shows the structure of an organization resource:

```
{
  "displayName": "myorganization",
  "organizationId":"34739118321",
  "createTime": "2016-01-07T21:59:43.314Z"
  "owner": {
    "directoryCustomerId": "C012BA234"
   }
}
```

 NOTE Some GCP services require that an organization be created before they're allowed to be leveraged. Shared VPC is an example of this.

Having an organization resource is necessary to manage resource life cycles. It's also important in identity management, recovering organizations in the event of an account recovery, and giving all your resources one central point of ownership. With an organization, there is always a mechanism to track accountability for resources in Google Cloud. Imagine, for example, that an employee who created an important project leaves your company. What happens to the user's project when her account is deprovisioned and deleted? Imagine that the employee's projects were deleted. That would be a sight to see. A better idea is when an employee leaves your company, their projects follow the organization's life cycle policies. Take a look at Figure 4-1 for a visual representation of this resource hierarchy.

Suppose there is a major US bank called BankyBank. Let's say Product 1 is Banky-Bank's flagship mobile banking app. Team A is the Data Science team, Team B is the Mobile Banking dev team, Credit Card users are Dept X, and Dept Y is the Retail Banking department. From an IAM perspective, you can get an idea here of how access is managed:

- The most obvious point, users who do not have access to the organization will not have access to anything within the organization.
- Credit Card (Dept X) users will not have inherent access to the Retail Banking (Dept Y) resources.
- BankyBank's Data Science team (Team A) does not have inherent access to the resources of the Mobile Banking team (Team B).
- BankyBank's flagship mobile banking application is in a separate folder (Product 1) that is PCI-compliant, and their back-office applications are in a separate folder (Product 2). These are two separate groups of developers.
- Development, test, and production support teams are all prevented from accessing one another's environments by default. It just so happens, however, that the dev/test teams share the same IAM policy, so those users can access both the dev and test projects. We've also not applied any nonprogrammatic IAM access to the production environments, because there is an approval process in place to request break-glass access when a production issue managed by the support team occurs.

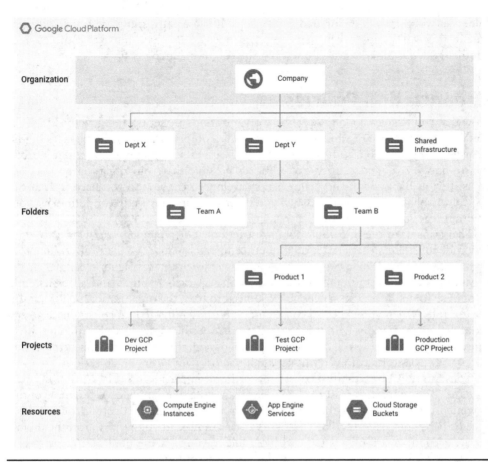

Figure 4-1 Sample resource hierarchy in GCP

As you know, with regard to the concept of defense-in-depth, least privileges, and separation of duties, this organization hierarchy now enables your business to have a multifaceted approach to how it designs, operates, and secures its applications. By not allowing any users to access the production environments, we've already eliminated the possibility of a nonprivileged user compromise from potentially harming the business. BankyBank also does not use live production data in its dev/test environments. So if a developer were to be pwned (aka compromised) in the dev or test environment, much of the risk has been minimized. Now you can imagine that when users get promoted or move to different teams, their privileges must be removed to eliminate privilege creep. Can you imagine what happens when a long-tenured employee who has played a pivotal role across the enterprise and accumulated permissions across all the businesses gets pwned? Not good!

Lastly, it's important to hammer the point that the IAM policy hierarchy follows the path of the resource hierarchy. If you make changes to your resource hierarchy, the policy hierarchy will also change. Here's an example of this: If you move a project between folders, it will change the inherited permissions. If those permissions are from a different parent, they will be lost when that project is moved. Once you move that project into another folder, it inherits everything from the parent hierarchy.

Organization Policies

Now that you've got a good grasp of how organizations are set up and governed in GCP, you've probably started to think about how your company most likely manages or will manage its organization in the Cloud. We've discussed how proper organization enables you to have a stronger security story. But it's possible that your organization may not be as strict as BankyBank and really wants developer freedom. So you need to factor in the culture of your organization when you determine how restrictive or permissive your environment will be.

That leads us to the next topic about restrictions. *Organization policies* are a configuration of constraints that are set on a resource hierarchy node (at the project, folder, or organization level). These organization policies enforce the restrictions defined in the organization's policy and enforce the restrictions on each resource and all of its child resources. To define and set the policy, you need to have the organization policy administrator role. When you choose a constraint, you can configure that constraint against a set of desired restrictions (run this constraint on a specific folder). All the child resources inherit that organization policy. If you apply an organization policy to your organization node, you've basically enforced this constraint across your entire organization.

Constraints can be either list constraints or Boolean constraints. List constraints evaluate the constraints with a list of allow/deny values that you provide. An example of this is whitelisting IP addresses that can connect to a VM. Boolean constraints can govern specific behaviors via a true/false restriction. For example, if you want to run the disable service account creation constraint within a folder, you'd set the Boolean to true to prevent users within that folder from creating service accounts.

It's also important to know that when an organization policy is applied, it is not retroactive. If you set an organization policy in a folder to restrict a certain behavior that is already occurring, you'll see that your policy is in violation, but it will not stop that behavior from happening. You'll need to remediate that behavior manually. Imagine, for example, that your organization decides it no longer wants to allow users to leverage CloudSQL and deploys this in an organization policy without giving its users ample time to migrate from CloudSQL—that could be disastrous! In such cases, you won't be able to use organization policies as a mechanism to stop behaviors from preexisting resources; you'll need to remediate those yourself when you see the retroactive violations.

Best Practices

When you're building a cloud environment for your enterprise, there are several considerations to think about as you're defining this organization structure—how you're going to automate your project creation, what naming convention will be associated with your resource containers, whether you'll use many projects or few projects, and so on.

It's much easier to do your due diligence at the beginning and try to predict what the future of your business will look like, instead of going through an entire rework a few years down the road. The cloud is agile, though, and if you follow infrastructure as code (IaC) as a best practice, it won't be too difficult to manage when things change (as they should) in your organization's future.

Considerations with regard to how you'll be separating resources into projects include the environment that your projects will be operating in, the roles that will be assigned to users within the project (aligned to a strong separation of duties model), how you plan on doing billing, some of the quotas and limits that will be tracked by your projects, and what could go wrong if a project were to be compromised. As a best practice, you should use a many projects approach, rather than few, as you'll end up doing the heavy work up-front. This will serve you well from a change management, access, and configuration standpoint in the future. If you automate your project factory, it will make your life even easier. For example, you probably would not want to design a structure with just three projects that are for each environment (development/test/production). Instead, use a hierarchy similar to what was described earlier, creating projects for each one of your applications in each environment. This will make governing your access model a lot easier. It will also make it a lot easier to label projects properly, to identify what's costing you the most money, and to minimize the amount of harm if a single project were to be exposed. If you follow the basic security principles in the design of your cloud, you will be very successful!

Lastly, there is the concept of a project lien, which is a function that will protect your projects against project deletion. This is important, especially for your production environments. You don't want someone accidentally deleting your project and shutting your business down due to a clerical error!

Exercise 4-1: Creating a Project

1. Head to Cloud IAM and ensure you have the resourcemanager.projects.create permission, which is included in the roles/resourcemanager.projectCreator role.

2. Open the Cloud Console and go to the Manage Resources page.

3. Select the organization for which you want to create a project. If you're a free trial user, this list will not appear, so, you can skip this step.

4. Click Create Project.

5. In the New Project window, enter a project name and select an appropriate billing account.

6. In the Location field, enter the name of the folder in which you want to add the project.

7. When you're finished, click Create.

Chapter Review

Well done! You're on your way to becoming a Google Cloud Architect. Feel free to practice your learnings in projects and QwikLabs, but think about scaling your actions in an enterprise fashion.

In this chapter, we started off discussing the importance of organization and how some of the best-run businesses around the world have earned their standing by being organized. Organization enables your developers to thrive without being cluttered by the fears of technical debt or restrictions. In today's world, it's important to adopt the mind-set of continuous iteration and continuous deployment. That can be effectively done only by having a very well-organized technology stack from the start. As you begin building your company's GCP environment, think about how all the little design items will need to adapt to a growing business model. Think about how you can enable your company to maintain its agility in the cloud by the way you architect cloud deployment.

We also explored the Cloud Resource Manager and discussed how this service is one of the core elements of designing your GCP environment, because it provides the ability to manage your organization through an organization hierarchy. The Cloud Resource Manager can be managed programmatically via the API as well, and it should certainly be managed programmatically for the modern enterprise.

Organization hierarchy is an important element that enables you to build in strong governance, security controls, and administration of your cloud. The organization hierarchy is governed in a top-down fashion. There are two major considerations of the resource hierarchy in GCP: to provide a hierarchy of ownership that binds your resource life cycle to its immediate parent in the resource hierarchy, and to provide points to attach and inherit access control and organization policies. The organization hierarchy starts with resources, which are the lowest-level component in GCP. Think of things like VMs, BigQuery datasets, and GCS buckets.

Resources feed up into projects, which are the first grouping mechanism for the resource hierarchy. Projects can contain multiple resources and are not tied into one another to enforce access control separation. Projects provide a point to attach ACLs, and it's best to leverage a many-project approach to allow for ample segregation of duties, minimize the blast radius in the event of a project compromise, provide enough granularity with your billing data, and govern/manage your GCP environment.

Projects roll up to folders, logical containers that group similar projects. Folders can stack ten high, but quite often they're stacked three or four tiers high. Folders are typically organized by applications, products, business units, environments, and so on. Folders also act as a policy inheritance point for IAM and organization policies.

Folders roll up into an organization, which is the root node and top-level governing element of the hierarchy. All resources that belong to an organization are grouped under the organization node. It's necessary to have an organization in place to manage resource life cycles, and also for doing proper identity management, account recovery, and ensuring ownership of all resources in an organization.

Organization policies are a configuration of constraints that are set on a resource hierarchy node, either at the project, folder, or organization level. Organization policies enforce restrictions defined in the policy on the resource and all of its child resources. Organization policies are important to secure and harden your cloud by preventing unintended behaviors from occurring. Google Cloud continues to iterate and improve the amount of organization policies that are available and their functionality. Think of organization policies as pre-deployment checks, where a build will be prevented from happening if it doesn't meet the criteria of the restrictions. Organization policies are not applied retroactively, so you'll see a violation of the organization policy for things that were occurring before the policy was set. You'll need to correct that behavior manually to remove any violations.

Additional References

If you'd like more information about the topics discussed in this chapter, check out these sources:

- **Cloud Resource Manager Concepts**   https://cloud.google.com/resource-manager/docs/concepts
- **Google Cloud Platform Resource Management**   www.youtube.com/watch?v=MzclA_hdNLY

Questions

1. In the organization hierarchy, how are policies applied?

   A. Top-down through an inheritance model, in which the child resources inherit their parents' policies

   B. Bottom-up through an inheritance model, in which the child resources inherit their parents' policies

   C. Top-down through an inheritance model, in which the parent resources inherit their children's policies

   D. Bottom-up through an inheritance model, in which the parent resources inherit their children's policies

2. What are resources?

   A. Minerals and gas that need to be mined by probes or SCVs

   B. The lowest-level component in GCP that includes things like projects, folders, and your organization node

   C. The lowest-level component in GCP; example resources are VMs, BigQuery datasets, and pub/sub topics

   D. The usage-based egress charges for your company when doing yum updates

3. What is the primary purpose of projects?

  A. They physically group GCP resources that enable you to manage a set of resources effectively.

  B. They logically group GCP resources that enable you to organize for policy enforcement and governance.

  C. They spread the amount of duties to complete a business-critical task across multiple users to minimize the amount of risk in the event a single user is compromised.

  D. They require that many people be hired in various roles to separate the duties of a security operations team.

4. A carefully designed organization hierarchy enables businesses to do all of the following *except*:

  A. Improve the speed of innovation.

  B. Have more granular billing data.

  C. Govern and secure the organization in a more managed and centralized fashion.

  D. Minimize the amount of projects needed to leverage GCP effectively.

5. What are folders?

  A. They are resources that control how your organization model will be structured for sandbox, development, staging, and production project environments.

  B. They are logical containers or groupings of projects that can be stacked ten high.

  C. They are logical containers or groupings of projects that can be stacked four high.

  D. They are resources you want to use to organize your files.

6. You're working on designing the gaming infrastructure for Duty Calls, a popular multiplayer video game, and you've been tasked with building the organization's resource hierarchy. Duty Calls has several applications running on Compute Engine that provide the gaming infrastructure for the computing clusters and storage, their analytics platform, the servers, and the matchmaking system. Two teams of developers comprise a team that focuses primarily on development and testing and a production support team that needs direct production access to be able to handle production issues in real time. How would you suggest they organize their resource hierarchy?

  A. Use the organization policy service to restrict access to APIs and services that are not in use by the company.

  B. Ensure that their developers have administrator roles over the main folder that hosts all of these projects and call it a day.

C. Leverage separate projects based on the development, test, and production environments for their computing and storage, analytics platform, servers, and their matchmaking system. Apply the same IAM policy for their dev/test projects and a separate IAM policy for their production project.

D. Leverage three separate projects based on the development, test, and production environments for their applications to minimize overhead. Use all the resources from the applications in each project to simplify things. Apply the same IAM policy for their dev/test projects and a separate IAM policy for their prod project.

7. Duty Calls has deployed several applications running on Compute Engine that provide the gaming infrastructure for the computing clusters and storage, their analytics platform, the servers, and the matchmaking system into a well-architected organization hierarchy. They have two teams of developers: a team that focuses primarily on development and testing, and a production support team that needs direct production access to be able to handle production issues in real time. The development team wants to combine all development resources for all applications into one project. Is this an appropriate pattern?

A. Yes; it simplifies the amount of management so that the development teams have a lot more freedom in owning their resources.

B. Yes; it is an anti-pattern to separate applications into multiple projects.

C. No; they should leverage a many-projects approach and create a separate environment and project for each application.

D. Yes; managing access is quite the pain and this would cut down all the support tickets their IT team gets.

8. Your development team is building a new business-critical application using virtual machines to be deployed in a dedicated production project. As part of this effort, the team is looking to implement a dedicated application testing environment within a development project. After a centrally managed infrastructure team provisions its new development project using infrastructure as code, the development team members realize that they cannot access the new environment, but their production support team can. Upon investigating, they do not see any discrepancies in the roles that their users have in Cloud IAM. What is likely the issue?

A. They likely used the wrong **--folder** flag when they were creating the project and inherited the wrong permissions in the hierarchy. Take a look at the code snippet they used to provision the project.

B. They likely used the wrong **--devtestprod** flag when they were creating the project and inherited the wrong permissions in the hierarchy. Take a look at the code snippet they used to provision the project.

C. They granted the wrong permissions to their users. Their development team should have both development and production roles.

D. The development team should not be working in this environment if they don't have access. There's probably a reason why they don't have access in the first place.

9. What are organization policies?

   A. A configuration of constraints that are set on the organization node, enforcing the restrictions defined in the policy

   B. A configuration of constraints that are set on the folder node, enforcing the restrictions defined in the policy

   C. A configuration of constraints that are set on the project node, enforcing the restrictions defined in the policy

   D. A configuration of constraints that are set on the project, the folder, or the organization node, enforcing the restrictions defined in the policy

10. What is the organization node?

   A. The top-level node shows policies are inherited by all the child resources below it

   B. The bottom-level node that has full ownership of all the child resources above it and propagates upward

   C. The domain name of your organization

   D. The node that you apply organization policies to when you need to prevent a certain behavior from happening within your organization

Answers

1. **A.** In the organization policy service, the hierarchy is applied through a top-down mechanism in which all the children below a logical container inherit all of the policies above them.

2. **C.** Resources are the lowest-level components in GCP. Some example resources are VMs, BigQuery datasets, Pub/Sub topics.

3. **B.** Projects are a logical grouping of GCP resources that provide a point at which to apply policies and inherit policies. Projects should be organized in a mechanism that makes the most sense for the business, based on certain design considerations and the culture of how the business develops and deploys its applications.

4. **D.** Minimizing the amount of projects leveraged in your GCP environment is not a goal of designing an effective cloud development and deployment strategy. The goal of governance in the cloud is to be able to apply policies consistently across the entire enterprise and also minimize the blast radius. You can do this using a many-projects approach. Minimizing the amount of projects does not enable you to segregate duties and manage access control properly.

5. **B.** Folders are logical groupings of projects, or subfolders, and they're allowed to be stacked ten high. Use folders iteratively, because you can always modify them later.

6. C. You would want to leverage projects here based on the application and the environment: dev/test/prod-matchmaking, dev/test/prod-analytics, dev/test/prod-servers, dev/test/prod-computing. That's a total of 12 resource containers. You can manage permissions accordingly, based on the dev/test users who should only have access to their respective applications and the production support team.

7. C. Minimizing the amount of projects you have increases your blast radius by enabling applications to have more access within its project or ACLs, disregarding the principles of separated duties and least privilege. Don't be afraid to use a many-projects approach. The cloud enables you to manage governance much easier than traditional on-premises environments.

8. A. Since their roles all appear to be functioning properly and are not misconfigured, the most logical answer is that their infrastructure as code likely used the wrong **--folder** flag. Since the production support team can access it, it's likely that they accidentally put this environment in the production folder!

9. D. Organization policies can be applied at project, folder, or top-level organization node.

10. A. The organization node is the top-level node, and all children below it inherit its policies.

Cloud Identity and Access Management

In this chapter, we'll cover
- Best practices for authorizing users to access resources using Cloud IAM
- The three main parts of the Cloud IAM: members, roles, and IAM policies
- The differences between users, groups, and service accounts
- How to use IAM conditions
- The importance of security principles in the context of user and programmatic accounts

It's an incredible time to be in cybersecurity, largely due to the fact that human beings consistently are the weakest link to and cause of environmental security compromise. If you think about some of the largest cyberattacks that have occurred in recent history, they all seem to have resulted from some aspect of overprivileged users or accounts, lack of multifactor authentication, or inconsistent configuration management, especially with regard to how access to applications is managed. An exploit is useless if an attacker can only manage to get into a low-level account with no access to sensitive data. In theory, following the principles of least privilege and separation of duties seems to be quite straightforward and easy, right? But making sure your organization follows these best practices is like trying to ensure that your parents aren't hoarding unused items in their garage. They may come up with a reason why and when they'll need these things, but in reality, they haven't used that antique dinnerware to serve their guests since 1995.

Humans are poor predictors; we often predict futures in ways that benefit us in an effort to minimize any potential risk. A common risk that we face is the very mild inconvenience of having to open a support ticket if we can't access a system we need to do our job. Risk management is, in fact, something that we all do all the time, especially when it means protecting ourselves and those who mean the most to us. But in the enterprise? It's easy to get so caught up in the mix of working at a giant conglomerate that your unrealistic optimism assumes that everything will be okay and your network won't get breached. But the truth is this: we all need to think about risk management in the sense of protecting the business that provides our paychecks.

Why am I talking about security so much? Well, being a security guy, I may be a bit biased. I realize that we cannot win the fight to secure our organizations by just being security professionals. Security is the responsibility of every single human being on this planet, whether it pertains to securing corporate machines or securing aspects of our own lives.

In a business, following proper access management best practices can mitigate much of the risk. After all, the cost of a breach is usually significantly more than the cost and time it will take you to design a system properly. It is your responsibility, dear Cloud Architect, to be "awake" on the importance of security in every aspect of your system design. We discussed the shared responsibility model earlier, and that will come up throughout the book. Even though Google Cloud may be the most secure cloud platform that exists, it is still up to cloud architects to responsibly bake in security best practices across their organizations. Consider the importance of your access model, and don't take this one lightly.

We've all experienced some nightmares in our current or former jobs. Think about your first day on the job as a systems administrator at an old Windows-based company. If you're a new SysAdmin, you're probably feeling excited. If you're a seasoned SysAdmin, you're anxiously opening up Active Directory, waiting to discover what's underneath. What you find is pure trauma: Why does a finance intern have the domain controller role and full access to all domain controllers? How did this even happen? So you write some PowerShell scripts or make some manual changes to the GUI; whatever your solution was, it was probably cumbersome and ineffective.

Lucky for us, Google Cloud and other cloud providers have made administration so much easier by baking in security via infrastructure as code (IaC). You simply manage the templates and build some monitoring and detection alerts to ensure that mistakes don't accidentally happen. Maybe you'll even build a corrective control to mitigate anomalous grants when they happen.

In this chapter, we'll talk about the access management system in Google Cloud and Cloud IAM and discuss the various complexities and considerations of building a robust access management program. Remember that Cloud Identity or your identity provider (IdP) handles your authentication aspect. Once your users are authenticated, their access is managed inside of the cloud environment.

Cloud IAM Overview

Cloud Identity and Access Management (Cloud IAM) is an enterprise-grade access control service that enables administrators to authorize who can take actions on certain resources and what conditions must exist before they can take action. The goal of a cloud administrator is to have full visibility and fine-grained, centrally managed, access control capabilities that span all cloud resources. Quite often, enterprises have massively complex organizational structures with hundreds of working groups, many projects, and very intricate access control requirements. Cloud IAM gives you the ability to manage all the access policies across your organization with its built-in auditing capabilities.

You can create and manage your IAM policies through the Cloud Console, the API, or the command line.

 EXAM TIP Remember the difference between Cloud Identity and Cloud IAM. Cloud Identity is the source of truth for handling authentication by creating or synchronizing user accounts, setting up single sign-on (SSO), and leveraging 2-Step Verification (2SV), and it is managed from the Admin console at admin.google.com. Cloud IAM handles access management, including creating and managing all the roles for your applications and environments, following the role-based access control (RBAC) model.

The purpose of having a strong access management model is to ensure that you are granting the right roles to the right users and minimizing their privileges so that they're using only what they need. As a cloud administrator, you'll probably be required to provide audit reports for internal or external compliance reasons and security monitoring. Remember the AAA security model: authentication, authorization (or access), and accounting (or auditing)? You need to manage AAA efficiently—the last thing you want to do is block your users from doing the work that they should be authorized to perform, especially in the cloud, where business and innovation are supposed to be exponentially accelerated. Your users don't care about the security model. They don't care about how many privileges they should have. They just want to be able to do their jobs without running into insufficient privileges errors.

What about your security operations team? Have you considered their feelings when you built your IAM architecture? After all, they have needs too! They hold you accountable for aligning to the information security policies of your organization. One of the biggest challenges I've seen is a lack of engagement between the folks who create the policies, the folks enforcing them, and the folks who are leading the cloud migrations and engineering work. When your work is in security operations, you're often down in the trenches building the capabilities to detect malicious activity or you're responding to potential incidents. Aside from having a say on the policies, it can be quite difficult to be a part of the cloud engineering or migration efforts.

When you're designing your IAM architecture, take a close look at your enterprise security policies around access management as you're working through the many considerations of a well-architected access model. For new cloud organizations, it's more than likely that they'll need to revisit their security policies around IAM and rework them as they understand how the model evolves in the cloud. For information security teams, it's important to dictate what users and how users can access resources in the cloud. How and when do they need to rotate their keys? Also, you need to have an inventory of all the resources that can surface the data to their security monitoring tool to ensure that everyone is compliant with their requirements. If your system gets breached, you are liable for all your customers' data. You have a duty to protect them, because mom won't be there to protect you!

Members, Roles, and Policies

The model for access management in Cloud IAM has three main parts: members, roles, and IAM policies.

- A *member* can be a Google account (human users), a service account (programmatic account for applications and virtual machines), a Google group, or a Google Workspace or Cloud Identity domain that can access a resource. The identifier for a member is the e-mail address associated with the type of account or the domain name associated with the Google Workspace or Cloud Identity domain. It's common to hear the term "users" used as a blanket statement to cover members. Just remember that Google Cloud refers to all of these as *members*, and each is treated distinctively according to the member's appropriate title.

- An *IAM role* is a collection of permissions that determines what operations are allowed on a resource. When you grant a member a role, all of the permissions contained within that role are granted to that member.

- An *IAM Policy* is a configuration that binds together one or more members and roles for the purpose of enforcing only approved access patterns through a collection of statements. It basically ties the "who" and the "what" together—*who* needs to access a resource, and *what* do they need to do? After you create an IAM policy, you attach it to the resource—or you can attach them to those logical resource containers (project, folder, and organization).

In Figure 5-1, you can see the various elements of an IAM policy.

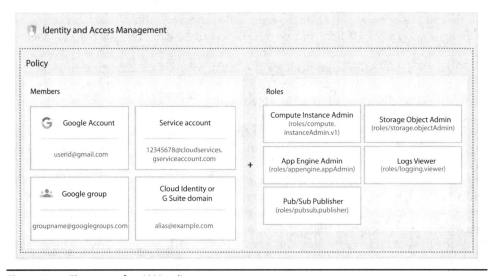

Figure 5-1   Elements of an IAM policy

TIP When you're defining the duties that any member will perform, an easy way to determine whether you've given your member too many roles is to imagine what would happen if the member were compromised. What is the extent of the damage that could happen? If you haven't mitigated the risk to an acceptable position, you may have to separate duties across various members. This is actually a great tip for everything you architect in the Google Cloud Platform (GCP).

Google Accounts

Google accounts are human users (members) authenticated from your identity provider that can be entitled to perform certain roles or actions in GCP. As discussed in earlier chapters, your users are typically provisioned in Cloud Identity, where users are defined along with the criteria for authenticating into GCP. User accounts should be individually provisioned and not managed by multiple humans, because you need to ensure accountability for every action that is performed in GCP. Remember the third A of the AAA security model—accounting (auditing).

Google accounts are typically developers, administrators, and other users who interact with Google Cloud. Any e-mail that is associated with a Google account, including Gmail addresses, can be an identity. You sign up for a Google account at https://myaccount.google.com.

This last point brings up an important topic: *conflict accounts*. These occur when a user creates a personal Google account with the same domain name as your organization. When your organization signs up for a managed Google account and attempts to add those users, a conflict will occur: users cannot use the same e-mail address for their personal and work accounts. This happens more often than you might think. Think about someone who signs up for a YouTube account with their work e-mail address. So what happens when you try to create an account for this user to your organization when there is already an existing account? The user with the existing account will be asked to rename their account. Once that account is renamed, it will continue to be managed *outside* of your organization.

Groups

Users and service accounts can be added to *groups*, which are logical containers or groupings of one or more accounts that define clear roles and ensure ease of manageability of your cloud access model. Groups are also provisioned in Cloud Identity. Imagine, for example, that your small organization is hiring DevOps engineers to work on the developer environment for its core application. It's much more difficult to track each and every developer's name and grant each individual access to that environment than it is to track developers by their role in the company and allocate them appropriately. That role probably will be applied to other applications in the group in which that team will be working. By using groups, you don't have to grant new permissions for each of your 300 developers; you can just add their role to the group policy.

Service Accounts

While users, or members, are the individual human accounts in Google Cloud, you'll often need to be able to perform certain actions without human involvement, but you'll still need to be able to trace where the action was performed. In this case, *service accounts* can be used in GCP. These programmatic accounts can be granted roles and privileges to perform certain actions on behalf of an application. Think about a bank running a batch job to process checks and sending the ledger of each transaction to a regulating agency every night. You can't expect your users to perform this action every single night. You can automate this instead by creating a service account with the appropriate permissions to access the database of posted transactions that can perform the batch job and send the transaction ledger to the agency.

When you run code on GCP, that code is run as the service account that you specify. There's no limit to how many service accounts you can leverage, and you should not be afraid to use as many service accounts as you need, as long as you have the appropriate oversight in place to manage them all. The principles of separation of duties and least privilege apply to service accounts as well as all members.

 NOTE Service accounts can be thought of as both a member and a resource. As a member, when you grant roles to a service account, you can allow it to access a resource. As a resource, when you grant roles to other members, you can allow those members to access or manage the service account.

Service accounts are not generated from your identity provider, whether it is Cloud Identity, Okta, or another provider. Service accounts are created within projects, so the management of these accounts falls directly to GCP. Authentication uses an X.509 private key to obtain OAuth2 tokens. You can also generate an external RSA private key if you need to authenticate to Google Cloud as the service account. Protecting this external RSA private key is important, because if this key is compromised, an attacker will have full access to all the resources that the service account is authorized to access.

Service accounts are an incredibly important aspect of the cloud. Any application that needs to access Google Cloud APIs will be leveraging service accounts. Imagine, for example, that your application needs to upload data to a storage bucket. How do you expect that application to upload the data? The application needs to be able to authenticate, to be authorized to perform the action in the target resource, and to programmatically perform a desired action. Service accounts can also be leveraged to run workloads in on-premises workstations or data centers that call Google Cloud APIs. Your application will assume the identity of the service account when it performs the action.

Managing Service Account Keys

In GCP, there are two types of service account keys:

- **GCP-managed keys** These keys are used by Google Cloud APIs such as Google App Engine, Google Cloud Storage, and Google Compute Engine.

You can't download these keys, and they're automatically rotated approximately once a week and are used for signing for a maximum of two weeks. (I won't get into Kubernetes here because it takes a much deeper dive with respect to key management than what this exam covers. So you can research that on your own.)

- **User-managed keys**   These keys are created, downloadable, and managed by your users. Once these keys are deleted from a service account, you can no longer use them to authenticate. If you're using user-managed keys, you need to think about some of the top key management requirements such as key rotation, storage, distribution, revocation, recovery, and access.

 NOTE   Keys that are stored in code by developers seem to be one of the hottest security weaknesses in the last few years. Every few months, we hear about a developer who stored a key in code and published the code to GitHub, where hackers and bots scour every new code change for explicitly stored keys. It's important that developers be taught to use best practices when managing keys, especially to ensure that they don't paste keys in their code.

You can create a process to use the IAM service account API to rotate your service account keys automatically. Most enterprises use some type of vault system to manage their keys. HashiCorp Vault is a top third-party solution in this space that has a close integration with GCP. With Vault, you can use its secrets engine to generate service account keys and OAuth tokens dynamically based on IAM policies. There is typically a secrets engine and a storage backend that is built to handle most of your key management tasks.

You can also create short-lived service account credentials, most commonly OAuth 2.0 tokens or OpenID Connect (OIDC) tokens if you need short-term elevated privileges. Imagine, for example, that you're fighting a production issue and need to troubleshoot it by impersonating a service account to determine the root cause.

Default vs. Custom Service Accounts

In GCP, there are two types of service accounts: default service accounts and custom service accounts. *Default service accounts* are automatically generated for Compute Engine instances upon project creation. Compute Engine needs service accounts to access other GCP resources. Upon project creation, these service accounts are entitled to a privileged editor role by default. Don't use the default Compute Engine service account because it's overly permissive, and you can do a better job of separating duties and minimizing privileges by creating your own application-specific service accounts. Instances depend on service accounts to access other resources. So be very certain that you've modified these dependencies before you delete a service account, because you might accidently break some of your VMs. *Custom service accounts* are user-created service accounts that can be used for various applications, including applications running on-premises or from another cloud environment.

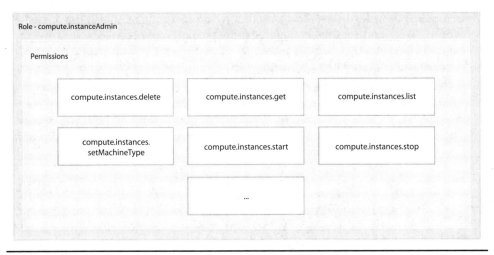

Figure 5-2 A set of permissions with the compute.instanceAdmin role

IAM Roles

In the RBAC model, users are not granted permissions directly to their user accounts, based on the discretion of the application owner, or based on security labels. Users are granted access based on a role in the organization that they perform. As mentioned earlier, a role is a collection of permissions. Roles are bound together with members inside an IAM policy, which is attached to a resource or an enforcement point. You cannot grant users permissions directly in GCP as you can in traditional, on-premises computing environments. When you grant users a role, they get access to all the permissions granted for that role. There are three types of roles in GCP: primitive roles, predefined roles, and custom roles. In Figure 5-2, you can see how the compute.instanceAdmin role is a collection of many permissions.

Primitive Roles

Primitive roles are historically available in the Cloud Console. These include roles such as Owner, Editor, and Viewer. These roles are no longer recommended to use today, and you should avoid them where possible because they are overly permissive.

Predefined Roles

Predefined roles offer finer-grained access control than primitive roles and are preconfigured by GCP to accomplish certain common functions. An example of a predefined role is a Pub/Sub Publisher, which in the console is shown as the roles/pubsub.publisher role. This role grants access to publishing messages with a Pub/Sub topic. Imagine, for example, that you have an Editor primitive role in a GCP project, which basically grants permissions to do any sort of editing across all of the resources within your project. It is recommended that you use predefined roles where you can.

Custom Roles

You can use a custom role to create a set of permissions that are tailored to the needs of your organization when the predefined roles do not meet your criteria. Given the careful development and criteria of predefined roles, custom roles aren't really used too often in GCP. There is usually a predefined role available to perform any desired action that meets the principle of least privileges and separated duties. Use these as needed.

IAM Policies

As discussed earlier, an IAM policy is a configuration that binds together one or more members and roles for the purpose of enforcing only approved access patterns through a collection of statements. These policies are represented by a Cloud IAM Policy object, which consists of a list of bindings. A *binding* binds a list of members to a role.

In Figure 5-3, you can see how a policy consists of one or more bindings; within each binding are members bound to roles, and the roles consist of a set of permissions. This policy can be attached to the various points of the organization hierarchy.

- A role is specified as *role/service.roleName*. Here's an example of an object creator role in Cloud Storage: role/storage.objectCreator
- Members are identified with a prefix:
  - Google Accounts = user:
  - Service account = serviceAccount:
  - Google Group = group:
  - G Suite or Cloud Identity domain = domain:

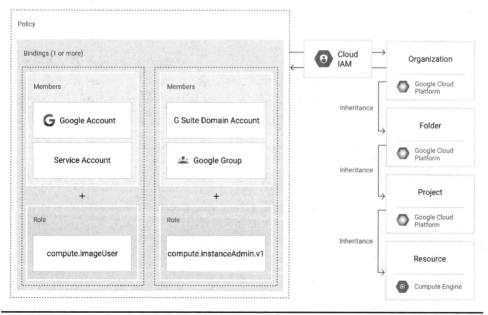

Figure 5-3 An example of IAM Policy binding

Here is an example code snippet of a Cloud IAM policy:

```
{
  "bindings": [
    {
      "role": "roles/storage.objectAdmin",
      "members": [
        "user:ali@example.com",
        "serviceAccount:my-other-app@appspot.gserviceaccount.com",
        "group:admins@example.com",
        "domain:google.com"
      ]
    },
    {
      "role": "roles/storage.objectViewer",
      "members": [
        "user:maria@example.com"
      ]
    }
  ]
}
```

IAM Conditions

The next evolution of a RBAC is the ability to augment your RBAC model with conditions in which a user can access a resource, such as what time of day a user can access a resource, which IP ranges they're permitted to originate from, and how long they're permitted to access a system. This is where IAM Conditions comes into play. *IAM Conditions* is an attribute-based access control model that lets you define the conditions in which a user is able to be authorized to access a resource. Today there are a few conditions that you can implement, but GCP continues to evolve and grow this feature with new request attributes. Conditions are added to your role bindings of your Cloud IAM policy, and you use the Common Expression Language (CEL) to specify the expression in the Cloud IAM Condition.

 EXAM TIP   You most likely won't see anything about IAM Conditions on the exam, because it's a recent generally available (GA) feature. It's a critical feature to use, though, especially for your highly sensitive crown jewel projects.

BeyondCorp

I'll preface this section by saying that it's unlikely you'll see much about Beyond-Corp in the exam. But BeyondCorp is certainly an access model that the most elite organizations implement and companies are striving to achieve.

BeyondCorp is Google's internal implementation of the zero trust security model that builds on best practices regarding how employees are authenticated and authorized internally. It is based on years of zero trust research and technologies and is intended to enable every employee to work from an untrusted network without the use of a VPN. Today, it is used effectively by Google users around the world.

It's almost impossible to assume that every user will be working from a secure location, and the use of a VPN can be a bottleneck in itself. In the BeyondCorp access model, Google has shifted access controls from the network perimeter to the users and devices. The high-level components of BeyondCorp include an SSO implementation, an access proxy, an access control engine, a user inventory, a device inventory, a security policy, and a trust repository.

Having never used a VPN at Google myself, I can say that I do not miss VPNs whatsoever. Being able to access any resources with biometrics from wherever in the world I am working has been a blessing in terms of productivity. I strongly encourage the strongest innovators to do a deep dive into the BeyondCorp zero trust model to see if it's something that is worth implementing at your organization. Google has a list of major partners, and one in particular, Dito, champions its ability in implementing the BeyondCorp model at the most complex of enterprises.

Accounting and Technical Compliance

The third A in the AAA security model is...? You guessed it: accounting (or auditing). I've said it so many times by now that even I'm sick of hearing it! I'm going to use auditing from this point on in the book. Another part of having a strong identity and access model is having the necessary telemetry data to ensure that you are monitoring for security and technical compliance. Who did what, where, and when? The Cloud Audit Logs security tool helps you get all of this data. Cloud Audit Logs are, well, exactly what they sound like: audit logs that provide the necessary authentication and access information for each Google Cloud project, folder, and organization.

There are three types of Cloud Audit Logs:

- **Admin Activity audit logs**   These contain log entries for API calls and other administrative actions that can modify configurations or metadata of resources. Log entries are generated, for example, when a user makes a modification to an IAM policy.

- **Data Access audit logs**   These contain API calls that read the configuration or metadata of resources and user-driven API calls against user-provided resource data. The logs are disabled by default because they are large, and large means expensive. It's highly recommended, however, that you enable these logs in your most critical environments.

- **System Event audit logs**   These contain administrative actions that modify the configuration of resources. They're generated by systems, not by user actions.

As a cloud administrator or security professional, you probably want to ensure that your configurations are not modified. Here's another big vulnerability of the day: customer-made misconfigurations are the leading causes of security breaches that happen in the cloud. To prevent this, you probably need to have a third-party vendor solution that helps you identify misconfiguration, such as Prisma Cloud from Palo Alto Networks or open-source Forseti Security. Both solutions offer a means to scan against misconfigurations in the cloud. In Forseti, you can build custom scanner rules or utilize ones that are on public GitHub pages. These scanners can, for example, ensure that there are no IAM policies on "All Users," ensure that service account keys are being rotated, or ensure that no Google accounts have access to production systems.

Chapter Review

In this chapter we discussed the importance of identity and access management, especially because it is one of the most critical security controls in protecting your intellectual property in GCP. There's no way I can emphasize this enough: truly embedding the AAA security model and principles of least privilege and separated duties into your IAM architecture alone will be effective in securing and hardening your cloud. It's like the Battle of Helm's Deep in the second *Lord of the Rings* movie—that gigantic wooden door (your IAM model) withstood an entire army of orcs (hackers) trying to smash the wooden tree stump (brute-force attack), until that one uruk hai (1337 leetsauce hacker) charged the castle's sewage system (unpatched vulnerability) with a bomb and threw the entire architecture out of whack. You're designing that same Helm's Deep when you are a Google Cloud Architect. Security is a responsibility of every single user in the cloud, and it starts with each chapter of architecture here.

We then went into Cloud IAM, which is the access control service that enables administrators to authorize who can take actions on what resources in GCP. In Cloud IAM, your users and groups are synchronized from Cloud Identity, which handles the authentication element of your cloud. Cloud IAM has three main components: members, roles, and IAM policies. Members can be categorized into five different types of users: Google accounts or human users, service accounts or programmatic users, Google groups or a grouping or set of users, Google Workspace domains, or Cloud Identity domains. The unique identifier for a member is the e-mail address associated with the account. IAM roles are a collection of permissions that determine what operations are allowed on a resource. There are three types of IAM roles: primitive roles, which are classic roles that are overly permissive and should never be used; predefined roles, which are curated roles by Google Cloud that define a duty aligned to a least privilege model on a certain function in GCP; and custom roles, which give you the ability to create your own set of permissions if nothing else meets your criteria. IAM policies are configurations that bind together one or more members and roles for the purpose of enforcing only approved access patterns through a collection of statements. This is done via a binding that binds a list of members to a role within a policy.

IAM conditions are the more advanced iteration of access control through an attribute-based access control model, with which you can not only define who can access a resource and what resource they can access, but you can also define the conditions in which that user can access the resource. Things such as time of day, time to live, geographic location, and a lot more will continue to come through the pipeline.

BeyondCorp is a zero trust access model that abstracts the authentication aspect of logging into the cloud away from the network and to the users and devices. The goal of a zero trust security access model is not to trust anything inside or outside an organization's network perimeters and to use a higher level of scrutiny to determine whether a user is who they say they are and if they are on a safe device to access a resource. Zero trust security models are great, so learn more about them at your leisure!

Lastly, we discussed the importance of following the third aspect of the AAA security model: auditing. Yep, I said we're going to use "auditing" from this point on and not "accounting." They mean the same thing, but let's just keep it easy. Auditing is your ability to ensure that your users—whether they be humans, service accounts, or other members—are meeting all of your technical compliance needs and that your security team is equipped with the right tools to ensure that everything is in order. We'll spend a lot more time on logging, monitoring, and auditing in Chapter 10.

With respect to IAM, just remember that there are certain types of logs that provide the data your security teams will need to ensure that the authentication and authorization elements of your IAM model are in line with your organization's requirements.

Additional References

If you'd like more information about the topics discussed in this chapter, check out these sources:

- **Cloud IAM Overview** https://cloud.google.com/iam/docs/overview
- **BeyondCorp** https://cloud.google.com/beyondcorp
- **Audit Logging** https://cloud.google.com/iam/docs/audit-logging

Questions

1. Your security team wants detailed visibility of all resources in your organization. You use Resource Manager to set yourself up as the organization admin. What Cloud IAM roles should you give to the security team?

   A. Org viewer, Project admin

   B. Org admin, Project browser

   C. Org viewer, Project viewer

   D. Project owner, Network Admin

2. GCP resources are managed hierarchically using organizations, folders, and projects. What is the effective Cloud IAM policy at a particular node of the hierarchy when there are multiple policies at varying levels of the hierarchy?

   A. The effective policy is determined only by the policy set at the node.

   B. The effective policy is the policy set at the node and restricted by the policies of its parent nodes.

   C. The effective policy is the combination of the policy set at the node and policies inherited from its parent nodes.

   D. The effective policy is determined from the nodes at the bottom of the resource hierarchy.

3. IAM policies are:

   A. A collection of statements that define who has what type of access

   B. A logical grouping of GCP resources that enable you to organize for policy enforcement and governance

   C. A method for tying a list of members to a role via a binding

   D. A configuration of users that are able to authenticate into the cloud

4. Your organization wants to centrally manage IAM policies for different departments independently. Which approach should you take?

   A. Create multiple organizations for each department and use your IAM policies on each folder.

   B. Use a single organization with folders for each department.

   C. Create multiple organizations, one for each business function.

   D. Use a single organization with multiple projects, each with a central owner.

5. You have an outage in your Compute Engine–managed instance group, and it seems that all instances keep restarting after five seconds. You have a health check configured, but autoscaling is disabled. Sydney, your engineer, needs to make sure that she can access the VMs. What should you do?

   A. Grant Sydney the project.Viewer IAM role.

   B. Disable the health check for the instance group and add her SSH key to the project-wide SSH keys.

   C. Restart the servers.

   D. Disable autoscaling for the instance group and add her SSH key to the project-wide SSH keys.

6. All of the following are recommended best practices for IAM *except* which one?

   A. Grant roles the least amount of permissions needed to perform the role.

   B. Treat each component of your application as a separate trust boundary.

   C. Use primitive roles by default.

   D. Restrict who has access to create and manage service accounts in your project.

7. You have an application that needs to interact with Google Cloud Storage and a few other Google Cloud APIs. This application needs to authenticate and be authorized to perform actions with these other services. Which type of account would you use in code when you want to interact with Google Cloud services?

   A. Google group

   B. Service account

   C. GitHub account

   D. Google account

8. Your client is migrating to the cloud and needs a solution to manage their secret keys for their service accounts. They need to interact with their Google Cloud services from their on-premises applications, and they also have Compute Engine instances in the cloud that need to talk with other GCP services. What service account key-management strategy should you recommend?

A. Provision service account external private keys for both on-premises and Cloud services.

B. Authenticate the on-premises infrastructure with a user account, and provision service account keys for the VMs.

C. Provision service account external private keys for the on-premises infrastructure, and use GCP-managed keys for the VMs.

D. Deploy a custom authentication service on Google Kubernetes Engine (GKE) for the on-premises infrastructure, and use GCP managed keys for the VMs.

9. Which of these is *not* a recommended method of authenticating an application with a Google Cloud service?

A. Embed the service account's keys in the source code.

B. Use the **gcloud** and/or **gsutil** command-line interface.

C. Request an OAuth2 access token and use it directly.

D. Use one of the GCP client libraries.

10. A user is troubleshooting the following code snippet to figure out what went wrong when putting together the IAM binding. What is likely the cause?

```
{
  "bindings": [
    {
      "role": "roles/storage.objectAdmin",
      "members": [
        "user:joetheboss",
        "serviceAccount:my-other-app@badcompany.gserviceaccount.com",
        "group:admins@badcompany.com",
        "domain:badcompany.com"
      ]
    },
  ]
}
```

A. The service account is not provisioned to the right domain address.

B. The member's code is blank.

C. The username needs to be an organization e-mail address and not just a username.

D. The user forgot to deploy the code.

Answers

1. **C.** Org viewer grants the security team permissions to view the organization's display name. Project viewer grants the security team permissions to see the resources within projects. You don't want to give editor privileges, especially because editor privileges are so permissive, unless it is absolutely required.

2. **C.** The policy set at the node automatically inherits the policies set by its parent nodes. So it will be a combination of both the inherited parent policies plus the policy set at the node.

3. **A.** IAM policies determine who (which user) has what type of access (is authorized to access which resource). A policy consists of a binding, which ties members to roles.

4. **B.** An effective way to do this is to use a single organization and multiple folders to separate your different departments. That way, you're empowered to define independent policies for each department according to their needs. You're also able to manage these policies centrally, as folders are all seen as points or nodes to attach IAM policies to.

5. **B.** The best answer is to disable the health check and add her SSH keys to the project-wide SSH keys. The question is asking for access to VMs that require SSH, so project.Viewer will not help there. The other issue is that the VMs keep restarting every five seconds, which is a function of a health check triggering a restart.

6. **C.** Primitive roles are overly permissive and should not be leveraged at all, if possible. Your goal is to ensure that you're following the best practices of least privilege, separation of duties, and the AAA security model to ensure that authentication, authorization, and auditing are properly defined and in place.

7. **B.** Service accounts are leveraged by your applications to perform programmatic actions on behalf of an application. Use service accounts, and don't store your secret keys in code.

8. **C.** If you're using an application on the premises, you won't be able to use GCP-managed keys on GCP. So you will have to generate an external private RSA key to grant access there. For your GCE to GCP APIs access, you will want to leverage GCP-managed keys.

9. **A.** Never—I repeat, *never*—embed your service account keys or any credentials directly into your source code.

10. **C.** Identifiers are always e-mail addresses, not usernames. The user should be granting the storage/object.Admin role to joetheboss@badcompany.com.

Networking

In this chapter, we'll cover

- How network constructs are built in Google Cloud Platform
- The various options for connecting to your cloud, including where and when they should be used
- Best security principles to defend your network against internal and external attackers
- A story about networks in a post-apocalyptic world

Evidence shows that the earliest human beings existed more 3 million years ago. These human beings had no concept of a network. Evolution had not enough time to grow and develop their brains to think about things like language and connections, and they were unable to think beyond their instincts for staying alive—find food and eat food or you'll die. About 2.5 million years ago, the first networks were formed as evolution began to progress, as humans realized that having other people around would be more resourceful and could help increase the probability of living another day. It took 2.5 million years to get to where we are today, after humans iteratively improved their capabilities by developing more complex thought patterns, understanding the necessities of life, learning how to communicate, developing technology, and then starting to learn empathy.

It has been a fascinating journey. Networking has enabled humans to progress in virtually every single aspect of our human development. It's easy to see how important it is to be resourceful and build connections in our lives. The "do it all alone" mind-set doesn't scale—not in personal development or from a technology standpoint.

As with human history, in the early history of computing, there was no such thing as a network. It wasn't until 1969 that the first form of computer-to-computer connection was born with the creation of ARPANET, which enabled the successful transmission of the word "login" from one computer to another. ARPANET was the precursor to the Internet. By enabling computers to communicate with one another, we unleashed a major evolution in technology. This technology has since been scaled exponentially by leveraging as many resources (or computers) as these networks could support to share data and iterate.

The Internet, in my opinion, is the single most impactful human invention in the past 3-plus–million years. With the advent of the Internet, we took networking from being confined to knowledge and data that could be mined in a local vicinity, to sharing and iterating data and knowledge collaboratively with billions of individuals and who-knows-how-many machines around the world, and even beyond. Think about life before the Internet. How did you source your knowledge? From the radio? From TV? From the nearest library? Internet networking has enabled you to connect with people all over the world and learn about their cultures, their beliefs, and their research. And it's networking that enables you to watch memes endlessly on Instagram, sharing them directly with Grandma at the click of a button.

Networking has evolved so much since the first network in 1969. In traditional computing, we used the castle-and-moat philosophy of protecting our organizations. Today in the cloud, we can rapidly deploy and delete an endless amount of castles and moats on demand, connected as necessary and when necessary, to spread resources for efficiency and to diversify risk. Safe perimeters can be logically extended across the world to provide instantaneous communications and resourcefulness across all of our castles. If we are even more advanced, we can follow a zero trust philosophy that assumes that nobody in the castle is a safe actor. This new paradigm gives us the power to leverage resources at massive scale (infinite scale is not correct, however, because there are only so many data centers that exist or will exist in the world) to solve the most complex of problems.

Be forewarned that this is a long and dense chapter. I recommend loading YouTube as you read so you can watch some videos if you need clarification on some topics—visual knowledge can be much more attainable at times. We're going to dive into all things networking.

Take off your on-premises hats and don't try to apply every traditional concept here. With the cloud, networking can operate in an entirely new and fundamental way that differs from traditional environments. Finally, security is still a feature that needs to be baked into every single design consideration. As you ponder how you're going to design your network in the cloud, wear an attacker's hat and think about how you can break into this architecture. That will help you right-size security patterns and controls into the way you design your architecture.

Networking Deep Dive

Networking in Google Cloud, or in the cloud in general, operates from a fundamentally different point of view than networking in traditional environments. Amazon Web Services (AWS) has been in the cloud space since around 2008 and has commanded a large market share because of its presence and timing on the market. Google's massive global infrastructure has been in place to serve content to billions of users worldwide. This move to the cloud was a no-brainer for Google, because all they had to do was externalize their infrastructure. Think about Google's massive global content delivery network that serves billions of users around the world with YouTube, Google Search, and Gmail; sharing this already established infrastructure to the world makes perfect sense.

Google's Global Network

Google Cloud's worldwide network serves content to billions of users, from internal applications for employees, to Google-developed public applications such as Gmail and YouTube, to customer applications built on their own infrastructure such as Spotify.

Hundreds of thousands of miles of fiber-optic cables connect this entire backbone of data center regions across land and under oceans. To date, Google has data centers and networking sites spanning over a total of 22 regions, 67 zones, 140 edge points of presence, and more than 800 global cache edge nodes. These numbers grow every month as Google is in a constant state of expansion because of the rapid growth of its business-to-consumer (B2C) technologies as well as its cloud business.

An *edge point of presence* (POP) is a location where Google connects its network to the rest of the Internet via peering. *Edge nodes*, also known as content delivery network (CDN) POPs, are points at which content can be cached and served locally to end users. The user journey starts when a user opens an application built on Google's infrastructure, and then their user request is routed to an edge network location that will provide the lowest latency. The edge network receives the request and passes it to the nearest Google data center, and the data center generates a response optimized for that user that can come from the data center, an edge POP, and edge nodes.

This entire infrastructure supports Google Cloud's custom Jupiter network fabric and Andromeda virtual network stack. The *Jupiter network fabric* is Google's system of networking hardware, represented as a fabric that provides Google with a tremendous amount of bandwidth and scale, delivering more than 1 petabit per second (Pbps) of total bisection bandwidth. This is enough capacity for 100,000 servers to exchange data at 10 Gbps each. To visualize the depth of this bandwidth and scale, the network could read the entire contents of the Library of Congress in less than 1/10th of a second. Insane networking throughput! *Andromeda* is Google's software-defined networking (SDN) stack that provides an abstraction on top of all of the underlying networking and data center hardware for Google and its cloud tenants to conduct business securely, privately, and efficiently. Google continually iterates its hardware and SDN—for example, the company saw a 3.3× latency improvement from virtual machine–to–virtual machine network latency from its release of Andromeda 2.1 over Andromeda 2.0. With this SDN stack, Google can offer endless cloud networking possibilities for GCP customers. Google is able to provide the most complex and innovative networking solutions as its world-class engineers continue developing new technologies in GCP.

 EXAM TIP Google's SDN and network fabric are all behind-the-scenes features made available to customers of GCP. You will not see anything about them in the exam, but it is quite fascinating to know how Google Cloud runs and operates its technology stack, especially if you are trusting GCP with your business.

Encryption in Transit

Encryption in transit is an important topic for cloud customers. Google encrypts and authenticates all network data in transit at one or more network layers when that data flows outside physical boundaries not controlled by Google; data in transit within GCP is not necessarily encrypted, but it is generally authenticated. This usually triggers some questions for security professionals, as they would imagine that in a multitenant cloud environment, they'd like all their data to be encrypted in transit and protected against packet sniffing or Address Resolution Protocol (ARP) cache poisoning attacks across the entire network, end to end.

Although Google encrypts all traffic outside its boundaries, Google employs many other security controls within its boundaries to ensure that customer data is private and protected from access by other Cloud customers. There are a few things to unpack here. The *Google Front End* (GFE) is a reverse proxy that protects the backend Google services. When a user sends traffic to Google, it hits the nearest edge node that routes the traffic through the GFE; then the GFE authenticates the user, assures integrity, and employs encryption in transit by default using Transport Layer Security (TLS)—specifically, BoringSSL, which is an open source version of OpenSSL. Once you are proxied by the GFE, you are under the purview of GCP.

Once your data is inside Google, varying levels of protection are available, depending on whether or not the data goes outside of the physical boundaries protected by Google. When data goes outside of that physical boundary, the network is semi-trusted, and Google enforces authentication and encryption in transit for that connection. For application layer, or layer 7 security, Google uses Google Remote Procedure Calls (gRPCs) from service to service that are authenticated, tamper-evident (maintains integrity), and encrypted in transit using Advanced Encryption Standard (AES) for calls that leave the physical boundary. Within Google's physical boundaries, data is authenticated and assured to be tamper-evident. Google attests to rigorous internal security controls and maintains the highest level of audit and compliance for them in order to prevent insider threats. Moreover, based on the inner workings of the software-defined network, there is no way that tenants sharing a physical host would be able to listen to other tenants' traffic. You still have the ability to employ additional secure measures on the application layer if you want or if your compliance and regulations require it, but for most organizations, using the default encryption in transit is sufficient.

Network Tiers

Since Google owns its entire network end to end, it is able to offer its customers the concept of *network service tiers*. Google offers two network service tiers: a default Premium network service tier and Standard network service tier. The *Premium tier* is the default setting for GCP customers, offering users access to high-performance networking using Google's entire global network, as described previously. In the Premium tier, Google uses *cold potato routing*, a form of network traffic routing in which Google will hold onto all network packets through the entire life cycle until they reach their destination. Once inbound traffic reaches Google's POP, Google will use cold potato routing to hold onto packets until they reach their destination. Outbound traffic will be routed through Google's network until it gets to an edge POP nearest to the user.

The *Standard tier* is a more cost-effective, lower-performance network that does not offer access to some features of Cloud networking (such as the ability to use a global load balancer) to save money. In the Standard tier, Google uses a *hot potato routing* method, whereby Google will offload your network traffic as fast as possible and hand it off to the public Internet to save you money.

NOTE In cold potato routing (Premium tier), Google will hold onto your network packets until they get as close to the user as possible. In hot potato routing (Standard tier), Google will offload your packets as close to the source, not the user, as possible so that the public Internet can handle the rest, which means you save some money on GCP.

Standard tier offers much lower performance and is less secure than Premium tier, and as a result, most GCP users do not use the Standard networking tier. Actually, the Premium tier is unique to GCP, because Google has its own massive private global network. Other cloud providers do not have a global network of fiber-optic cables connecting their data centers, so they have to use hot potato routing. This is one of the major reasons why GCP is a more secure cloud by default.

Virtual Private Cloud, Subnets, Regions, and Zones

We discussed all the things outside of your purview in Google Cloud—the magic behind the scenes. Now let's get into some details of the network constructs within your GCP environment.

Virtual Private Clouds

The fundamental network in the cloud is a *virtual private cloud* (VPC), a virtual version of a physical network built on Google's software-defined network stack, Andromeda. A VPC provides connectivity for your virtual machines (VMs), Google Kubernetes Engine (GKE) clusters, App Engine flex environment instances, and any other products that are built on Google Compute Engine (GCE) VMs. VPCs offer native internal TCP/UDP load balancing and proxy systems for internal HTTP(s) load balancing, as well as the ability to leverage a variety of connectivity options, from VPN tunnels to Cloud Interconnect attachments that connect to your on-premises environments. VPCs are global resources and are not associated with a particular region or zone; they are built inside of projects and by default do not permit cross-project communication.

Subnets

You can create your VPC in two ways, and your choice is determined by the way you create your subnets, which we'll dive into in the next paragraph. A *subnet* is a subnetwork, or a logical subdivision of your RFC 1918 IP space. An *RFC 1918 IP range* is simply a private network that uses both IPv4 and IPv6 specifications to define the usable private IP addresses in your network. In layman's terms, your RFC 1918 IP range is just your private network. Think about all the internal applications and devices that are hosted in your organization; they all have IP addresses on your RFC 1918 IP range (your private IP space) that is associated with your subnets. Subnets exist to make your network infrastructure more efficient, more manageable, and more secure. Subnets are also regional resources, whereas VPCs are global resources. Think about a company like Google.

Can you guess how many devices and servers those nerds have? All of those devices and servers need a unique name (an IP address) to talk to one another, and you can't shout at Habib the Database Server and expect a timely response in a single room full of a billion other servers.

You can't have a VPC network without at least one subnet in it, so you can either use auto mode VPC networks or custom mode VPC networks to provision your network. An *auto mode VPC network* is the default network that is created when you create a project. In this configuration, each region automatically gets a default /20 subnet created in it. *Custom mode VPC networks* do not come with any subnets, giving the network administrator full control to define the subnets and IP ranges before the network is usable. Custom mode VPC networks are the more likely choice of provisioning a network, especially because most enterprises are building their infrastructure with code. They do not come with any firewall rules by default. Many companies want to extend their private network from on-premises to the cloud, or between clouds. When you're defining your subnets, you want to be cognizant of things like the private IP ranges of your other private networks to avoid conflicts and right-sizing your subnets to make them most efficient. It's also very important to avoid overlapping IP addresses, and leveraging custom mode VPC networks enables you to have that full end-to-end control over your subnet creation. Auto mode networks are good if you just need to build and tear down a quick environment to do a proof of concept (POC), for example.

 EXAM TIP   Remember that VPC networks are global resources and subnets are regional resources. This design is one of the more significant advantages to using GCP over other clouds, because the global end-to-end physical network is fully owned by Google.

Regions and Zones

You probably already know the difference between a region and a zone if you're studying for this certification, but if not, let's do a quick refresher. A *region* is a collection of zones. A *zone* is an isolated location within a region. For example, in Northern Virginia, the us-east4 region is located in Ashburn and consists of us-east4-a, us-east4-b, and us-east4-c zones—which are typically individual data centers within the Ashburn, Virginia, geographical location. When you're building critical applications, you want to avoid any single points of failure, which could result from building applications in one zone or even building in one region. As you do with security, you imagine the worst will happen, and that will give you the north star for how to build your applications and networks to be fault tolerant, redundant, and highly available. Outages occur, and you should never believe otherwise; this is why service level agreements (SLAs) are so important. But there can be further outages beyond those anticipated in the SLA, for which you'd typically be eligible for financial credits from Google Cloud or whatever is determined as compensation in your SLA.

Two Outrageous Outages

A few years ago, in 2017, AWS experienced a major outage of its Amazon Simple Storage Service (S3) environment in Northern Virginia, which is commonly referred to as the "backbone of the Internet." Although S3 provides storage, similar to Google Cloud Storage (GCS), many other elements of web applications depend on S3 to surface data. This outage took down Medium, Slack, Reddit, and even the AWS cloud health status dashboard. In total, the four-hour outage resulted in a loss of approximately $150 million to the aggregate of the S&P 500 companies that were affected.

There was another outage caused by extreme winds in Northern Virginia later that year. I was sitting in a testing center across from Capital One in McLean, Virginia, taking the—wait for it—AWS Solutions Architect Associate certification exam. The wind took out power for the whole testing center, and there was another massive AWS outage. Luckily, the testing center providers had designed a strong disaster recovery system, and 25 minutes later, everything came back up with the answers still intact. That was a really tough exam.

For the context of your networks, VPCs are global resources, but the subnets themselves are regional objects. Your subnets can be assigned to one or multiple zones, but you cannot assign a subnet across multiple regions. The region you select for a resource determines the subnets that it can use. Let's say, for example, that you create a VM instance in the us-east4 zone. You can assign it an IP address only within the subnets that span across that zone. In Figure 6-1, you can see an example of a custom mode VPC network with three subnets in two regions.

Subnet Ranges and IP Addressing

You should be familiar with *Classless Inter-Domain Routing* (CIDR) and subnetting by now, but don't stress the nitty-gritty details of subnet ranges for the exam, because it's unlikely that you'll see questions about calculating subnet ranges and whatnot. CIDR is the guiding standard for Internet Protocol (IP) that determines the unique IP addresses for your networks and devices. These IP ranges are typically referred to as *CIDR blocks*. GCP has certain ranges that are restricted for its Google APIs, Google services, and other things.

When you create a subnet, you must define its primary IP address range, and you can optionally add a secondary IP range that is used only by alias IP ranges. Both IP ranges for all subnets in a VPC network must be a unique and valid CIDR block. For your RFC 1918 address space, it's the same as it would be in your on-premises environment, where you can use a 10.0.0.0/8, 172.168.0.0/12, or 192.168.0.0/16 IP range. The primary internal addresses for VM instances, internal load balancers, and internal protocol forwarding comes from the subnets' primary range.

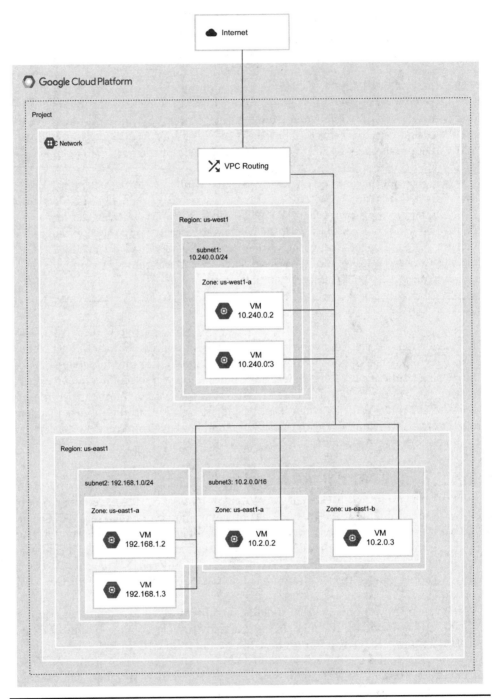

Figure 6-1 Custom mode VPC network with three subnets

External IP addresses are accessible to the public Internet. These addresses are not on your RFC 1918 IP address range. You can use external IPs on VMs and external load balancers. If you want your VM to be directly accessible from the outside (which you should avoid at all costs unless you have a need for public-facing endpoints), you would request a public IP as part of your VM creation. Google will then assign your VM a public IP address from its pool of available external IP addresses.

Keep in mind that externally accessible IPs are one of the biggest threat vectors for malicious actors, so you should be very aware and deliberate regarding what you're exposing to the outside world and how you're exposing it. Although there are many incredible Internet visitors who deserve praise for using the Internet ethically, there are an equal number of not-so-nice humans who are actively seeking out vulnerable people and technologies to exploit to gain a reward—even if that reward is simply bragging rights on 4chan. There are many use cases for external IPs—game servers, web applications, other consumer-facing applications, and more. However, you'll avoid much pain by simply asking this question: Who needs access to these machines and how can I reduce or avoid attack risks from those who don't?

To Expose, or Not to Expose

Following are some considerations to ponder when you're deciding whether or not to use an external IP:

- If you want to open an internal instance of Jira to your internal users who are working remotely, you don't need to expose it to the Internet.

- If you want your contractors to access an HVAC system application remotely, you don't need to expose it to the Internet.

- If a bunch of VMs need to perform updates from the Internet, you don't need to expose them to the Internet directly. Use network address translation (NAT) instead.

- If you need public users to access a web application, you should serve static content through your content delivery network (CDN) and put your application behind an external load balancer and/or a web application firewall (WAF), such as Cloud Armor.

- If users need to access a production game server, use public IPs and put them behind a proper security stack.

- If there are API calls to and from your network, rather than using public IPs, put them behind an API gateway and leverage whitelisting and proper firewall rules to allow communication.

(continued)

- If you are evaluating a marketplace application in a sandbox project that uses a public IP address as part of its deployment, consider adding a firewall rule to allow traffic only from known IP sources (such as your company's external IP CIDR block or the IP address assigned by your home service provider).

- Finally, if you absolutely need to expose a VM to the Internet and you can't properly secure that machine (and you should assume that you can't), then isolate your VM from the rest of your network. Basically, if machines need direct access to the Internet, you should limit the blast radius to those minimum resources. Don't let a breach of these VMs extend beyond those resources.

There are many ways to expose an application to the public without granting users direct access to the application instance itself. Adding layers of abstraction such as a load balancer, a CDN for static content, or an API gateway always adds an additional layer of security to the underlying application.

We'll dive into network security best practices later in the chapter, but for now, note that everything is always easier in theory. In practice, when you're facing large and complex migrations and hard deadlines, you'll have to play a role in prioritizing the most important controls to protect your enterprise and to minimize risk. As a cloud architect, you must clearly gather the requirements for a desired network pattern and maintain a set of approved patterns, documented clearly alongside a risk assessment and clear usage criteria that is accessible to your users internally.

Routes and Firewall Rules

When it comes to routing, you should know the simple difference between ingress and egress traffic. From a routing efficiency, security, and cost perspective, knowing how to optimize your network routes is key to building a well-architected network. *Ingress traffic* refers to packets that have a destination inside of your network boundary. *Egress traffic* refers to packets that originate inside of your network boundary but have a destination outside of your boundary. In this context, your network boundary is not necessarily Google's data centers. You can have many network boundaries, depending on how you set up your VPC. Here are a few examples:

- Egress traffic between zones in the same region on your RFC 1918 address space.

- Egress traffic between regions within the United States and Canada, or other continents, on your RFC 1918 address space.

- Egress traffic between GCP and on-premises RFC 1918 CIDR blocks.

- Egress traffic between regions across continents on your RFC 1918 address space.

- Egress traffic through external IP addresses.

- Internet egress.

Ingress traffic is free, whereas egress traffic has costs associated with it, depending on the usage and the services being used. Quite often during the sales cycle, enterprises and Google Cloud sales teams are gathering networking usage details to estimate the cost of traffic routing. It's not the ingress traffic that costs ISPs a lot of money; it's always the egress traffic. On Google Cloud, it's very much the same. Imagine all of the traffic that flows between data centers, between regions, and between continents—somebody has to pay that bill, and when your meme-generator company has petabytes of internal traffic flowing across the world, it's not going to be cheap!

Routes define paths for egress traffic. Think of your network like a combination of highways and roads sprawling across the country. The roads themselves (like physical network cables) don't know where drivers are going. Luckily, however, signs on the road tell drivers which exit and paths to take if they are going toward a specific destination. Network routes act like the signs on the road, helping a packet get from one place to another. Routes define how individual packets will travel across the network, depending on where they are going. This can get rather complicated because, unlike modern roads, these routes know about only the next exit junction. They don't see "the big picture." So, if you are going toward X, Y, or Z, they'll tell you to get off this road at this exit; otherwise, you should stay on this road to the next exit. With modern networking, these signs can be either *static* (hardcoded) or *dynamic* (updated behind the scenes). The trouble with networking, and what drives architects, developers, and cloud operators crazy at times, is that when your car/packet runs into a dead end, it is eliminated/dropped. Talk about a bad road trip! Networking concepts can get very deep and go way beyond the requirements for this certification. However, it is very important that you understand that if you don't set up the signs on the road correctly, your drivers will get lost and will be terminated! Thankfully, configuring networks on public cloud platforms are, relatively speaking, much less painful than what your typical Cisco Certified Internetworking Expert has to deal with.

In GCP, there are two categories of routes: system-generated routes and custom routes. Every new network starts with two types of system-generated routes: a default route and a subnet route. The *default route* is a system-generated route that defines a path for traffic that meets Internet access criteria to leave the VPC. Now this is important. What does it mean to leave the VPC in your architecture? Within GCP, it is assumed that you will exit to the Internet through GCP resources such as a cloud NAT or Internet gateway. But many enterprises, as a security policy, do not want GCP resources to have their own Internet traffic routes. Such access to the Internet adds points to the attack surface area. Any one of these Internet access points could be used to launch a direct attack on all GCP networked resources and even on-premises resources. So instead, such access is often routed to explicit destinations such as back to the on-premises network (which already protects Internet access) or to a dedicated environment such as a DMZ (demilitarized zone) within GCP to provide a single point of entry/exit to protect properly.

For the sake of simplicity, let's assume that your VPC projects are isolated and self-contained. For these environments, the *default route* criteria would have traffic that has to do the following:

- Have a default Internet gateway route that provides a path to the Internet
- Have firewall rules that must allow egress traffic from the instance
- Have an external IP or be able to use NAT

The *subnet route* is created for each of the IP ranges associated with a subnet, with each having at least one subnet route for its primary IP range. These routes define paths for traffic to reach instances that use the subnets. This extends across your entire RFC 1918 private IP network (on GCP, on premises, multi-cloud, and so on). Let's go back to the road concept. Think of subnet CIDR ranges as the most granular level that road signs understand. Inside an individual subnet, all the "homes" can easily reference one another by their home address (IP address). But when they need to "drive to another home" outside their current subnet, the network needs to find the best road/path to the destination egress address. It does this by using the destination subnet CIDR. From a network engineering perspective, as your network gets more complicated, this is the configuration you need to ensure is correct to enable individual subnets across your network to communicate with one another. If your machines are unable to communicate across multiple subnets, you likely have a misconfiguration in your subnet routes or a firewall misconfiguration.

Right-sizing your subnets is incredibly important when you're designing your network. You can always expand IP addresses on subnets, but you can't shrink and repurpose the IP ranges elsewhere. There is a finite amount of addressable IPs in IPv4, and if you're expected to build only 1000 homes in your neighborhood, you don't want to provision a subnet range for 100,000 homes. Right-size your subnets to the best of your ability, because you can always expand them and cross that bridge when you get there; but you cannot do the opposite!

 TIP Once you create a primary IP range for your subnet, you can't modify it on GCP. If you need to add IPs to your subnet, you first need to configure alias IP ranges and then use those as secondary IP ranges for your subnet. This is how you can expand your subnet IPs on GCP.

Firewall rules are your first perimeter boundary to protect yourself to and from the evil world. (Treat the world as evil. I don't care how many nice, wholesome videos you saw on Reddit today. In 2020, a 17-year-old kid hacked Twitter. This is unrelated to firewalls, but the message is the same: trust nobody! This is the Internet, where everybody gets pwned.) Firewall rules are leveraged to allow or deny traffic to and from VPC networks. When a rule is created, you specify a VPC network and a set of components that defines what the rule does. You can target certain types of traffic based on protocols, ports, sources, and destinations.

One of the items you'll see on the test on a question or two will have something to do with network tags. *Network tags* are strings that are used to make firewall rules and routes applicable to specific VM instances; they are added to the tags field in any resource, such as a compute engine instance or instance templates. Here are a few examples of when to leverage network tags:

- You want to make a firewall rule apply to specific instances by using target tags and source tags.
- You want to make a route applicable to specific instances by using a tag.

EXAM TIP   You may see a scenario in which a web application has VMs running inside of a VPC, and you're asked to restrict traffic between the instances to specific paths and ports that you authorize. The application autoscales, so you can't route based on a static IP address. In this case, you'd use firewall rules to authorize traffic based on network tags that are attached to your VMs.

Private Access

A VPC is your virtual private cloud. It is private, where you manage IP addressing and your entire infrastructure. Google Cloud uses many public API endpoints for its managed services such as Google Cloud Storage and BigQuery. If you have an instance that needs to communicate with these services, you would need to have an external IP address to communicate with the resources outside of its network. This is where Private Google Access and Private Service Access come into play.

Private Google Access

Private Google Access enables instances without external IP addresses to access resources outside of their network inside Google Cloud. This was created to avoid security concerns for sensitive workloads where you did not want to have to assign your VM an external IP address and have it communicate over the Internet to communicate with Google Cloud's managed services. You can extend this access through your on-premises network if you have a VPN or an interconnect setup.

Private Google Access enables you to use Google managed services across your corporate intranet without having to access the Internet and exposing your GCP resources to Internet attackers. Remember that RFC 1918 is your friend from a security perspective. The fewer public IP addresses you are dealing with, the lower your external attack surface area. Private Google Access can be used to maintain a high security posture using private IP addressing within your network, while leveraging Google services and resources that live outside it but still inside Google Cloud. Google Cloud acts as a sort of DMZ in that you can leverage these services to bring assets (such as data files into GCS, public repositories in BigQuery, Git repositories in Cloud Source Repositories, and so on) into your ecosystem without actually exposing your network to the outside world. This significantly reduces your exposure to a network attack. You don't always need to access the Internet from your environment to keep it up-to-date. You can have the Internet come to you via Google Cloud services and then access those resources indirectly through Private Google Access.

Imagine a scenario in which you need to install software on your VMs, and the content is located in an on-premises file server, but your organization does not permit or have connectivity (VPN or Interconnect) between your Google Cloud environment and your on-premises network. Moreover, your Google environment needs to install this software securely without accessing the Internet as per security requirements. You can enable this capability securely using Private Google Access. You can establish a secure TLS session from your on-premises environment to GCS when you need to upload your files using **gsutil**. Then you can set up Private Google Access on the GCP project's subnet that your VM is located on, and just use the **gsutil** tool to download your content to the VM from GCS on GCP. It's like a secret backroad to Google Cloud public endpoints, and Google acts as your security guard.

Private Service Access

Private Service Access enables you to connect to Google and third-party services that are located on other VPC networks owned by Google or third parties. So imagine a company that offers a service to you, hosted on its internal network on GCP, and you want to connect to that service without having to go over the public Internet. This is where you'd want to leverage Private Service Access. This sounds a bit more risky, but Google has many controls to ensure privacy between tenants to prevent security incidents. Still, you should assess each offering with the lens of your organization's risk tolerance. This security model is similar to how AWS implemented a dedicated GovCloud for government agencies wanting a more secure cloud. The idea is that by never leaving the Google Cloud network and using trusted and certified third parties, you are able to leverage best-of-breed Software as a Service (SaaS) services or partner services without having to host these applications yourself in your own cloud.

Cross-Project Communication

We discussed in Chapter 4 (Resource Management) that it's a best practice to follow a "many projects" approach. Oftentimes, you'll need to communicate between VPCs that are used on separate projects. Even if you created two VPCs on the same project, they won't be able to communicate with each other by default. You've got options for how you want to enable cross-project communication. You can use these communication approaches beside one another, as some network complexities will require multiple communication mechanisms between VPCs. In this section, we'll discuss the usage patterns for a shared VPC, when to use VPC peering, and when you want to leverage a VPN gateway between VPCs.

Shared VPC

Some enterprises want strict control over all of the happenings inside of the cloud, and other organizations want to enable full developer freedom. Shared VPC provides a happy medium. It enables an organization to connect resources from multiple projects to a common VPC so that they can communicate securely on the same RFC 1918 IP space while still having a great amount of freedom and ownership over their projects. In the shared VPC model, a host project essentially becomes your control plane, and service projects give your developers freedom to build while still being confined to the constraints defined in the control plane. Your host project is where your VPC gets provisioned, including all of the networking elements. Your service projects are attached to the host project, where you can provision resources and allocate them internal IP addresses from the shared VPC.

In a shared VPC model, billing is attributed to the service project. Think about a large enterprise with a variety of revenue-generating business units that wants to use Google Cloud, but the company wants all of its business units to adhere to the organization's governing model. In such a case, you'd want to use a shared VPC, so that each business

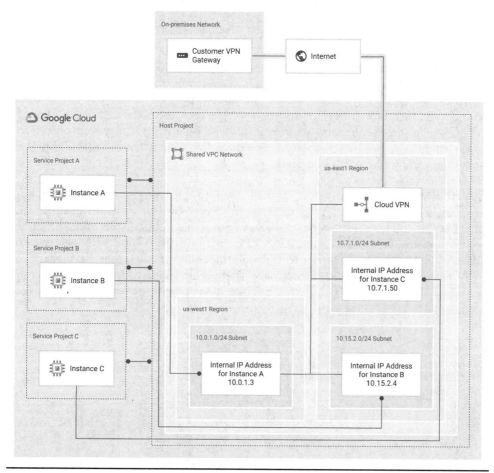

Figure 6-2 Sample shared VPC network

unit owns a portion of the bill and has more freedom to develop and build, and your centralized network and security administrators define the policies that govern the entire enterprise. In Figure 6-2, you can see an example of a shared VPC deployment.

You can have multiple shared VPCs inside a host project, but a service project can be connected only to one host project. This is becoming a much more common pattern, especially with large enterprise organizations, as they are federating the cost of cloud computing to their teams who want to leverage the cloud. In most enterprises, if any of the businesses want to migrate, they can administer most of their infrastructure, communicate to other business units securely, and also pay their portion of their bill themselves.

NOTE   Shared VPC is typically referred to as "XPN" in the API.

VPC Peering

VPC peering enables two separately managed VPCs to communicate with each other. These connections are nontransitive, meaning that multiple VPCs cannot communicate through a common VPC unless they are explicitly peered with each other. This is great for organizations that federate the governance and ownership of their projects to their teams to own their project and VPCs fully, but their projects still need to communicate with one another. From a performance perspective, there are no latency issues, as peering a VPC would provide the same performance they'd experience if they were on the same VPC network. In Figure 6-3, you can see a case of an ingress firewall that allows traffic only from certain source IPs in a peered network.

Cloud VPN

You can leverage the cloud VPN to connect VPC networks in hybrid environments. Imagine that you have a network in AWS and you'd like to build a network pattern that connects your GCP VPC to your AWS VPC environment. Cloud VPN is a transitive IPSec VPN tunnel. This is a more scalable solution, but it requires that you manage your VPN tunnels and network configurations. There is also limited throughput—you only get 1.5 Gbps over the Internet and 3 Gbps over direct peering or between GCP projects.

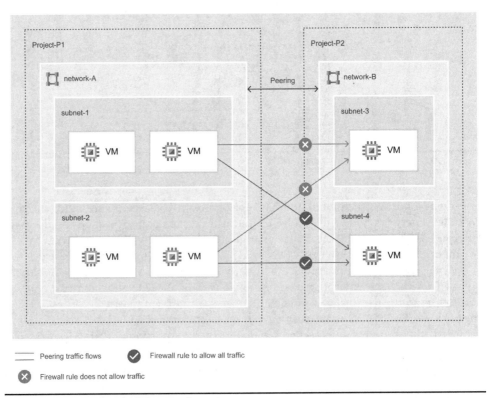

Figure 6-3 Firewall with VPC network peering

It is likely that you'll see improvements to this technology in the future, with Google Cloud and other cloud providers offering VPN solutions that significantly improve throughput.

 EXAM TIP Know the difference between transitive and nontransitive peering. If, for example, VPC-A is connected to VPC-B using VPC peering, and VPC-B is connected to VPC-C via peering, VPC-A will still explicitly have to be connected to VPC-C to communicate—hence it being nontransitive. In the transitive model, as long as routes and rules are properly configured, you can communicate across to any other connected networks, which is typically the pattern desired in a hub-and-spoke model.

Cloud DNS

If you have a web server running your startup's website with an IP address of 72.44.923.12, good luck trying to get anyone beyond you and your co-founder to memorize that address. The Domain Name System (DNS) solves this by translating domain names to IP addresses so your web browser can load Internet resources. It's the phonebook of the Internet. You should have a strong understanding of DNS by this point in your career, so we'll skip the basics. (If you don't, I recommend that you brush up on how DNS works online.)

 EXAM TIP You likely won't see anything too complex on the test about DNS, except maybe some questions about troubleshooting, where the answers could have to do with incorrect DNS records or setup.

In the world of the cloud, with hybrid environments consisting of multiple clouds and on-premises environments, DNS records for internal resources typically need to be accessed across environments. Traditionally, in on-premises environments, these DNS records are manually administered using an authoritative DNS server. When you run DNS in Google Cloud, it's important to be familiar with a few concepts:

- **Internal DNS** This service automatically creates DNS records for VMs and internal load balancers on GCE with a fully qualified domain name.
- **Cloud DNS** This managed service provides ultra–low-latency and highly available DNS zone serving with 100-percent SLA. It can act as an authoritative DNS server for public zones that have Internet visibility or private zones that are visible only within an internal network.
- **Public DNS** This is a Google service, not Google Cloud, offering an open, recursive DNS resolver—you've probably seen 8.8.8.8 and 8.8.4.4 in your technology life at some point.

It's possible that an organization may want to hold off migrating their DNS service to Cloud DNS for public zones but may want to use Cloud DNS just for their private zones. If you're using Cloud DNS for your internal-facing DNS records, you'll need to configure private zones to manage all of the internal records. The VPC must be in the same project and authorized to use the private zones in order for this to work properly, and if you're working across projects, you'll need to configure DNS peering. DNS peering enables you to query private zones across VPC networks without having to connect the networks. This is especially useful in a hub-and-spoke model, where you'd want to forward queries from a hub project on GCP to your on-premises environment. Let's think about that for a second.

- Imagine you have a hub-and-spoke model for your company, Covfefe, where your hub (VPC-A) is a VPC that is connected to your on-premises environment via an interconnect.

- Your spokes are separate VPC networks (VPC-B and VPC-C) that are peered to your hub (VPC-A).

- Since peering is nontransitive, you can't automatically resolve DNS queries across VPC-A to the on-premises environment.

- You'd want to leverage DNS peering to peer your private DNS zones on VPC-B and VPC-C to your peering zone (gcp.covfefe.com) on VPC-A. Then you could use a DNS forwarding zone to forward those queries to your on-premises (onpremise.covfefe.com) environment.

As mentioned earlier, don't worry too much about diving deeply into DNS if you're really focused on passing the exam. Just think about what could happen in the event of a missing record—what types of errors you'd run into. Could the lack of a DNS record or an improper zone configuration be the answer to your problem?

Connectivity to Your Cloud

Most organizations are not cloud-native. Most are running either their own data centers or are working with third-party providers that provide the organization space to own its physical infrastructure (the not-so-cloud cloud). As you can imagine, if you've already been running technology for so many years, it isn't easy to jump ship and rebuild or migrate everything to Google Cloud. For many organizations, including cloud-native ones, there are always aspects of connectivity requirements between data centers, other cloud providers, and Google Cloud that come into play. It's very rare to see an organization put all its eggs in one basket, and that's not a best practice from a risk-management standpoint. So oftentimes you need connectivity to provide critical services access to others across this multi-cloud or hybrid environment.

Imagine, for example, that you're running a machine learning environment that is processing data and needs to ingest streaming data from an on-premises application in a secure fashion. How would you set up this ingestion pipeline securely without having proper connectivity in place between your on-premises data center and GCP? As a cloud architect, if you're building these network pipes, you'll want to gather some information about the bandwidth, SLA, and redundancy requirements. You'll want to know the use case, where your data centers are located, and how to leverage the right connections in the most operationally efficient and cost-efficient way. In this section, we'll talk about using a VPN, using the various Cloud Interconnect options, and peering your networks with GCP. But, first, let's discuss the most important foundational element here, which is Cloud Router.

Cloud Router

Cloud Router is a managed service that dynamically exchanges routes between your VPC and your on-premises network using the Border Gateway Protocol (BGP) via a Dedicated Interconnect or Cloud VPN. This router is the foundational element of using the Cloud VPN and Cloud Interconnect.

BGP is a very complex exterior gateway path-vector routing protocol that advertises routing and reachability information among autonomous systems on the Internet. Virtually the whole Internet runs on BGP. There are two flavors of BGP you should be aware of—external BGP (eBGP) and internal BGP (iBGP).

Let's imagine we have five large companies that have their own networks full of computing systems: Froogle, Tastebook, Netzeroflix, Bamazon, and Microdelicate. The collection of each of their public networks is considered an independent autonomous system (AS). eBGP enables each of those autonomous systems to advertise to its connected peers and say, "Hey world, this is Froogle, I'm right here! This is my Public IP network." eBGP lets all of these systems announce themselves to the world as their assigned AS number and what IP ranges their networks own. eBGP then propagates these details across the global network, with each node calculating best paths to optimize traffic routing with this new information. eBGP is the mechanism that enables the Internet to propagate public IP addresses across the globe. iBGP, on the other hand, is a mechanism to provide detailed private IP network information within an AS. So when you connect two separate ASs with a solution like Cloud VPN, their private network details are exchanged using iBGP. Obviously, Froogle can't access Tastebook's internal networks, because these are only aware of each other's public IP network via eBGP.

So in the context of the cloud, the Cloud Router provides a managed service that exchanges private network routes between your VPCs and your on-premises networks using iBGP. You can do this on a regional level by sharing routes only for subnets in the region where you have leveraged a Cloud Router, or you can leverage global routing to share the routes for all of your subnets inside of your VPC. When these routes are advertised, by default, they advertise subnets according to the regional or global routing option. If you want more control, you can use custom advertising to decide which IP ranges and subnets to advertise. Imagine that Froogle and Bamazon partnered up and ran a multiorganizational infrastructure with shared resources across the cloud, and you have to connect to your on-premises environment but you don't want to share Bamazon's subnets—this is where you'd use custom advertising. In Figure 6-4, you can see an example of what a regional dynamic route would look like.

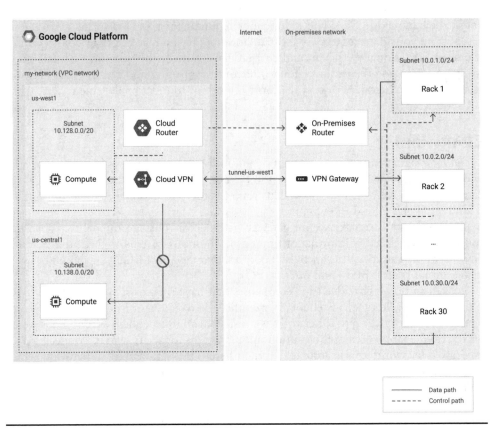

Figure 6-4 Cloud Router with regional dynamic routing

Cloud VPN

I would imagine that by this point in your career, you know what a VPN is. If you don't, that's alright; there's always next year. Kidding. Let's do a five-second refresher. A VPN lets you create a secure tunnel over an unsecure channel to avoid people sniffing and snooping on your packets. Cloud VPN is a solution that enables you to connect any of your peer networks to your VPC securely through an IPSec-encrypted tunnel. IPSec, Internet Protocol Security, is a secure network protocol that authenticates and encrypts the packets of data between two endpoints. This includes data that flows between a pair of hosts (host-to-host), between a pair of security gateways (network-to-network), or between a security gateway and a host (network-to-host).

You can use Cloud VPN to secure access from other clouds or your on-premises environment to GCP. But it has its limitations, particularly around bandwidth, because it supports only 1.5 to 3 Gbps per tunnel, depending on your peering location. There are two types of Cloud VPNs: Classic and High Availability (HA). Classic VPN supports static routing in addition to dynamic routing. As you can imagine, if you're using static routing, you've got to have an external IP and interface for each VPN gateway you set up. There's really no reason to use Classic VPN. If you don't have any need for static routing, leverage the HA VPN. With the HA VPN, you can do dynamic routing and you can connect as many on-premises VPNs to your HA VPN gateway without having all of the overhead of managing several VPN gateways in GCP. Many companies have not adopted the BeyondCorp zero trust access model and still have a need to use Cloud VPN to secure their on-premises traffic to GCP; sometimes it's easier and more cost-effective to spin up a Cloud VPN if it meets your use cases to secure traffic between sites as well, rather than having to provision an interconnect.

Cloud Interconnect

You know you're a born engineer when you have a story about how you got so tired of your awful Wi-Fi, especially after ISPs started doing multimedia-over-coax in their router/modem combos. Since you were too lazy to bridge your custom-flashed DD-WRT router, you instead decided to run a 100-foot cable through the crevices of your house just so that your Internet friends wouldn't hate you for lagging everyone up in a StarCraft match. Cloud Interconnect is similar to this but better, because it offers a low-latency, highly available network connection to transfer data and connect your RFC 1918 address space between your on-premises environments and GCP VPCs. Cloud Interconnect offers two options for extending your on-premises network: Dedicated Interconnect and Partner Interconnect. *Dedicated Interconnect* provides a direct, dedicated physical connection between your on-premises network and GCP. *Partner Interconnect* provides a connection between your on-premises and VPC networks through a supported service provider.

Dedicated Interconnect

Dedicated Interconnect is a dedicated line that connects your on-premises environment to your VPC network, enabling your private RFC 1918 space to communicate while bypassing the Google Front End (GFE). Dedicated Interconnect can use either 10 or 100 Gbps lines (commonly referred to as network pipes) that provide a 99.9 percent or 99.99 percent SLA and can attach to multiple VPCs by creating a VLAN with VLAN attachments in your Cloud Router. This line is dedicated to your traffic only, so it is not encrypted. Whenever security architects hear "not encrypted," they panic, so let's backtrack a bit to see exactly how this is set up.

First, Dedicated Interconnect is not available everywhere, because your physical network will need to meet Google's network in a colocation facility. Inside of Google's colocation facility, you'll be providing your own routing equipment that must support a 10G or 100G circuit and some other requirements. This is called a *cross connect*, because it connects your on-premises router (essentially your on-premises network) to Google's peering edge network inside of the colocation facility via a dedicated 10G link, a 100G link, or a bundle of links—this is your Dedicated Interconnect. You would then use interconnect attachments (VLAN attachments) to create an 802.1q VLAN to your Cloud Router that can be attached to multiple VPCs. Each attachment can be connected to a single VPC only, and only within the regions that the colocation facility serves; you can see those details online. Here are the essential details:

1. You bring your own trusted hardware into a colocation facility owned by Google that extends your on-premises network into Google's colocation facility.

2. From there, you cross-connect to a Google peering edge via a Dedicated Interconnect line(s) that Google reserves for you.

3. From this Dedicated Interconnect, you create interconnect attachments to configure a VLAN and associate it with a Cloud Router in the regions that the physical colocation facility supports, bypassing the GFE entirely, and avoiding any multitenant concerns.

4. Your Cloud Router is then attached to multiple VPCs.

5. At this point, you essentially have a full extension of your private RFC 1918 into Google Cloud. I hope you properly defined your VPCs' RFC 1918 IP ranges and subnets to avoid overlapping and conflicts with your internal network. Otherwise, you'll need to solve that problem now.

In Figure 6-5, you can visualize this configuration. You can see that at no point do you have to worry about any other cloud tenants or malicious users sniffing your unencrypted traffic, as long as you trust Google enough—and I doubt you'd be hosting your data with them if you didn't. Some organizations need to encrypt traffic among themselves because of compliance regulations. For this use case, you can use any third-party IPSec VPN to encrypt traffic inside of your interconnect. You can't use Cloud VPN, though. Imagine, for example, that your company is trying to build a backup replica of its on-premises MySQL database on GCP. It's a large 25TB database and updates multiple times a day, and it requires RFC 1918 space. Cloud VPN won't have enough bandwidth here. You'll need to use a Dedicated Interconnect.

When you use a Cloud Interconnect, traffic between your on-premises network and your VPC network does not traverse the public Internet, and that means fewer network

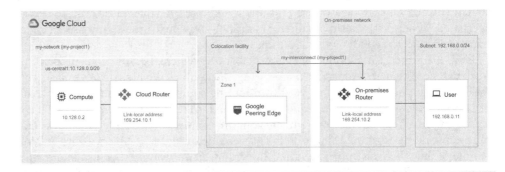

Figure 6-5 Sample Google Dedicated Interconnect configuration

hops and fewer points of failure where your traffic might get dropped or distributed. You also won't need to use a NAT or VPN to reach internal IP addresses. Using Cloud Interconnect is a great way to reduce your egress costs, as you still have to worry about egress costs when you use a Cloud VPN. Also, don't forget Private Google Access, because you can still use it in conjunction with Cloud Interconnect so that your on-premises hosts use internal IPs to reach Google APIs and services. If you don't use Private Google Access, your hosts will still be leveraging TLS when they're accessing Google APIs and services through the GFE.

Partner Interconnect

You get the gist of how the interconnect works. So I'll keep this section short and sweet. Dedicated Interconnect costs more, and it isn't available unless you are geographically near a Google peering edge. You also don't need to spend the money for a 10G Dedicated Interconnect if you only need bandwidth between 50 Mbps and 10 Gbps. So it can be more cost-efficient. Partner Interconnects are available in a lot more parts of the world. With this type of connection, instead of connecting your on-premises network to a Google peering edge, you connect your on-premises router to a partner peering edge that is connected to a Google peering edge, which then connects to your Cloud Router via the same attachment mechanism described in the last paragraph.

 EXAM TIP Don't forget the bandwidth constraints of the various connectivity options. Cloud VPN only supports up to 3 Gbps per tunnel, Partner Interconnect supports up to 10 Gbps, and Dedicated Interconnect supports up to 100 Gbps. If you get a question on the exam about speed, privacy, and connecting between on-premises to GCP—you know what to do.

Cloud Load Balancing

One of the major benefits of using Google Cloud over other cloud solutions is Google's fully owned global infrastructure. Other cloud solutions offer regional infrastructure. With Google Cloud, this plays a significant role for load balancing. Think about it: Google has had to load-balance global traffic for billions of users using Gmail, YouTube, and Google Search worldwide for 20 years now. They're experts! The cloud uses the same infrastructure that serves Google and the world.

Cloud Load Balancing is a fully distributed, high-performance, software-defined, managed load balancing service that dynamically distributes user traffic across your infrastructure to reduce performance and availability issues. Offering a variety of load balancers, with global load balancing you get a single anycast IP that fronts all your backend instances across the world, including multiregion failover. There also is software-defined load balancing services that enable you to apply load balancing to your HTTP(S), TCP/SSL, and UDP traffic. You can also terminate your SSL traffic with an SSL proxy and HTTPS load balancing. Internal load balancing enables you to build highly available internal services for your internal instances without requiring any load balancers to be exposed to the Internet.

Imagine, for example, that you have a website serving up millions of users or clients worldwide, and on the backend of the website, you have many VMs that are autoscaling to meet user demand. It's great for the VMs to autoscale on user demand, but how do you actually distribute the load between those servers? Imagine the servers keep running at full capacity and spinning up new ones to support additional users, but every time a server maxes out, it crashes. This is where load balancing comes into play: it helps spread the load to the backend evenly based on capacity and the health of the servers. You'd much rather have 20 servers running at 50 percent instead of 10 servers running at 100 percent, potentially bottlenecking your application and causing reliability issues.

 NOTE Remember that reliability is the most important objective for businesses! How do you plan on running a business if your service is having availability issues? Reliability is one of the biggest reasons for customer churn.

Overview

There are many types of load balancers with varying categories of configuration options. In Table 6-1, I've outlined the various types of load balancers. Take a look at the table and get familiar with the current list.

External load balancers balance the load of external users who reach your applications from the Internet. As described earlier, this can be for TCP/UDP, HTTP(S), or SSL traffic. The TCP/UDP external load balancer is a pass-through load balancer and is commonly referred to as a network load balancer. Pass-through means that the client retains its IP address instead of getting proxied by the server (or load balancer in this case).

Load Balancer Type	Traffic Type	Internal or External	Regional or Global	Supported Network Tiers	Proxy or Pass-through
Internal TCP/UDP	TCP or UDP	Internal	Regional	Premium only	Pass-through
Internal HTTP(S)	HTTP or HTTPS	Internal	Regional	Premium only	Proxy
TCP/UDP Network	TCP or UDP	External	Regional	Premium or Standard	Pass-through
TCP Proxy	TCP	External	Global*	Premium or Standard	Proxy
SSL Proxy	SSL	External	Global*	Premium or Standard	Proxy
External HTTP(S)	HTTP or HTTPS	External	Global*	Premium or Standard	Proxy

*Global in Premium tier only; otherwise, they are effectively regional in Standard tier.

Table 6-1 Types of Load Balancing Options in Google Cloud

Recall the MountKirk Games case study described in Chapter 1. Their CTO is looking to provide low-latency load balancing across to their users worldwide, and they want to get rid of their physical servers and move their game servers to VMs. Think about a game like Fortnite; what kind of load balancer would you use to distribute traffic worldwide across your VMs?

Internal load balancers distribute traffic to instances inside of GCP. Your load balancers periodically need to check on the instances to see how they're doing before the load balancers shovel more traffic onto their instances. These load balancer *health checks* determine whether the backends, such as instance groups, properly respond to traffic. They say, "Hey, instance group, are you dead yet?" and the instance group will respond, "I'm alive, buddy" or as you can imagine, dead instance groups provide no response. Based on a few details of how fast instance groups respond and how many times they respond successfully, the load balancer keeps an accurate tab on how they're doing. In order for these health checks to work properly, there needs to be a firewall rule that enables the load balancer health checks to reach the instances in the instance group. Otherwise, you can get HTTP 502 and 503 error codes, timeouts, and other issues. The health check may also tell the VM to restart itself if the instance groups continue to fail.

TIP When it comes to health checks, you need to ensure that the firewall rules are properly set up, and it's a best practice to check health and serve traffic on the same port. If you spin up an instance group behind an HTTP(S) load balancer and you notice that the VM instances are being terminated and relaunched every minute, it's probably not your VMs that are broken; you're missing a firewall rule.

Cloud CDN

Cloud Content Delivery Network (CDN) is a fast, reliable web and video content delivery network with global scale and reach through Google's global infrastructure. It provides edge caches peered with nearly every major ISP worldwide, and it leverages an anycast architecture to give you a single global IP address for global distribution. A lot of organizations use Cloudflare or Akamai for their CDN, which can all integrate with Cloud CDN. You'd want to use this to cache content from instances and storage buckets. How do you think companies like YouTube, Instagram, and TikTok are able to serve you photos and videos in near real time across the world? Global content caching is incredibly powerful and powers much of the content on the Internet today.

Network Security

With the old castle-and-moat belief system in the trash, and the post-apocalyptic architecture scenario that you'll see in the next section, you should ground yourself with the many common fundamental network security principles as well as new principles you can follow to secure your network. In this new shared responsibility model, depending on whether you use Infrastructure as a Service (IaaS), Platform as a Service (PaaS), or

Software as a Service (SaaS) solutions, you're benefiting from a varying level of default security that Google provides. But you also need to establish strong security controls in many other areas. It just so happens that networking is up there as one of the most important areas in the cloud, including from a security perspective, hence this dense chapter. (Honestly, this chapter is really designed to prepare you for the MCAT and the GRE at the same time, while you're preparing to self-nominate for a Nobel Peace Prize.) Let's talk about network security.

Network Security Principles

I will preface this by saying that when you're involved in a highly complex implementation, it's very important that you understand the core principles of designing a secure network. However, when you're reading a certification book, it sounds a lot easier than it is in real life. Oftentimes, you'll run into highly sophisticated projects that have incredibly meticulous requirements that you'll continually discover, with engineering challenges that prevent you from applying certain controls and best practices. So although you need to understand security very well, you should also work alongside your information security team to ensure that they're doing risk assessments and providing advice for every bit of architecture work that is going into your GCP environment. For that reason, we won't dive too deep into the most advanced network security controls, and we'll focus instead on the foundational principles of designing a secure network. This is subject to change in complexity based on the industry you work with, specific compliance and security requirements you're beholden to, and your organization's overall risk posture.

If you've read any security book, you know about the *CIA triad*, the most foundational information security model, which refers to *confidentiality*, *integrity*, and *availability*. This basic model will give you guidance when you're designing any system in the cloud. It's also important that you know the *shared responsibility matrix*, because Google will provide protection to many areas in the cloud based on IaaS, PaaS, or SaaS, and you'll need to step up. It's a partnership, so don't slack on securing your network. Most cloud security breaches you hear about in the news happen because of a mistake that the cloud tenant made. Very rarely are they caused by failures of cloud providers.

The principle of *confidentiality* refers to protecting your sensitive and private data from unauthorized access. If someone sees your data but shouldn't see your data, even if they see it at the wrong time, that's a breach of this principle. The principle of *integrity* refers to the protection of data against modification from an unauthorized party. Think of hashing algorithms like SHA1 and MD5, calculating a hash, and appending it to a message so that the recipient of the message knows that it has not been tampered with. The principle of *availability* refers to ensuring that authorized users are able to access your service or data when needed. Availability is not binary—whether something works or doesn't. When you think of availability, especially around networks, not only do security mechanisms protect against availability, but fundamental issues with how you've designed your cloud with anti-patterns can also prevent it from scaling. It can also be affected by attacks against your cloud provider or outages.

When you think about the concept of prevention, detection, and response with respect to networks, you and your cloud provider both have roles to play in the shared responsibility matrix. The way you design your network, the network patterns that are risk-assessed and approved, the exceptions with mitigating controls, and all the configurations associated with it are preventative controls. Setting up your network according to best practices, as I've outlined in this chapter, is all preventative work—it will prevent bad behavior.

You'll also need both your platform folks and security operations folks to be able to detect faults and malicious activity. For the networking folks, their detection is centered around ensuring the availability of a system, improving the performance of a system, and tangentially detecting security issues. For the security operations folks, their role is purely focused on detecting malicious activity. This could include attacks against availability such as DDoS attempts, unauthorized network traffic patterns, open firewall rules, and much more. Having all your network logs exported to both teams monitoring systems and also having visibility over misconfigurations will provide this level of visibility to detect faults and malicious activity.

Lastly, from a response aspect, both teams will need to define what is needed to recover from an event. If there is malicious activity going on inside of a project and your security operations team identified it, what actions are taken to validate that this is an incident and then contain the activity? Should the teams have privileged access to perform actions, or should they have to work with the project owners? Shadow IT continues to be a problem, especially when the security operations folks know little about the engineering behind the network but everything about detection and response. So the platform teams continue to roll over them.

My recommendation is to understand the shared responsibility matrix and your organization's security requirements and to ground yourself in these principles when you're designing your network. That will be a great start. Take the initiative when nobody else does to talk about network security requirements during a meeting and find the right folks who you can partner with to help protect your business. A breach can result in loss of customers, leading to layoffs, or shutting down an entire product. It's in everyone's best interest to take part in designing a secure cloud. Also, infrastructure as code is king. When you have documented configurations adhering to sound governing principles, a process to build and deploy, and a mechanism to prevent misconfiguration, you are less likely to encounter many network security issues in the cloud. Google Cloud does a phenomenal job of doing most of the work in defending against sophisticated network attacks. Think about how these principles have applied to the previous chapters, organization design, identity, and identity and access management (IAM), and also consider these same principles as you continue throughout the book.

Google Front End

We discussed a bit about the GFE earlier in the chapter. The GFE is a smart reverse-proxy that is on a global control plane in more than 80 locations around the world, all interconnected through Google's global network. When a user tries to access an address on Google's infrastructure, the GFE authenticates the user and employs TLS to ensure confidentiality and integrity. The load balancing algorithm is applied at the GFE servers to find an optimal backend, and then the connections are terminated at the GFE. After the traffic is proxied and GFE has determined an optimal backend, it will leverage a gRPC call to send the request to the backend. You get DoS protection from the GFE and DDoS protection from the GLB. It's basically a traffic cop that decides who to route where in an orderly fashion.

Firewalls

Firewalls are among the most important elements of network security. The purpose of your firewall is to monitor and control incoming and outgoing network traffic based on rules you determine. Nowadays, there are next-gen firewalls that provide capabilities beyond port/protocol rule-based traffic matching and do L7 (layer 7, or deep packet) inspection, intrusion prevention, and more intelligence-based services. A significant amount of incidents occur because of misconfigured firewalls. We've all heard or seen cases of this. Even the most talented folks can make the mistake of improperly opening up a firewall. So the more you can automate this and get human hands off of making firewall changes, the better your life will be.

Managing firewall rules can be cumbersome, especially with large organizations. It's almost impossible to manage firewall rules manually in a clean, organized fashion when you're scaling and growing many teams, many applications, and many solutions. Anyone who works on a traditional enterprise knows that there is a massive risk register full of old firewall rules that need to be deleted. Most of the cloud-native companies look to manage firewall rules in an automated fashion by employing tools like Terraform to do everything as infrastructure as code (IaC), creating a central policy repository for approved firewall patterns, and allowing developers to do pull requests when they want to leverage an approved pattern. This enables organizations to keep tight governance controls over what rules are approved in the repository, to detect anything that violates the policy repo, and to update and delete rules in a more centrally governed fashion. It's similar to our conversation about network patterns—all network patterns should include required firewall rules so that security architecture and information security can review the risk, tag the pattern accordingly, and keep it centrally stored so developers don't need to bug security every time they want to reuse a pattern and so security can use tools to automate the configuration enforcement and detection.

Web application firewalls are L7 application layer firewalls focused on protecting web applications by filtering and monitoring HTTP traffic between a web app and the Internet. The WAF technology should be implemented in front of any of your external IPs, without a doubt. Don't forget that most cybersecurity attacks happen on external IPs, as you're exposing your technology to all of the 1337 h4x0rs in the world. The issue is that configuring and managing WAF rules is a lot more complicated than just firewall rules. Cloud Armor is Google Cloud's solution to WAF. WAF will protect against common attacks such as cross-site forgery (CSRF), cross-site-scripting (XSS), SQL injections, and others.

CAUTION Do not expose your public IPs without adequate security to protect them from the world!

VPC Firewall Rules

You use *VPC firewall rules* to allow or deny connections to or from your VMs based on a configuration that you specify. These rules are always enforced. In GCP, every VPC network functions as a distributed firewall, where rules are set at the network level and connections are allowed or denied on a per-instance basis. You can set rules between your instances and other networks and also between instances within your network. Firewall rules can apply to an ingress or egress connection, but not both. The only action you can take is to allow or deny. (I wish "New phone... Who dis?" was an option. That would be nice if you're testing a rule.) You must select a VPC when you're creating a firewall rule, because they're distributed firewalls across VPCs. You can't share a rule among VPC networks; you'd have to define a separate rule in other VPC networks. When it comes to shared VPC, your firewall rules are centralized and managed by the host project. Firewall rules are *stateful*, meaning that after a session is established, bidirectional traffic flow will be permitted. A few components of a firewall rule are described in Figure 6-6.

Most of the items in the figure are pretty straightforward, but let's rehash a few. Priority is sorted from 0 to 65535 in ascending importance, where 0 is the highest priority.

Ingress (inbound) rule					
Priority	Action	Enforcement	Target (defines the destination)	Source	Protocols and ports
Integer from 0 to 65535, inclusive; default 1000	allow or deny	enabled (default) or disabled	The *target* parameter specifies the destination; it can be one of the following: • All instances in the VPC network • Instances by network tag • Instances by service account	One of the following: • Range of IPv4 addresses; default is any (0.0.0.0/0) • Instances by network tag • Instances by service account	Specify a protocol or a protocol and a destination port. If not set, the rule applies to all protocols and destination ports.

Egress (outbound) rule					
Priority	Action	Enforcement	Target (defines the source)	Destination	Protocols and ports
Integer from 0 to 65535, inclusive; default 1000	allow or deny	enabled (default) or disabled	The *target* parameter specifies the source; it can be one of the following: • All instances in the VPC network • Instances by network tag • Instances by service account	Any network or a specific range of IPv4 addresses; default is any (0.0.0.0/0)	Specify a protocol or a protocol and a destination port. If not set, the rule applies to all protocols and destination ports.

Figure 6-6 The components of a firewall rule

You can target the destination based on all instances in a VPC, or you can use network tags, or you can apply it to instances by service account. If you use network tags, you have to create and manage the tags, which may make it easier to apply firewall settings. If you target instances by service account, then when a cloud application scales up or down and new VMs are added and removed, you won't have to make any firewall modifications, which may drastically simplify managing IP address–based firewall rules. You still need to specify a protocol and port.

You need to consider a few *implied rules*, which are firewall rules that are built in to VPC Firewall by default; you cannot change them, but if you need to make a pattern that goes against the implied rule, you can give it a higher priority and it will take precedence. Implied rules were created to prevent a default, new project from being exposed to the world. There are two rules:

- **Implicit Ingress Deny** This rule will deny any ingress traffic to your VPC by default. You don't want to open up your VPC to the outside world unless you really need to!

- **Implicit Egress Allow** This rule will allow your instances inside your VPC to send traffic to any destination if it means Internet access criteria (that is, it has an external IP or uses NAT).

Google is also releasing a new feature called *hierarchical firewall policies*, which solve a lot of challenges when it comes to building more consistent, yet granular firewall policies and applying them at various parts of the resource hierarchy. With hierarchical firewall policies, you can assign firewall policies at the organization level node or to individual folder nodes. Managing firewall rules can be tough to centralize and approve in a stream-lined fashion, even through Terraform. Using hierarchical firewall rules enables you to give your teams more freedom to open up firewalls as they need to, but you can still apply critical policies to allow or deny certain high-risk traffic. All that said, do not open your firewall accidentally to the world!

TIP If you are running a multitier web application and you need to determine the direction in which traffic should flow, add tags to each tier and set up associated firewall rules to allow the desired traffic flow.

Simple Solution to a Major Misconfiguration

There are times that your users will want to deploy prepackaged solutions from Google Marketplace or simply deploy a proof-of-concept (POC) application whose installation instructions recommend the use of a public IP address. We have all seen this, and it is often the leading cause of successful attacks within public cloud networks. Although we will mention more hardened solutions for this later, when it comes to firewall rules, what can you do to minimize risk? A very successful strategy in dealing with those use cases is to enforce firewall rules that follow a least privilege configuration approach, even in sandbox environments. Basically, the way to achieve this is simply never to permit ingress "allow 0.0.0.0/0" in your firewall configuration! This will save you a ton of hurt! Sometimes that means allowing only your corporate public IP CIDR block access to your resources, or your test users' home IP addresses, or the entire RFC 1918 range. It's just rarely the case that any self-managed resource you deploy in a public cloud should ever need to be exposed to the entire Internet directly via its public IP address. So why are you allowing users to configure their firewalls as such?

Cloud Armor

Cloud Armor is a managed WAF that integrates directly with external HTTP(S) load balancers for any applications that you are exposing to the world through an external IP. As mentioned earlier, you should not expose your external IPs directly to the world. Instead, use an external HTTP(S) load balancer and leverage Cloud Armor to provide WAF capabilities to protect against attacks beyond just the default DDoS mitigation that you get with the external load balancers. In fact, Cloud Armor provides both L7 application security and layer 3/4–enhanced DDoS protection in the form of WAF capabilities via preconfigured rules, custom rules, and access control restrictions that are attached to your external HTTP(S) load balancer by a security policy. When you have a Cloud Armor security policy on your external HTTP(S) load balancer and external traffic hits the GFE when a user is going through the proxying process, your Cloud Armor policies are assessed against that user as well.

Here are some of the key things to note around Cloud Armor WAF:

- IP-based and geographic requirements can improve access to backend services.
- Preconfigured rules provide protection against XSS, SQL injection, local file inclusion, remote file inclusion, and remote code execution attacks. These rules are based on the OWASP ModSecurity Core Rule Set.
- Custom rules can be written through a Common Expression Language (CEL) format.
- You can preview the effect of a rule before enforcing it.
- All logs are logged against your external load balancer, and your security team will want these.

CAUTION   Do not open your external IP addresses to the world without proper protection! Put them behind an external load balancer, and leverage Cloud Armor or a WAF of your choice to protect against attackers.

Cloud NAT

Cloud NAT is a managed network address translation service that enables VMs and GKE clusters to connect to the Internet without having external IP addresses. Yep, the key theme of this chapter is to minimize your threat surface and avoid using external IP addresses where possible! With Cloud NAT, outbound communication is permitted from an instance that is only on your RFC 1918 space, and inbound communication is permitted only when it's a response to a request. So imagine, for example, that you have a bunch of servers that need to reach out to a public address to request updates, such as a Windows Update service. You can use Cloud NAT to enable all of your internal instances to do their updates without having to give them external IP addresses.

VPC Service Controls

We talked about how you have your internal RFC 1918 space, but Google offers managed services that are hosted on their public API endpoints. These particular managed services, such as BigQuery and Google Cloud Storage, do not sit inside of your VPC network. If you're using Private Google Access to connect to these services through the secure backchannel route that Google provides, that's great! But how are you able to prevent your own users or compromised users from exfiltrating data when it's outside of your VPC?

This is where *VPC Service Controls* come into play. They enable security administrators to define a security perimeter around managed services, such as GCS and BigQuery, to mitigate data exfiltration risks and keep data private inside of your defined perimeter. When you create this service perimeter, it effectively isolates resources of multitenant services and constrains the data from these services to fall under the enforcement boundaries that you create to protect your VPC. VPC Service Controls are awesome, but they are quite complex when you're implementing them, so be patient and deliberate with your use case here.

 NOTE Mukesh Khattar, security consultant at Google Cloud, has put together a phenomenal blog series on Medium titled "Mitigating Data Exfiltration Risks in GCP Using VPC Service Controls." This is an amazing reference guide. The link is in the "Additional References" section at the end of the chapter.

Identity-Aware Proxy

Google follows a zero trust access model called BeyondCorp that shifts access controls from the network perimeter to individual users and devices, challenging users through a highly sophisticated authentication and authorization mechanism. This enables employees, contractors, and other users to work more securely from virtually anywhere in the world without the need for a traditional VPN. Identity Aware Proxy is one of the building blocks to building a zero trust model. *Identity-Aware Proxy (IAP)* is a mechanism to control access to your cloud-based and on-premises applications and VMs on GCP that uses identity and context to determine whether a user should be granted access.

In 2021 and beyond, we're in a world where users want to be able to work wherever they are, and dealing with managing a VPN involves way too much overhead. We still want to be able to trust our users and ensure that they are securely accessing internal resources. The most advanced organizations are all headed this route, so if you're ahead of the curve here, this will greatly simplify user productivity.

The secret sauce of BeyondCorp is the integration of Cloud Identity with Identity-Aware Proxy. Cloud Identity allows for managing user identities along with the endpoint devices they use such as iPads, iPhones, laptops, and so on. When you use an endpoint device to connect to IAP, the proxy authenticates and authorizes your identity, your device, and the context of the session (where you are coming from, what time of day, device security posture, and so on). Based on that information, IAP identifies explicitly what set of internal resources you are allowed to access at that moment. So, unlike the perimeter-protection solution that VPN offers, IAP allows for in-depth protection of all your resources inside your private network with context-aware access.

Network Logging

It's critical that all of your network logs are required to be enabled at the organization level, are output to your key monitoring services, and are actively being monitored by your application and security teams to ensure that anything that shouldn't be happening in your environment is in fact not happening. You need these logs to follow the CIA triad principles. We're going to do a deeper dive into each type of log in Chapter 10, but, for now, just note the importance of viewing all your telemetry data and preventing it from being tampered with.

Explain Like I'm 5 (ELI5)

The castle-and-moat analogy of computing is old news. After 2021, anything goes, so here's a better story to tell. Let's have some fun! Disclaimer: There is no underlying meaning here, it's intentionally bizarre, enjoy the read, and tag me if it helped break down the complex concepts of networking in GCP!

In January 2020, the passing of the late, great basketball giant Kobe Bryant began a year filled with a series of disastrous world events. As 2020 progressed, we faced political warfare, the COVID-19 virus, a rising income inequality gap, unprecedented racial tension, record-breaking Tesla stock surges, and a devastating explosion in Beirut, while humans continue to ignore the abnormal trajectory of world climate and increasingly severe weather patterns that are signaling the beginning of the end. Increasing ocean temperatures continue to kill marine wildlife, which triggers food shortages in the entire global ecosystem. Year upon year, as temperatures continue to fluctuate beyond their normal millennial thresholds, they cause weather pattern changes that typically took thousands of years to appear in just a hundred years. Predictions indicate that the Arctic will see ice-free summers by 2050.

(continued)

Now let's do some time-traveling into the future. The traditional form of government has just collapsed, along with the Federal Reserve, because traditional resources such as oil and gold became seemingly extinct. The remaining Earth societies have survived on the last source of energy, which is now dependent on precious metals. Since Google, Amazon, and Microsoft spent decades mining these metals for the purpose of amassing data centers next to everyone and their babushka, they have become the New World Order. Bitcoin is the standard form of currency, and the new monetary system is owned by those three companies, as they have used their massive computing power to mine the last of the remaining Bitcoin. Jeff Bezos, Elon Musk, and Bill Gates moved to Mars, where they beam TikTok streams of their perfect lives back to the inhabitants of Earth. We are back to serfdom in a post-apocalyptic world, and tribes begin to form and need places to live and re-create society.

Most of the pre-apocalyptic cities that still exist are barren, desolate wastelands, with remnants of buildings and towns (on-premises environments) haphazardly running operations to the best of their abilities. You're the leader (cloud architect) of your tribe (your company), and you're deciding where to build your encampment. Three world superpowers (Google Cloud, AWS, and Microsoft Azure) all provide a safe space for tribes to live and innovate, each with its own pros and cons. You've decided to lead your tribe to build an encampment on GCP, as you believed that the services GCP provides in its shared responsibility matrix are the most secure, cost-effective, and scalable for your tribe's needs.

You are offered an empty plot of land and are allowed to do whatever your tribe wants to do (for a fee, of course). On your new land, you build a town (VPC) inside of a geographical boundary (project) that has sections (subnets) for housing and businesses (resources). These sections are categorized based on their proximity to one another, within a neighborhood (zone) or within a postal code (region). The addresses for the homes (RFC 1918 private IPs) are known only to the inhabitants of the town. Businesses (external IPs) have addresses as well, but they have stricter requirements for allowing customers in, since they have precious goods. The roads were paved by the federal government/superpower (physical network), and you have to put up the traffic signs that provide directions to navigate the town (routes); otherwise, your tribe members won't know where it's safe to go. They don't want to fall off a cliff (dropped packets) accidentally!

You have only a finite amount of resources for your citizens to build homes and businesses, so you need to plan your zones properly to ensure that your community can grow efficiently (right-sizing subnets). In this neighborhood, you don't allow anyone to leave as they want. They're all quarantined inside the neighborhood (no public IPs), as mandated by your state government (your company's governance policies). The federal government/superpower has provided a safe mechanism for you to communicate with other neighborhoods without having to worry about any other tribes interfering. If you want to communicate with their federal resources (Google Cloud APIs), you would normally have to leave the government boundaries and go through their front door (through the Internet). Even though they will ensure that you know the secret handshake (TLS), you'd much rather go directly to their resources without all the border security guards constantly patting you down. So they offer a secure back-channel for you to go directly to their federal resources (Private Google Access) while you're still within their boundaries.

On the perimeter, security guards have a list of who is allowed to come in and leave (firewall rules). While individuals go through Customs and Border Patrol (GFE), there are traffic cops (external load balancer) who show these people the right way. Even within your local boundaries, you've hired security guards and traffic cops (internal load balancer) to ensure that people inside and across your neighborhoods are going only where they're allowed to go (internal firewall rules). It's a cold world out there, and you can't even trust everyone inside of your own neighborhood. Who knows, someone could be a mole or could be compromised! If you want to market your business to the outside world, you aren't just going to pave a road to the outside. When the wandering *Mad Max*–esque freaks notice that some Customs and Border Patrol agents aren't protecting your road, you hire a special detective (Cloud Armor WAF) and advertise your business through Customs and Border Patrol and the traffic police.

You believe you did a great job setting up and running your old city (on-premises environment), and you intend to migrate all of the resources you had there to your new city, but you are afraid of doing this over the public roads. The federal government/superpower (Google Cloud) said they'll pave an expressway toll road (Dedicated Interconnect) just for you if you can meet them in their colocation facility. You trust your citizens in the old city enough to let them work directly with the folks in your new city, so you extend the boundaries of your old city to the colocation facility and agree to have this private toll road set up.

But wait! Things are heating up! Someone just launched a massive distributed attack against you. Luckily, the federal government/superpower is protecting your borders! You also notice that one of your businesses is using 200-percent more energy than usual. So you inspect your traffic logs (VPC flow logs) and see that something funky is going on. The business isn't just seeing a lot more customers, it is actually exfiltrating your intellectual property! Someone went rogue and social engineered your security guard to open up a path to the outside world, and now an attacker has made it to the inside! Immediately you start the incident response process. You analyze this behavior, shut the business down, close your borders, arrest the perpetrators, and then reconvene with your police force (Security and Governance) to do a "lessons learned review" and figure out how to prevent this from occurring again. Luckily, you're able to recover and get back to normal, and you followed best practices in securing your town and realize you shouldn't take these security topics lightly. The good news is that everyone in your city has a chip implanted in their body, so if you need everyone to abide by a new law, all you have to do is click a button and deploy it (centralized governance).

(continued)

Ultimately, your tribe is growing at a rapid pace, and the federal government/superpower has your back as they continue beefing up their innovative offerings and security. You realize that this model makes so much more sense from a total cost of ownership perspective. All your money is no longer tied up in capital expenditures. You've been able to achieve feats that would never have been possible in your old city—so much so, that you've decided to deprecate your old city entirely and build a beautiful new world the way you envision it. Your citizens are happy, your government is empowering you, and your tribe has learned how to sustain and thrive. You wake up one morning and hear the birds chirping, looking out the window to a beautiful vista of farmland and nature. You feel safe and secure. You have a growing population of beautiful new families, shelter, water, food, and technology, all built on a strong, secure, and efficient network that you architected—and world peace is finally achieved.

Chapter Review

In this chapter, we discussed the importance of networking and dove into the deep subject areas of networking in Google Cloud. Networking is the most complex and important topic of cloud computing, as the entire cloud is a massive global system of networks designed to give your organization a cutting edge in building the most innovative, cost-efficient, and operationally effective solutions for your customers worldwide. We started with the history of networking and why it has played the most pivotal role in the growth of society. Then we went into a technical deep dive into Google's global networking concepts. Google is the only cloud provider to offer a full end-to-end global network at scale, and that gives their cloud the competitive edge over other clouds to offer things like cold potato routing, global load balancing, encryption in transit by default, and encryption at rest by default.

We talked about the fundamental networking constructs and that your Virtual Private Cloud is a virtual form of your data center, hosted in Google's software-defined global network. We talked about subnets, routes, IP addressing, and the importance of your RFC 1918 address space and why it's so critical to minimize your threat surface by avoiding unsecured external IP addresses. Private Access offerings are a competitive offering by Google to provide a more secure, advanced transportation method for communicating with Google Cloud's public API endpoints, from which most of their managed services operate. We discussed the shared VPC model and when it's used, including some of the best practices around using VPCs and/or shared VPCs.

Next, we discussed the various ways you can provide connectivity to your cloud. In an increasingly multi-cloud and hybrid-cloud world, it's very important to know how you can connect all of your intellectual property across the world in a safe, fast, and secure fashion. We also went into load balancing, discussing how to handle load effectively to provide the highest availability objectives to your customers. Remember that reliability is the most important metric in the world; you have no business if your product is not available.

We dove into the key elements of network security, including some of the foundational security elements that should be applied across any cloud architecture, such as the CIA triad. Confidentiality, integrity, and availability are the fundamental principles that you need to ground yourself with when you are designing any architecture in the cloud (or anywhere for that matter).

Lastly, we had some fun and imagined a story analogy of networking and cloud computing in an alternate universe and post-apocalyptic world. It's okay to have some fun learning how networks operate in GCP without being bored down into the weeds. Try making a fun story in your next meeting! And don't forget the history and power of networking. From the earliest form of a network to where we are today, networking with one another is what created the beautiful world we live in. Building strong, positive relationships with those around us and extending our networks to uplift one another will get us through to our next human evolution. Keep on being a positive force in the world, and keep on finding ways to leverage technology to improve the lives of your loved ones and the ones who need it most.

Additional References

If you'd like more information about the topics discussed in this chapter, check out these sources:

- **VPC Overview**   https://cloud.google.com/vpc/docs/overview
- **Best Practices and Reference Architectures for VPC Design**   https://cloud.google.com/solutions/best-practices-vpc-design
- **Mukesh Khattar - Mitigating Data Exfiltration Risks in GCP Using VPC Service Controls**   https://medium.com/google-cloud/mitigating-data-exfiltration-risks-in-gcp-using-vpc-service-controls-part-1-82e2b440197

Questions

1. You're an engineer troubleshooting a network issue. Network traffic between one Compute Engine instance and another instance is being dropped. What is likely the cause?

   A. A firewall rule that the instances depended on was deleted.

   B. The instances are on a default network and nobody created additional firewall rules.

   C. Network bandwidth is low.

   D. Your TCP/IP settings are improper.

2. You're working at a top eSports company that has a PostgreSQL database on-premises that handles user authentication to their training platform. You'd like to build a backup replica of this database on GCP. The database is only about 10TB, and there are frequent large updates. Replication requires private address space communication, and you're looking for a secure solution. What networking approach would you use?

   A. Use a Dedicated Interconnect to enable your on-premises traffic to have a steady and high-bandwidth line directly to your GCP environment.

   B. Use a Google Cloud VPN connected to your data center.

   C. Use a Compute Engine instance with a VPN installed connected to the data center.

   D. Use NetZero or AOL. (Seriously, don't you miss the good ol' days before Facebook?)

3. Your security team discovered a rogue network that was created in your project. This network has a GCE instance with an SSH port open to the world. They're working on identifying where this network originated from. Where should they look?

   A. Look in the Cloud Monitoring console in your project.

   B. Connect to the VM and look at the system logs to identify who logged in to the environment.

   C. Look through the logs in the console and specify GCE Network as the logging section.

   D. Look at the Cloud Audit logs and determine which user accessed this environment the most. Then interrogate that user.

4. Your organization needs a private connection between its Compute Engine instances and on-premises data center. You require at least a 20 Gbps connection and want to follow the best approach. What type of connection should you set up?

   A. Create a Virtual Private Cloud (VPC) and use a Dedicated Interconnect to connect it your on-premises environment.

   B. Create a Virtual Private Cloud (VPC) and use a Partner Interconnect to connect it your on-premises environment.

   C. Create a Virtual Private Cloud (VPC) and use a Cloud VPN tunnel to connect it your on-premises environment.

   D. Use a Cloud CDN to store content to the nodes closest to your on-premises data center and connect it from there.

5. You're running several Compute Engine instances and want to restrict communication between the instances to the paths and ports you authorize. You don't want to rely on static IP addresses or subnets, because you are working on a web app that is intended to autoscale. How should you restrict communications?

   A. Use firewall rules based on network tags and attach them to the instances.

   B. Use service accounts to delineate this traffic.

C. Use Cloud DNS and allow connections only from authorized host names.

D. Create separate VPC networks and authorize traffic only between those VPCs as needed.

6. You have an application running on a Compute Engine instance in a single VPC spread across two regions. This application needs to communicate over VPN to an on-premises network. How would you deploy the VPN?

A. Expose the VPC on-premises using VPC sharing and proper access controls.

B. Create a global VPN gateway and create a VPN tunnel for each region to your on-premises environment.

C. Use VPC Network Peering to peer the VPC to your on-premises network.

D. Deploy a Cloud VPN gateway in each region and ensure there is at least one VPN tunnel to the on-premises peering gateway.

7. You have a few VMs that need to be able to reach the Internet to do yum updates. But you don't want to expose the VMs to the world. What should you do?

A. Assign the VMs a public IP address, but put IP blacklisting in place to prevent anyone from accessing it.

B. Create one server that can download all of the updates and store them locally in your cloud. Then have your VMs update from that server.

C. Set up a Cloud NAT gateway so that your VMs can send outbound packets to the Internet and receive the updates.

D. Properly configure your DNS settings so that the network domain name is accessible by the Internet.

8. You'd like to set up a system to enable your development teams to do firewalling in a much more automated fashion. Historically, you had to create firewall rules manually for different traffic patterns for each development team environment and go through a review for every firewall rule creation. What would be a great way to solve this challenge for your enterprise in the most operationally efficient and secure manner?

A. Create a firewall rule review process that streamlines the rule approval from your information security team(s); then task your developers to continue creating the requests as needed.

B. Use an infrastructure as code solution such as Terraform and build a system where there is a policy repository for existing firewall rules from which development teams can do pull requests to use in their environments. Also, create a mechanism to vet and approve new network patterns as needed into that policy repository.

C. Provision each development team leader with enough access to manage the firewall in GCP so that you don't have to do this yourself.

D. Deploy a WAF on your external IP addresses, and you should be good to go.

9. You have an application on VMs serving web traffic and you noticed that after you configured the VMs as a backend to an HTTP(S) load balancer, the VMs are being terminated and relaunched. What is most likely the best way to deal with the issue?

   A. Ensure that a firewall rule exists to enable the health check on the load balancer to reach the instances in the instance group.

   B. Assign a public IP to the instances and configure your firewall rules appropriately.

   C. Use network tags on each instance to route traffic from the instances to the load balancer.

   D. Allow the source traffic on the instances to reach the load balancer by using firewall rules.

10. A shared VPC is:

   A. A network construct that connects resources from multiple service projects to a common host project that contains the VPC network, so that they can communicate with each other securely and efficiently using private RFC 1918 address space.

   B. A network construct that connects resources from multiple projects to a common VPC network, so that they can communicate with each other securely and efficiently using public address space.

   C. A network construct that connects resources from multiple organizations to a common VPC network, so that they can communicate with each other securely and efficiently using private RFC 1918 address space.

   D. A network construct that connects resources from multiple projects to a group of VPC networks, so that they can communicate with each other securely and efficiently using private RFC 1918 address space.

Answers

1. **A.** From all the answers here, the most likely one is that a firewall rule was accidentally deleted or intentionally deleted because someone didn't understand the dependencies of the rule. Check to see if the instances are permitted to communicate with each other.

2. **A.** You need direct access to your private network in the cloud for RFC 1918 communication between your on-premises environment and GCP. You also need to transfer large amounts of data frequently, so being bottlenecked by the limitations of a VPN is not useful here. The best approach is to use a Dedicated Interconnect so you have a strong pipe, a private line, and continuous integration into your private RFC 1918 address space.

3. **C.** Your goal is to identify when a network was created. Look through the logs in the console and search for a Create Insert; it'll display the JSON code string that contains the e-mail used to create the network. Your security team can use this as part of their investigation to determine the origin and root cause.

4. A. The best approach is to use a Dedicated Interconnect, because you're looking to establish a 20 Gbps private connection. Cost is not a constraint in this question.

5. A. Network tags enable you to make firewall rules and routes applicable to specific VM instances without having to rely on static IP addresses.

6. D. VPC Peering is allowed only between VPCs, not from a VPC in the cloud to your on-premises network. The answer here is to deploy a VPN gateway in each region and deploy at least one tunnel to your on-premises environment, so that instances in other regions can use the tunnel for egress traffic and you can meet your high-availability requirements.

7. C. A Cloud NAT gateway will allow your internal IP addresses to reach outbound addresses without needing an external IP. This is helpful for things like updates.

8. B. The goal here is to give your developers more freedom to build and deploy faster and to automate as much as you can, while eliminating sources of bottlenecks. By using a system like Terraform and having a firewall rule policy repository with approved network access patterns, you can securely give your developers the freedom to open firewall rules as needed, while also ensuring that only approved access patterns are in place.

9. A. You are getting the appropriate web response from each instance, but the instances keep getting terminated and relaunched. The network pattern between the load balancer health checks and the instances may not be properly configured.

10. A. A shared VPC is used when you have multiple projects that need to leverage one VPC network so that they can communicate securely and efficiently without having to deal with too much network configuration between VPCs and other network constructs.

Compute and Containers

In this chapter, we'll cover
- Running computing workloads in the cloud and where the industry is headed
- Basics of the Google Computer Engine, App Engine, and Kubernetes Engine
- Googles IaaS, PaaS, SaaS, and FaaS offerings in the cloud
- How to manage your API endpoints securely and effectively

Computing enables us to surface our technological innovations to the world. We've leveraged computing to solve some of the most advanced, most complex, challenges that humanity has faced. As companies move to the cloud, the speed of problem-solving continues to grow at such a rapid pace that it defies Moore's Law, which states that the number of transistors on a microchip will double every two years, reflecting the speed of innovation. Moore's Law has always been an accurate historical observation of future projection in the computer industry, but as the pace of digital innovation has improved tenfold with cloud computing, hardware seems unable to keep up with it. For that reason, computing workloads are finding more ways to optimize and become more efficient, without depending solely on the growth of their hardware counterparts.

It started with buying servers and data centers and hiring the appropriate networking and technical staff to build, deploy, and manage all of this hardware. Then, we worked with third-party companies and placed orders directly through them, and their engineers would manage our physical infrastructures. Virtual machines then simplified this greatly by enabling organizations to do more with less, which translated to hiring more resources in-house to manage the hypervisor and the instances beneath it. Now, in the cloud, we are seeing a shift to fully managed services to solve some problems and semi-managed platforms to solve others, and customer-managed infrastructure to solve the remaining issues. As the strategy has evolved, the needs of businesses have evolved with new rapid development cycles and feedback loops. All of these solutions continue to optimize the rate at which computing can solve problems. In the last dozen years, we've seen the most significant evolutionary growth. What do the next dozen years hold for us? How can we pair the most effective computing technologies with the business challenges we are trying to solve to create innovations that remain unseen in society?

In this chapter we're going to dive into Google's Infrastructure as a Service (IaaS), Platform as a Service (PaaS), Software as a Service (SaaS), and Function as a Service (FaaS) offerings. We'll talk about how you manage virtual machines, Google App Engine

(GAE), Kubernetes, and other managed service offerings. We'll also discuss how you can effectively manage and secure your APIs in the Google Cloud Platform (GCP). Because there's never been a one-size-fits-all solution when it comes to computing, think about where you can leverage each of these products in your organization to improve your computing power.

Google Compute Engine

Google Compute Engine (GCE) is Google Cloud's IaaS solution that enables users to launch virtual machines on demand. With GCE, users must manage the entire underlying infrastructure associated with virtual machine (VM) instances, including the machine types. VMs can be launched on predefined or custom machine sizes. GCE supports live migrations, OS patch management, preemptible VMs (PVMs), and more, similar to Amazon Elastic Compute Cloud (EC2). GCE is a core element of computing in the cloud, and for most organizations, migrating completely to a container-based architecture is a major goal—but there is still a strong need for leveraging a standard computing infrastructure.

You can configure the underlying infrastructure on GCE to your liking. You don't have to worry about calling SoftLayer anymore and putting an order in for a ton of CPU, memory, and storage just to be on the safe side. With GCE, you can make adjustments as you need to. You also get to decide on what kind of operating system you'd like to run, how you want to log in, which images you want to leverage, what type of software you want to run on startup, and more.

Virtual Machine Instances

It's a good thing to know about a variety of possible configurations when you're configuring your VM infrastructure. Let's start with the basics.

An *instance* is a virtual machine that is hosted on Google's infrastructure. When you're creating a VM instance in Google Cloud, you first assign an instance name, then assign key/value pair labels, assign the instance to a region and a zone, and then select the machine configuration. Each of your instances belongs to a project, and you can have one or more instances in each project.

Your *machine type* is a set of virtualized hardware resources that includes your system memory size, virtual CPU (vCPU) count, and persistent disk limits for your VM instances. Machine types are sorted according to families, and there are subtypes within each family. Each family is organized in a manner that enables you to understand what the machine types are optimized for—general-purpose computing, memory-intensive workloads, or compute-intensive workloads.

You can manage your instances through the Cloud Console, by using the **gcloud** command-line tool, and via the Representational State Transfer (REST) API. You can also connect to your instances via Secure Shell (SSH) in Linux and Remote Desktop Protocol (RDP) in Windows Server instances. There are a variety of states that an instance can move through in the instance life cycle. Take a look at Figure 7-1 to get an idea of the various transitions between each instance state.

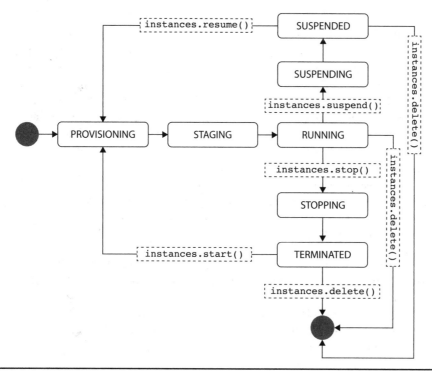

Figure 7-1 The various states of an instance

Machine Types

General-purpose machine types offer the best price-to-performance ratio for various workloads. There are four families of general-purpose machines: E2, N2, N2D, and N1. The E2 machines are typically used for day-to-day computing at a low cost, often for serving web applications, backend applications, small to medium-sized databases, microservices, virtual desktops, and development environments. The N2, N2D, and N1 general-purpose machines offer a balanced price-to-performance ratio and can be used for web applications, backend applications, medium-sized to large databases, caching, and media/streaming.

Memory-optimized machine types are optimized for memory-intensive workloads, and they offer more memory per core than other machine types (up to 12TB of RAM). There are two families of memory-optimized machines: M1 and M2. M1 and M2 machines are optimized for ultra-high-memory workloads—think of large in-memory databases such as SAP HANA, Redis, or in-memory analytics.

Compute-optimized machine types are optimized for compute-intensive workloads. They offer more performance per core than other machine types. These machine types offer Intel Scalable processors and up to 3.8GHz of sustained all core turbo, which essentially means that the chips will be able to run all of their cores at a consistent maximum rate. There is one family of compute-optimized machine types, C2, and they're typically used for high-performance computing, gaming, and single-threaded applications that are heavily CPU-intensive.

Shared-core machine types are optimized for cost. These are machine types that share a physical core and are often used for running very small, non–resource-intensive applications. Shared-core machines are available only in the N1 and E2 families. Within the E2 family are e2-micro, e2-small, and e2-medium shared-core machine types that have two vCPUs available for short periods of bursting. Within the N1 family are f1-micro and g1-small shared-core machine types that have only one vCPU available for short periods of bursting.

 EXAM TIP Take a look at the "Machine Types" public documentation page and get familiar with some of the common bounds of each machine type. You may see a question or two that has to do with optimizing your VM environment.

After you select your machine configuration, you can add GPUs for your compute workloads if you have a graphically intensive workload. These come in handy for things like processing rendering jobs, virtual applications, and machine learning. Google Cloud offers NVIDIA Tesla GPUs in its environments as of 2020. In Figure 7-2, you can see a few of the initial configuration options you have when creating your VM instance through the Cloud Console.

Preemptible VMs

You may have some workloads that don't necessarily need to be run with four nines of uptime. Saving money should always be at the top of your mind when you're building a cloud environment, and cloud computing can get very expensive. Running very powerful virtual machines can cost a lot of money over time, so think about some workloads that may not need the extremely high availability. Going back to the bank example from Chapter 4, imagine that BankyBank runs an application that processes mobile check deposits throughout the day. BankyBank provides its customers with a service level agreement (SLA) that ensures that their funds will be available to them within one business day but are subject to occasional holds. Does BankyBank really need to be running an expensive virtual machine all day to process these checks instantly? Here's where PVMs can be handy. These highly cost-effective instances are designed for non–fault-tolerant workloads that can withstand possible instance preemptions. Batch jobs are a great use case for PVMs.

 EXAM TIP If you see questions about the cost efficiency of your virtual machine environment paired up with no requirements for availability, think about how PVMs fit in.

It's also a great idea not to use PVMs for workloads that cannot be terminated. Compute Engine might terminate PVMs at any time because of system events. Compute Engine also terminates PVMs after they run for 24 hours. Also, PVMs are not covered by any SLA, and they are explicitly excluded from the GCE SLA.

Figure 7-2
Creating
an instance

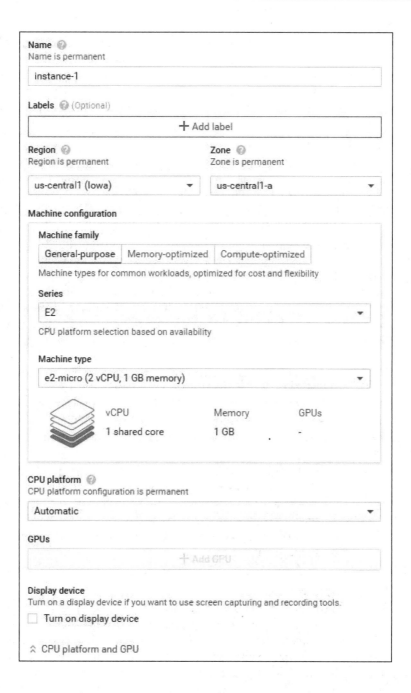

TIP When you're using PVMs, it's always wise to consider leveraging shutdown scripts so that a proper procedure can be followed when the instances are preempted. This way, you can ensure that your application is properly shut down and any cleanup actions are performed before the instance stops. You can add this shutdown script to your instance metadata.

Shielded VMs

Shielded VMs are a security feature designed to offer a verifiable integrity of your VM instances, so that you can be sure your instances are not compromised by boot- or kernel-level malware or rootkits. These are designed for more highly sensitive workloads or for organizations that have stricter compliance requirements. Shielded VMs leverage Secure Boot, with a virtual Trusted Platform Module (vTPM), and integrity monitoring to ensure that your virtual machine has not been tampered with.

Confidential VMs

Confidential VMs are a breakthrough technology that Google Cloud developed that offers to encrypt data that is in use. This technology has never before been available to this extent. Encryption traditionally has been permitted only for data at rest or data in transit. When you're actively using data or an application is processing data, you would have to decrypt the data in CPU and memory for your system to do anything with it. With Confidential VMs, GCE is able to work on encrypted data without having to decrypt it. This is possible by leveraging the Secure Encrypted Virtualization feature of second-generation AMD EPYC CPUs. Basically, the CPU natively encrypts and decrypts all the in-process memory. So if a bad actor were able to get a memory dump from your system, they would not be able to forensically make sense of anything.

NOTE You won't see any questions about Confidential VMs on the exam, but if you're working for a highly sensitive organization or you have highly sensitive workloads, think about how you can leverage them. It's incredibly simple to migrate to them, as there's no need for any special refactoring. When creating a VM, you just have to check a box. When migrating, it's a simple lift and shift.

Sole-Tenant Nodes

Some organizations, particularly those in the public sector, often require dedicated hardware to ensure that even the most sophisticated of attackers cannot access their computing infrastructure by exploiting Google Cloud and the VM's host environment. In standard GCE environments, your VM may run alongside other customers' VMs, all on the same hardware. This is called *multitenancy*. There is no reason to be alarmed, though, because Google Cloud has very strong security controls to ensure that other tenants cannot laterally move through or exploit the hypervisor to get access to another tenant's data or environment. For highly sensitive workloads, hardware isolation is important to ensure that other customer workloads are not running on the same physical server

Figure 7-3
Multitenant host
versus sole-
tenant host

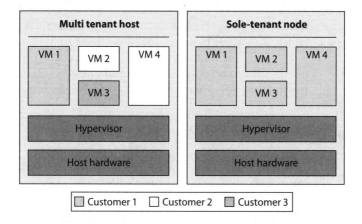

as yours. Sole-tenant nodes may also be beneficial for some workloads, such as gaming, where the performance requirements may benefit from being isolated on their own entire hardware stack. In Figure 7-3, you can see how a standard VM environment and a sole-tenant node are organized.

Images

You've set up your instances, but now you need to think about your actual virtual machine images. GCE offers both public images and the ability to leverage custom images. *Public images* are provided and maintained by Google, the open source community, or third-party vendors that are available upon image selection and also in the GCP Marketplace. There are a variety of public images, each with its own flavor, from various operating systems such as Debian, Red Hat Enterprise Linux, and Windows Server, to images optimized for SQL Server. Public images are typically hardened to an extent, with minimal services running on them. The benefit of leveraging public images is that they've already done most of the work for you, and the images are maintained through their life cycle, which also includes maintaining security updates and other updates for the operating system.

Custom images are boot disk images that you create, own, and control access to. You've probably heard the terminology "Golden Image" to refer to the hardened, secure, and optimized image used for respective applications in your organization. Most companies opt to leverage custom images, as they typically have their own software, services, and configuration that these images are optimized for. A lot of organizations would also like to manage the image life cycle themselves, often storing their images in a secure image repository (or image factory) so that they can maintain who has access to the image, who can authorize the image to be deployed, what characteristics are validated before an image is deployed, and the process of identifying and remediating vulnerabilities in the image. When you're building a custom image, your goal is to harden the image by minimizing the amount of services, functionality, and configuration that your business needs.

NOTE The Center for Internet Security produces "CIS Hardened Images," which are images that are hardened based on their benchmarks. Their benchmarks are known in the industry as the go-to vendor agnostic and internationally recognized secure configuration guidelines. They offer CIS hardened images for most major public cloud computing companies.

Instance Templates and Instance Groups

Instance templates are sets of configurations that define the machine type, boot disk image, labels, and other image properties that VM instances and managed instance groups (MIGs) can conveniently use to deploy the right configuration as needed. Instance templates are seen as resources in Google Cloud. You want to use instance templates when you need to create VMs from pre-existing configurations. It may be easy to use the Cloud Console to create a VM in 30 seconds or less, but don't forget the importance of infrastructure as code. When you standardize your deployments, it makes you more operationally efficient, and it enables you to manage change effectively. Since these are resources, you can control access to the instance templates, you can monitor them to prevent anyone from changing the configuration and detecting any misconfigurations, and you can store them in a repository to stay organized when you have a massive infrastructure that requires a variety of configurations for instance groups.

You would also need to use an instance template if you want to create a MIG. *Instance groups* are a collection of VM instances that you can manage as a single entity. There are two kinds of instance groups, managed and unmanaged. MIGs enable you to operate multiple identical virtual machines to make your workloads scalable and highly available. *Unmanaged instance groups* enable you to load-balance across a fleet of VMs that you manage yourself.

With MIGs, you can take advantage of some features such as autoscaling, autohealing, regional deployment, and automatic updating. Autoscaling MIGs automatically scale up or down by adding instances to meet demand or by removing instances to reduce your costs. Autohealing is a policy that relies on application-based health checks, similar to firewall health checks, which will periodically check whether your MIGs instances are responding or not. If a MIG is not responding, it will delete and re-create that instance. You can also launch MIGs across multiple zones to protect against zonal failures—that way, you're achieving higher-availability objectives to ensure reliability. MIGs also can use internal load balancing services to distribute traffic evenly across the instances in your MIG. You should be careful with health checks, though, because if you push an update that breaks connectivity to an instance, your health checks might trigger your instances to all be re-created endlessly until they start working again.

TIP You can create MIGs with a minimum and maximum instance count set to 1. This enables your MIG to guarantee that at all times one instance of your VM is up and running within a region. This is a very cost-effective way to enable high availability without incurring the extra costs of having to keep two or more instances running at all times.

Storage Options

You can leverage a variety of storage options in your VM instances, all of which have their own benefits and caveats. It's recommended that you dive into the various storage options on the public documentations site so you can get a deeper understanding of how your storage choices vary depending on the type of machines you leverage and their best use cases. But don't worry about diving too deep into the technicalities of storage for the exam.

Following are storage options you should be familiar with:

- **Persistent disks** These hard drives offer reliable, high-performance block storage for your virtual machines. You can attach persistent disks to provide storage for your instances. You can leverage zonal persistent disks or regional persistent disks that replicate your storage over two zones.
- **Local SSD** This local solid-state drive offers the highest performance, with transient, local block storage.
- **Cloud Storage buckets** This option can be leveraged to give your instances an affordable object-based storage option. It has to be created within the operating system by configuring Cloud Storage FUSE to mount the storage to your VM.
- **Filestore** This high-performance, network-attached file storage, like a traditional network file system, can be attached to your instances.

OS Login

OS Login is a mechanism to simplify SSH access management by linking your SSH users in Linux to their respective Google identities in Cloud Identity. If you aren't using OS Login, your users will need to have separate credentials to log in to their respective VMs. You use OS Login for the same reason you'd want to use single sign-on (SSO) to simplify access management for your users. It enables you to manage the full life cycle of your Linux accounts through the governance of your Google identities. That way, you can manage identity and access management (IAM) permissions centrally through Cloud IAM, you can do automatic permission updates, and you can also import existing Linux accounts from your on-premises Active Directory and LDAP servers to ensure that they are synchronized for VMs across your environments.

You can also enable an organization policy to enforce OS Login to prevent a malicious user who does not have proper authorizations through a Google identity from getting direct SSH access to your VMs. It's a lot more difficult to manage the full SSH key life cycle if you are manually provisioning privileged users on your VM instances.

Google App Engine

Google App Engine (GAE) is a PaaS solution that offers a fully managed serverless application platform on which users can build and deploy applications without having to manage the underlying infrastructure. There is no server management and no configuration deployments, enabling developers to focus on building. GAE supports popular development languages such as Go, Ruby, PHP, Java, Node.js, Python, C#, and .NET, and you can bring your own language runtimes and frameworks.

GAE is a great solution for development teams that want to build an application that is deployed and managed by Google. It's incredibly simple to leverage, and it was one of Google Cloud's most major offerings that a lot of organizations and development teams were initially interested in using. However, as the computing evolution continues and new offerings are being introduced, more organizations are moving toward models in which they still can maintain the right amount of control and also leverage fully serverless and ZeroOps solutions for workloads or events that don't necessitate the need for a platform. PaaS solutions often create vendor lock-in, making it difficult to port applications between cloud service providers in the event that certain vendors no longer meet new business objectives.

In GAE, you create apps that are composed of one or more services. Each service uses different runtime configurations and can operate with varying performance settings. Within each service, you can deploy versions of that service to manage version control, and within each version, there are instances that your user traffic can be routed to accordingly. This level of version control is great for testing, managing rollbacks, and other temporary events. Also, your instances will scale up or down on demand. In App Engine, you can also leverage a memory cache (memcache) service to minimize the number of queries to your database backend.

App Engine Flex vs. App Engine Standard

App Engine offers the ability to run applications in two environments, App Engine Flex and App Engine Standard. You can run your applications in either environment or in both at the same time, depending on your needs.

Here's when you'd use the standard environment:

- Instances run in a sandbox, using the runtime of a supported programming language
- Sudden spikes of traffic require rapid scaling
- You pay for only what you need and when you need it, and your application can scale to zero when there's no traffic

And you'd use the flexible environment in these conditions:

- Instances run within Docker containers on GCE VMs
- You have consistent traffic that deals with gradual scaling
- You're using a custom runtime and/or using an unsupported GAE Standard programming language
- You need better integration with your GCE environments
- You need to route traffic from another cloud or on-premises environment to a specific instance through a VPN

NOTE The standard environment can scale to zero, but the flexible environment must have at least one instance running for each active version.

Google Kubernetes Engine

Google Kubernetes Engine (GKE) is a managed Kubernetes solution for deploying, managing, and scaling containerized applications on GCP. *Kubernetes* is an open source container orchestration system intended for automating application deployment, scaling, and management. Google has been running Borg, a large-scale cluster-management system, for its internal applications before the advent of Kubernetes. From this experience, Google originally designed Kubernetes (commonly stylized as K8s), and now it's maintained by the open source community.

Turning the open source K8s product into an enterprise-grade solution is where GKE comes into the picture. This is where Google manages several aspects of the underlying GKE architecture while still giving organizations the responsibility to own the necessary elements of Kubernetes to build, deploy, and manage their applications securely. Kubernetes falls into an interesting space between IaaS and PaaS in that it's more of a hybrid between the two. As a cloud architect, you still have to concern yourself with the deployment, the services, and the overall architecture. However, applications are built cloud-native into containers such as Docker. Moreover, the development pipelines and solutions are supported across all cloud options, allowing for easy application portability and no vendor lock-in. This is a main business reason why Kubernetes is growing in popularity.

Before we dive into the cluster architecture, let's talk through the shared responsibility model for GKE. Some of the details may be hazy until you get through the rest of the GKE section, so feel free to return back here for a review.

At a high level, Google is responsible for protecting the following:

- The underlying GKE infrastructure that powers Google Cloud, similar to the underlying infrastructure Google manages in Compute Engine.

- The GKE nodes operating system, particularly for the public images, such as Container-Optimized OS (COS) images. If you have auto-upgrade enabled, your nodes will automatically upgrade as Google releases new patches to these images.

- The overall K8s distribution. Google takes the open source K8s distributions and provides many updates to them as they're leveraged across GKE.

- The control plane, including the master VMs, the API server, the etcd database, and other components running on the master VMs.

- Integrations into other Google Cloud services, such as IAM, Audit Logging, Cloud Key Management Service (KMS), and so on.

At a high level, GKE customers are responsible for protecting the following:

- The nodes that run your Kubernetes workloads, including any extra software or configuration you run on the nodes. You're responsible for keeping these nodes up-to-date, whether you're leveraging COS images or not.
- The workloads themselves, including your applications, container images, IAM configurations, network configurations, and any of the features you deploy across your GKE environment.

Cluster Architecture

A lot of the lingo used previously won't make sense until you understand what the GKE architecture looks like. Take a look at Figure 7-4 and reference that throughout this section.

As you can see, there are a few elements of GKE that are managed by Google and a few that are managed by customers. Let's walk through each of these:

- A *cluster* is the foundation of GKE. All Kubernetes objects run on top of your GKE cluster. Within each cluster is at least one cluster master.

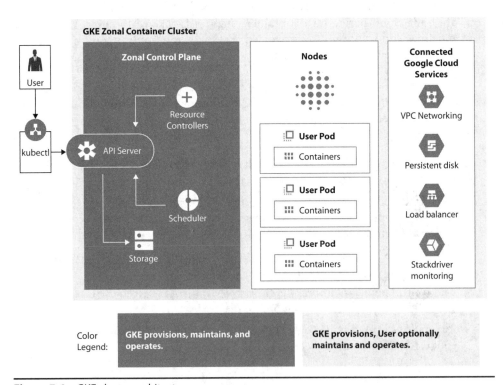

Figure 7-4   GKE cluster architecture

- A *cluster master* runs all of the K8s control plane processes, including the API server, scheduler, and resource controllers. This includes the updates to the K8s version running on your cluster master.

- The *K8s API server* is the endpoint for your cluster, where you can interact with the cluster via HTTP/gRPC API calls through the K8s command-line client **kubectl**. This K8s API server is the central hub for all communications within your cluster, including all requests sent to your cluster nodes, controllers, and system components.

- A *node* is known as your worker machine and runs your containerized applications and other workloads. Your node essentially is a Compute Engine VM instance. You can choose your machine type and your OS images, just as you do in Compute Engine.

- Within your nodes you will run *pods*, which are groups of one or more container applications, such as Docker, Containerd, or rkt. Your pod will also have an IP address and can have shared storage volumes and other configuration information.

- You can leverage GKE's native integrations that Google manages into other tools such as persistent disk, load balancers, and Cloud monitoring.

 EXAM TIP   Remember the command syntax **kubectl [command] [TYPE] [NAME] [flags]** that you use when interfacing with your Kubernetes environment. And **gcloud container** is the syntax of the command you use when you interact with GKE's clusters, node pools, images, subnets, and operations. These are the Google-specific infrastructure configuration parameters. Know when to use these versus **kubectl**.

Configuration

GKE is a revolutionary product that enables businesses to build highly customizable, scalable, and resilient applications while taking away much of the burden from managing the underlying elements of the GKE infrastructure. When you're building out your GKE environment, most of the work you'll do will involve designing a strong network, identity and access model, and operational management process for your GKE environment. I would recommend doing a proper GKE deep dive to understand most of the work that goes into building your GKE environment.

For the context of the exam, there are a few key configuration items you should be aware of that can be related to cluster-level configuration or pod-level configuration hosted in pod templates. Here are a few examples of items that would be useful to know:

- You can attach persistent disks to your cluster nodes and determine which pods can access these shared storage volumes as well.

- You can leverage StatefulSets, which are unique, persistent identities and stable host names that are maintained by GKE that you can use to deploy stateful applications and clustered applications that save data to your persistent storage.

- Your Kubernetes clusters can leverage the Horizontal Pod Autoscaler, which is an autoscaling feature that enables your workloads to increase or decrease the number of pods automatically based on demand.

- You can also scale your pods vertically using the Vertical Pod Autoscaler, which will make changes to your pods' CPU and memory as needed.

How Kelsey Hightower Solves Technology Challenges with Influence

Kelsey Hightower, one of the most prominent figures in the open source community and a developer advocate at Google, has led the force in the adoption of Kubernetes worldwide, and his influence is not solely based on his engineering depth. Kelsey proved to the world that it takes more than just technical expertise to influence adoption, and he did that by bringing passion and storytelling into his work to inspire technologists worldwide. As the founder of KubeCon, he continues to lead developer conferences and events across the globe. As technologists, we usually prioritize solving problems over building influence and soft skills, but Kelsey's approach to solving technology challenges worldwide is something that we can all learn from.

Node Upgrades

When you're doing rolling updates of your nodes, you can control how disruptive upgrades are to your workloads by leveraging two parameters, **MaxSurge** and **MaxUnavailable**. **MaxSurge** enables you to determine how many nodes GKE can upgrade at one time, and **MaxUnavailable** enables you to set a limit of the maximum GKE nodes that can be unavailable during an update. See Table 7-1 for an idea of three different settings you can leverage when doing upgrades.

Remember that reliability is one of the most important metrics for your business. When you're doing upgrades, you'll need to determine your performance needs and right-size to understand how you can provide minimally disruptive upgrades for the nodes that host all of your applications. Most organizations don't trust themselves enough to do auto-upgrades, but if you can build a habit of using auto-upgrades and maintaining your optimal surge configurations, you've solved one of the biggest challenges of patch management.

 TIP All new node pools are automatically configured to use **maxSurge=1** and **maxUnavailable=0** configuration specifications. You can modify these yourself.

Description	Configuration
Balanced (default), slower but least disruptive	**maxSurge=1 maxUnavailable=0**
Fast, no surge resources, most disruptive	**maxSurge=0 maxUnavailable=20**
Fast, most surge resources, and less disruptive	**maxSurge=20 maxUnavailable=0**

Table 7-1 Three Different Upgrade Settings for Node Upgrades

Cloud Functions

Not having to manage servers is great. Not managing platforms is even better. But not managing a single thing and paying only for the time your code executes and the duration it takes to run—well, that's priceless. *Cloud Functions* is a FaaS offering that is an event-driven serverless execution environment. With Cloud Functions, you can run your code locally or in the cloud without having to provision any servers. It scales up or down on demand, so it is cost-effective and you pay only for what you use. Developers write the code, and Google Cloud does the rest. Cloud Functions is based on an open source FaaS framework that enables you to run functions across multiple environments to prevent lock-in, including local development environments, on-premises, Cloud Run, and other Knative-based serverless environments.

FaaS has its limitations, though, and there are certain use cases for which you'd want to be leveraging Cloud Functions. It's event-driven, so you can use Cloud Functions to trigger single-purpose functions that are attached to events emitted from your environment. The code itself executes in a fully managed environment that falls under Google Cloud's purview in the shared responsibility matrix. You can use JavaScript, Python 3, Go, or Java runtimes to write your functions. Some of the use cases for which you'd want to consider using a Cloud Function include extraction, transformation, and load (ETL) jobs; building webhooks; creating lightweight APIs; or more common use cases like triggering a Cloud Function to perform an action when a certain message has been received on a Cloud Pub/Sub topic.

One of the most popular use cases for Cloud Functions is simply to extend the capabilities of GCP services. Basically, you can tap into any GCP event you want to react to. By default, Cloud Functions supports events natively from HTTP, Cloud Storage, Cloud Pub/Sub, Cloud Firestore, and Firebase. With Cloud Logging, you can forward log entries of interest to a Pub/Sub topic by creating a sink and then triggering a Cloud Function off that event. This gives you unlimited ability to react to anything generating a log within your environment. Think of all the possibilities of building automations that react to incidents or any unplanned events.

 TIP Talk about scaling up or down. Cloud Functions can literally scale to zero so you don't incur any costs when there is no activity. This is incredibly cost-efficient.

Cloud Run

Cloud Run is a serverless compute platform that enables you to run stateless containers, abstracting away all of the infrastructure management and built on an open source Knative framework. Essentially, you're bringing serverless to containers by not having to manage the entire container infrastructure. You probably won't see any questions about Cloud Run on the exam.

API Management

Creating, publishing, and managing APIs is quite a challenge for many organizations. If you're in the business of creating APIs, whether internal or external, it's not easy to govern and manage all of your API endpoints in a consistent manner. This is where using API management platforms comes in handy. Modern API management platforms offer the tools to develop, secure, publish, and manage your APIs in a consistent and often policy-based manner. API management platforms such as Apigee are fully developed platforms that will handle the full API life cycle, whereas other solutions such as Cloud Endpoints are not in parity when it comes to features and functionality.

Apigee

Apigee, a Google acquisition, is a full end-to-end OpenAPI-compliant API management platform that enables you to manage the full API life cycle in any cloud, including multi- and hybrid-cloud environments. This incredibly robust product was ranked by Forrester as a leader in API management solutions in Q3 2020.

The most useful capability that Apigee offers is the fact that it is an API proxy. As a result, for API clients, it presents your business services as managed "facades" for backend services. Technically, your backend need not support HTTP, be modernized, or even understand the concept of microservices. Apigee can act as a translation layer between the modern client-facing REST API presentation layer your business is exposing to its clients and whatever new or old technologies you have lurking in the back corners of your enterprise. Furthermore, as a proxy, it can control the end-to-end security, transaction rates, access controls, and so on, for your business-exposed APIs, enabling a company to modernize its business face without necessarily having to reinvent its backend.

Cloud Endpoints

Cloud Endpoints is an API management platform that enables you to secure, manage, and monitor your APIs on Google Cloud. This greatly simplifies the need to manage all of your APIs manually in Google Cloud. You can build all of your API documentation in a developer-accessible portal. With Cloud Endpoints, you can leverage three communications protocols——OpenAPI, gRPC, or Cloud Endpoints Frameworks for App Engine standard environments. This offering gives your development teams the ability to focus on developing their APIs instead of building custom frameworks.

Secure Your APIs

APIs expose application logic and sensitive data by their intended design, and this continues to become a target for attackers. Products such as Apigee and Cloud Endpoints can prevent a lot of these flaws by default or provide you the ability to configure your APIs in a consistent, secure manner. Here are some recommendations to leverage when you're thinking about securing your APIs:

- Classify your APIs and design a reference architecture for the required controls and approved patterns based on the classification of the API. For example, you can have public-facing APIs, internal APIs, and partner-facing APIs, each with a different level of security controls.

- Implement rate limiting to prevent denial-of-service attacks.

- Be aware of excessive data exposure, and think about how you can filter unnecessary data before it's displayed back to the end user of the API.

- Use a common configuration and monitor your APIs for security misconfigurations.

- Validate your inputs—ensure that your API is not the subject of injection flaws, such as SQL injections, to avoid malicious code being executed by an attacker.

- Leverage IP whitelisting where you can.

- If you're not using an API management platform that manages performance, scalability, and distribution, put your APIs behind a load balancer.

- Be very wary of how you're managing authentication tokens and other authentication mechanisms.

Chapter Review

In this chapter, we discussed the importance of computing and dove deep into the subject areas of IaaS, PaaS, SaaS, and FaaS offerings in Google Cloud Platform. While networking bridges the gaps and enables all of the brains to get to work, the computing itself is the brains that determine how we solve problems and surface innovations in the world. Google Cloud has many computing options that all have various use cases and can be leveraged as needed. As a cloud architect, you need to think about how you can optimize your computing needs based on the products associated in the cloud, while managing your costs, security, and ease of use for your development teams.

We talked about Google Compute Engine, which is Google Cloud's virtual machine infrastructure service. In GCE, it's important to know about how you can choose the appropriate machine types to balance your price-to-performance ratio. You can also leverage a variety of instance options for different use cases. Preemptible VMs are good for batch jobs because they can and will shut down at any given moment—it is recommended that you use a shutdown script for a graceful shutdown. Shielded VMs are good for ensuring that you're protecting your VMs against rootkits and bootkits.

Confidential VMs (or confidential computing) is a breakthrough technology that solves the encryption-in-use challenge that has historically been infeasible to solve. Sole-tenant nodes are dedicated hardware for organizations that do not want to share infrastructure with other tenants.

You can use custom images or public images to manage your operating system in the cloud. Instance templates give you a way to manage the configuration of your VMs, and instance groups can be used to manage autoscaling and clustering of your virtual machines. You can use a variety of storage solutions with VMs, and OS Login is a way to tie in your Linux users from your on-premises AD or LDAP directory to their Google Identity.

Google App Engine is a PaaS offering that abstracts the underlying infrastructure away from the development teams so that they can focus strictly on coding. It is great for certain use cases and has a really strong ability to manage deployments. App Engine Standard is an environment mode that is designed for sudden spikes of traffic that require rapid scaling. It can scale to zero when there's no traffic, and you can use it only with certain supported programming languages. App Engine Flex is an environment that allows instances to run within Docker containers on GCE VMs. It's helpful when you have consistent traffic that deals with gradual scaling and you prefer your instances to run in Docker containers on a VM rather than in a sandbox.

Google Kubernetes Engine is a managed Kubernetes solution that builds on Google's dozen-plus years running large-scale cluster management systems for use worldwide. With GKE, Google provides management of several elements of the open source Kubernetes solution to enable organizations to control only the things they care about and to focus on building modular, rapid-scale applications. The cluster master is managed by Google, and the nodes and below are managed by you. Nodes are VMs that hold pods, which contain your containerized applications. Pod templates and cluster level configuration are very important elements of designing a robust GKE platform on GCP. Most organizations are headed this route. I would recommend diving into Kubernetes in more depth if you're really interested in becoming a technical leader for your organization's computing goals.

Cloud Functions is a FaaS offering that is a serverless, event-driven function that can be leveraged when responding to various events in GCP. Cloud Run is a serverless computing platform that enables you to run stateless containers.

Lastly, when it comes to APIs, it's very important that you properly secure, manage, and govern your APIs in GCP so that you are not exposing sensitive data to the wrong people or potentially exposing your network to the world. Apigee is a full, end-to-end API management platform that was acquired by Google, and Cloud Endpoints is a GCP-built solution for managing your APIs in the cloud. Secure your APIs!

Additional References

If you'd like more information about the topics discussed in this chapter, check out these sources:

- **GKE Overview**   https://cloud.google.com/kubernetes-engine/docs/concepts/kubernetes-engine-overview
- **GCE Concepts**   https://cloud.google.com/compute/docs/concepts
- **Machine Types**   https://cloud.google.com/compute/docs/machine-types
- **Storage Options for Compute Engine**   https://cloud.google.com/compute/docs/disks

Questions

1. You're an architect designing an application that is going to be run for half of the day only. You need to process batch jobs and would prefer to leverage a serverless product that scales to zero so that you can save money. What service should you use?

   A. App Engine Flex

   B. Cloud Functions

   C. Kubernetes

   D. Compute Engine PVMs

2. You're looking for a solution to scale your node pool automatically based on its CPU and memory load. What would you use?

   A. Leverage Horizontal Pod Autoscaler.

   B. Leverage Vertical Pod Autoscaler.

   C. Leverage a Cloud Function to listen to a custom event created in your GKE environment that sends a message to Pub/Sub every time CPU/memory usage spikes.

   D. Right-size your cluster from the start and you won't have to worry about this.

3. You need to leverage a consistent set of host names for your pods. Which feature should you use?

   A. Persistent Volumes

   B. Persistent Disk

   C. Instance Templates

   D. StatefulSets

4. Your organization needs a cost-effective solution to building applications in the cloud that will be leveraged to process data from mobile networks. Google Compute Engine is being used, and the applications are designed to run on a virtual machine. Since the networks are slow, it's not too important to process this data instantly. What should you use?

   A. Use sole-tenant VMs so that the data from mobile networks does not get bogged down by other tenants.

   B. Use a Cloud Function to process the data and migrate off of GCE entirely.

   C. Leverage preemptible Compute Engine instances.

   D. Leverage nonpreemptible Compute Engine instances.

5. You're running several Compute Engine instances inside of a VM and need to design a solution to manage the SSH key pairs that developers use to log in to their VMs. What would you recommend?

   A. Inventory all SSH key pairs via their public key, have developers upload their public keys to a central repository, and send an automated notice for developers to rotate these keys.

   B. Use OS Login to integrate their Linux SSH access to their Google identities.

   C. Restrict access only to internal corporate networks and disable external IP addressing on their VMs.

   D. Provide developers with a central secure identity that they can share and you can monitor to ensure that you've simplified access for everyone.

6. What would you use to run virtual machines?

   A. Compute Engine

   B. Kubernetes Engine cluster master

   C. VM Engine

   D. Compute Container Engine

7. Your application needs to provide user inputs through an API tier that then gets routed to the database tier, but you don't want user inputs to flow directly to the database. How would you restrict this traffic flow?

   A. Assign the web applications a public IP address, but put IP blacklisting in place to prevent anyone from accessing it.

   B. Add tags and appropriate firewall rules from your web frontend to your API and from your API to your database backend.

   C. Define your routing in a way that would prevent this traffic flow from occurring in the first place.

   D. Use separate subnets for each tier.

8. You're planning on pushing a new deployment to an App Engine application. You'd like to test the update with a small set of live users before you migrate all of the live traffic to the new version. What do you do?

   A. Create a new application version in GAE and split traffic between the new and current version.

   B. Create a new App Engine instance group in GAE and target a small set of production users for your testing.

   C. Deploy the new update and migrate a set of your users to your old version before you migrate them back to the new version.

   D. Update your application version and create a firewall rule that restricts traffic from 75 percent of users to your new version.

9. BankyBank wants to create an API and manage it on Google Cloud. What service should be used?

   A. Cloud Endpoints

   B. Google App Engine

   C. Google Compute Engine

   D. Google Kubernetes Engine

10. BankyBank is using preemptible VMs and is having an issue with VMs not shutting down gracefully every time they terminate. What should be leveraged to solve this?

    A. Pod templates

    B. Instance templates

    C. Shutdown scripts

    D. YAML files

Answers

1. **B.** You would want to leverage Cloud Functions in this instance because it is serverless, it can be leveraged to respond to events, and it scales to zero. Preemptible VMs are commonly associated with batch jobs, but you don't get to decide when a PVM is going to be run or not, and PVMs don't scale to zero.

2. **A.** Horizontal Pod Autoscaler is used to scale your nodes. Vertical Pod Autoscaler is used to scale the CPU/memory within your node.

3. **D.** StatefulSets are used to assign a consistent set of unique host names for your pods.

4. **C.** Preemptible VMs are cost-effective solutions to building applications that do not have strict SLAs, especially with batch jobs like the one described in the question. You cannot run applications designed to run on VMs on Cloud Functions.

5. **B.** You can use the OS Login feature to tie in your Linux SSH users to their Google identities so that you can have one way to govern and manage all of their access.

6. **A.** You can run virtual machines on Compute Engine.

7. **B.** By leveraging tags and appropriate firewall rules, you can restrict the traffic flow to your intended patterns. You'd want to leverage them both from the users who are coming in through the web tier and routing their requests to the API layer and then from the API layer to your database backend.

8. **A.** In Google App Engine, there is a lot of built-in, inherent functionality to do proper testing. To do this, create a new application version and then split traffic to that new version's instances.

9. **A.** Although you can build APIs on a variety of services, the Cloud Endpoints tool can deploy, manage, and protect your APIs on Google Cloud. Apigee is a much more robust product than Cloud Endpoints, though it is not one of the choices here.

10. **C.** To ensure graceful shutdowns, it's recommended that you leverage shutdown scripts in your PVMs.

Storage, Databases, and Data Analytics

In this chapter, we'll cover

- Storage solutions and database offerings available to use with GCP
- Various tools to use for data analytics workloads, including industry-leading BigQuery
- Securing your data products and environments in Google Cloud

You know what's wild? DNA. Scientists have discovered that a single gram of DNA contains 215 petabytes (215 million gigabytes) of data. If we could find a way to encode digital data into an equivalent data storage system, every bit of data ever recorded by humans could be stored in a single room. In fact, scientists are currently working on creating the highest-density large-scale data storage scheme ever invented using DNA as a model.

Networking brought together the world's brightest brains. Computing brought phenomenal mathematical problem-solving power to the world. And data is the root of every evolutionary iteration. It's pretty crazy to compare old photos of the world's first hard drives, which were the size of a car and supported less than a megabyte of data, to today's USB sticks, which are the size of your finger and can store a terabyte of data. But when we compare a USB stick to the amount of data that is stored in our DNA, it's clear that we still have a magnitude of leaps to go until we can even come close to that capacity.

Data solutions in the cloud bring exponential scale and performance to storing, processing, and driving insights from the analytics of our data. This seems magnificent, but when I remember what the world was like before the cloud, I wonder what the world will be like when we have our next evolutionary breakthrough in data density and analysis. Quantum computing seems to be inching toward operational readiness, and it may be our next cloud-like evolution. When I say inching, I really mean inching. The current state of quantum computing is such that it won't be enabling any brute-forcing into your old Myspace account to find old cringe-worthy photos in a millisecond anytime soon—so don't worry.

We're going to spend a lot of time diving into data storage, databases, analytics, and data security solutions in Google Cloud. Along with networking, computing, and data, questions about these topics may make up a significant portion of the exam. Pay close attention to the key details of each service in this chapter and don't forget about each one's use cases. Look back at the case studies in Chapter 1, and think about what data solutions you'd implement in those scenarios.

Storage

In Google Cloud, there are a few types of storage options—block storage, object storage, and file storage. As a cloud architect, you'll hear these terms used quite often, and oftentimes incorrectly. Let's talk about each storage type.

Block storage refers to a data system in which the data is broken up into blocks and then stored across a distributed system to maximize efficiency. These storage blocks get unique identifiers so that they can be referenced in order to piece the data back together. Block storage systems are great when you need to retrieve and manipulate data quickly through a layer of abstraction (such as an operating system) that is responsible for accessing the data points across the blocks. The downside to block storage, however, is that because your data is split and chunked across blocks, there is no ability to leverage metadata. In the traditional sense, storage area networks and hard drives were associated with block storage. In Google Cloud, block storage is associated with technologies such as Persistent Disks and Local SSDs, which essentially are attached disk drives in their data centers. Think about a scenario, for example, in which your company wants to install a MySQL database on a virtual machine because they're not ready to fully migrate to a managed solution—or they just want to have full control. What type of storage would be the best solution for storing all of the underlying data from the database? This is a case in which an attached Persistent Disk or Local SSD would provide strong, durable block storage for a database stored on a virtual machine (VM).

File storage refers to a data system in which your data is stored in files, and those files are organized in a folder hierarchy, providing a simple user interface to organize and sort your data and the ability to leverage metadata within your files. File storage is great for use cases such as network-attached storage or for storing files within your operating system. Think about the Windows OS, with a file system that maps where your data is, but the underlying storage is chunked across block storage. In Google Cloud, file storage is associated with technologies like Cloud Filestore, which is a network-attached file storage solution in the cloud. If a bunch of your applications need to share a file server to share and access files commonly in a safe manner, this is where a solution like Cloud Filestore would come into play.

Object storage refers to a data system with a flat structure that contains objects, and within objects are data, metadata, and a unique identifier. This type of storage is very versatile, enabling you to store massive amounts of unstructured data and still maintain simple data accessibility. You can use object storage for anything—unstructured data, large data sets, you name it. However, because of the nature of this flat system, you'll need to manage your metadata effectively to be able to keep your objects accessible. In Google Cloud, object storage is associated with technologies such as Google Cloud Storage. For example, a mega-company like the National Football League (NFL) may have petabytes of game footage stored in an unstructured data store, but it most likely leverages a home-grown or third-party solution such as a media asset manager to add an organizational schema to make the data easily accessible, sortable, retrievable, and manageable.

EXAM TIP When you're taking the exam, knowing which Google Cloud storage technologies are related to file, object, and block storage may help you get to a more clear answer. Be careful, though, and don't assume a Google-managed service is always the answer. Read through each question very carefully for the requirements.

Google Cloud Storage

Google Cloud Storage (GCS) is a globally unified, scalable, and highly durable object storage offering in GCP. GCS is often used for content delivery, data lakes, and backup. Data in GCS is encrypted by default at rest. But you can also leverage all of the other Google Cloud encryption offerings on GCS.

It offers varying availability service level objectives (SLOs), depending on the storage class, ranging from 99.0 to 99.95 percent. GCS offers Object Lifecycle Management to move your data automatically to lower-cost storage classes based on criteria you define to optimize your costs.

TIP Durability refers to the ability for data to be protected from bit rot, degradation, or other corruption. Durability is also measured in nines, and GCS provides 11 nines of durability, or 99.999999999 percent annual durability.

In GCS, you store your *objects*, which are immutable pieces of data that can be any file of any format, in containers called *buckets*, which are associated with a project. Upon bucket creation, you select a globally unique name and a geographical location where you are going to store the bucket and the objects within it. That means your bucket name cannot be the same as any other bucket in the world, so you need to follow a strong naming convention. You also select a storage class that all of the files will be aligned to.

Figure 8-1 shows the hierarchy of GCS.

The four main storage classes offered by GCS affect an object's availability and pricing model. Table 8-1 summarizes these.

You should leverage the various storage classes based on your data's availability requirements:

- *Standard storage is great for data that is frequently accessed and needs the strongest availability.*

- *Nearline storage is a low-cost solution that is good for data that is infrequently accessed.* If you are okay with a slightly lower availability and a 30-day minimum storage duration, the lower storage costs can be a greater benefit than the increased costs for accessing your data. This is ideal if you want to read or modify your data once a month or less on average.

- *Coldline storage is a very-low-cost solution that is suitable for data that is infrequently accessed.* The at-rest storage costs are even lower than nearline. Coldline storage is great for data that you need to read or modify only once a quarter.

Figure 8-1
GCS bucket
hierarchy

- *Archive storage is the lowest-cost solution.* It has no availability service level objective (SLO), but its true availability is typically equivalent to nearline and coldline storage. This is good for data that needs to be accessed only once a year, and it has a 365-day minimum storage. If, for example, a compliance requirement necessitates that you retain audit logs for six years, you'd want to throw it in archive. The good thing about GCP is that, while other cloud providers offer similar storage classes, GCP can surface all of the data instantly when it is accessed. In AWS, if you store data in an equivalent archive solution, it may take hours or days to get your data out.

You can apply key-value pair labels to your buckets that enable you to group your buckets with other resources, such as VMs or persistent disks. You may want to use labels to classify data sensitivity according to your data classification model, to identify which team the data belongs to, or for other purposes. You can use up to 64 labels per bucket. Labels are often used for billing accounting purposes as well.

Storage Class	Minimum Storage Duration	Multiregion Availability	Regional Availability
Standard storage	None	>99.99%	99.99%
Nearline storage	30 days	99.95%	99.9%
Coldline storage	90 days	99.95%	99.9%
Archive storage	365 days	99.95%	99.9%

Table 8-1 Available Storage Classes in GCS

Object names are not globally unique, but because GCS is a flat storage, object names have to be unique within your buckets. For example, you can have two files named pwned.jpg in two different buckets, but they cannot be in the same bucket. You can also leverage object versioning to manage version control inside of your buckets. *Object versioning* is a feature that maintains old versions of files in your bucket when they are overwritten or deleted, based on parameters you set. Obviously, this will increase the cost of storage because you would be maintaining multiple versions of files, so you wouldn't want to use this feature if it's not needed.

CAUTION You cannot recover objects from a deleted bucket, regardless of whether or not you're using object versioning.

To manage cost effectively, you should leverage Object Lifecycle Management, which enables you to apply a configuration policy to your buckets to determine what actions to take automatically based on a condition your objects meet. For example, if objects haven't been accessed in more than 60 days, you may want to downgrade their storage class to coldline to save money, or you may want to delete them entirely. Your life cycle rule can be composed of two types of actions: **Delete** and **SetStorageClass**. As you can probably guess, you can either delete or change your storage class based on conditions such as object age, created dates, number of newer versions, and so on.

EXAM TIP When it comes to the exam, think about how you can leverage Google Cloud Storage in your architecture. It can be a great solution for both archival data, with its variety of storage classes, and for any applications that need object storage that is georedundant, with very strong service level objectives.

Imagine a scenario in which your compliance regulators require that you retain logs for six years. If your logs are not being accessed frequently, why would you want to store the data anywhere other than a long-term archival storage class in GCS? Or what about a backup data store for disaster recovery?

You can interact with GCS through the Cloud Console, through the **gsutil** command-line tool, using client libraries, and via the REST API.

EXAM TIP Remember the syntax for using **gsutil: gs://[BUCKET_NAME]/ [OBJECT_NAME]**. You can use this tool to do a variety of bucket and object management tasks, such as creating and deleting buckets; uploading and downloading files; moving, copying, and renaming objects; or editing ACLs.

You should remember that GCS is one of the most often used staging solutions for bringing data in and out of the cloud. When you use any data transfer solutions, it typically goes into GCS as its first step into GCP. When you move data between cloud services, it often is stored in GCS as an interim placeholder. When you need to move data out of GCP, GCS is the standard staging storage location for your processes.

Cloud Filestore

Cloud Filestore is high-performance managed file storage for applications that require a file system. Like the Network Filesystem (NFS) protocol, Filestore offers the ability to stand up a network-attached storage on your Google Compute Engine (GCE) or Google Kubernetes Engine (GKE) instances. Filestore is highly consistent, fast, fully managed, and scalable using Elastifile to grow or shrink your clusters. Filestore offers a 99.9 percent SLO.

When you create a Filestore instance, you're creating a single NFS file share with default Unix permissions. Filestore instances are required to be created in the same project and Virtual Private Cloud (VPC) network as the GCE or GKE clients that are connected to it (unless you use a shared VPC). Basically, you'd want it to be on the same RFC 1918 address space as your clients, and you can enable Filestore to select an available IP automatically in the RFC 1918 space that you designate to create the instances.

Persistent Disk

Persistent Disk (PD) is high-performance, highly durable block storage that provides solid-state drive (SSD) and hard disk drive (HDD) storage and can be attached to GCE or GKE instances. Storage volumes can be resized and backed up, and they can support simultaneous reads. The maximum size of a single persistent disk is 64TB, but you can use more than one disk.

There are three types of persistent disks:

- **Standard persistent disks** These are best for large data processing workloads that mostly leverage sequential I/Os.

- **SSD persistent disks** These are best for high-performance databases and applications that require low latency and more I/O operations per second (IOPS) than standard PDs. They provide single-digit millisecond latencies.

- **Balanced persistent disks** An alternative to SSD PDs, these are a great balance between performance and costs and suitable for most general-purpose applications.

If you need to modify the size of your persistent disk, it's as easy as increasing the size in the Cloud Console. If you need to resize your mounted file system, you can use the standard **resize2fs** command in Linux to do online resizing. PDs are not actually physically attached to the servers that host your VMs, but they are virtually attached. You can only resize up, but not down!

 TIP The command to modify the persistent disk auto-delete behavior for instances attached to VMs is **gcloud compute instances set-disk-auto-delete**. Auto-delete is on by default, so you will need to turn this syntax off if you don't want your PD to be deleted when the instance attached to it is deleted.

Local SSD

Local solid-state drives (SSDs) are high-performance, ephemeral block storage disks that are physically attached to the servers that host your VM instances. They offer superior performance, high IOPS, and ultra low latency compared to other block storage options. These are typically used for temporary storage use cases such as caching or scratch processing space. Think of workloads like high-performance computing (HPC), media rendering, and data analytics.

NOTE   Local SSDs disappear when you stop an instance, whereas all three types of persistent disks persist when you stop an instance—hence the name, persistent disk.

Each Local SSD is only 375GB, but you can attach 24 Local SSDs per instance. Because of their benefits and limitations, Local SSDs make a great use case for temporary storage such as caches, processing space, or low-value data.

Databases

There are a variety of database solutions in GCP, from installing your own database servers on virtual machines and using persistent disks to store your data, to leveraging a variety of managed services on GCP. For most cloud-native organizations, migrating to managed databases is a no-brainer, especially with the feature parity that GCP's database offerings have been able to achieve over the last few years compared to traditional databases. Managing and scaling a database operationally have quite the overhead. Why not let your cloud provider handle all of that work for you? Databases in GCP offer flexible performance and enormous scalability. They are often highly compatible with a broad set of open source technologies, and they are strongly integrated with key analytics and ML/AI products. Google Cloud's relational database offerings are Cloud SQL and Cloud Spanner, and its NoSQL/nonrelational database offerings are Cloud Bigtable, Cloud Firestore, Firebase Realtime Database, and Cloud Memorystore.

NOTE   The atomicity, consistency, isolation, and durability properties of database transactions are commonly referred to by the acronym ACID. The sequence of database operations that satisfies the ACID properties is called a transaction. Not all database offerings fulfill all ACID requirements, nor are they intended to do so.

Cloud SQL

Cloud SQL is a fully managed relational database for MySQL, PostgreSQL, and SQL Server that offers a simple integration from just about any application, similar to GCE, GKE, and Google App Engine (GAE). You can use BigQuery to query your Cloud SQL databases directly. Cloud SQL offers a 99.95 percent availability SLO and supports standard SQL queries.

When you're deploying a Cloud SQL instance, you get to choose between the three database servers: MySQL, PostgreSQL, and SQL Server. You can also select the region where the instance and its data are stored, as well as the zones. Ideally, you'd want to choose the same region for your data and the applications interfacing with it to minimize latency.

Replicating your instances between zones can be done by configuring Cloud SQL for high availability (HA). When you deploy an HA configuration, commonly known as a cluster, you're providing data redundancy across zones. An HA configuration typically has a primary instance in one zone and a standby instance in another zone. All of the data from the primary instance is stored in a regional persistent disk, which then uses synchronous replication to persistent disks attached in each zone. The standby instance is activated only if the primary instance becomes unresponsive, and it will automatically failover to the standby. After a failover happens, you'll need to perform a failback manually to resume serving data from your primary instance's zone after you are able to get it back up and running. In Figure 8-2, you can see an example HA architecture with Cloud SQL.

. You can also configure your instances to support read replicas to offload traffic from a Cloud SQL instance for read-heavy workloads. You cannot write to read replicas.

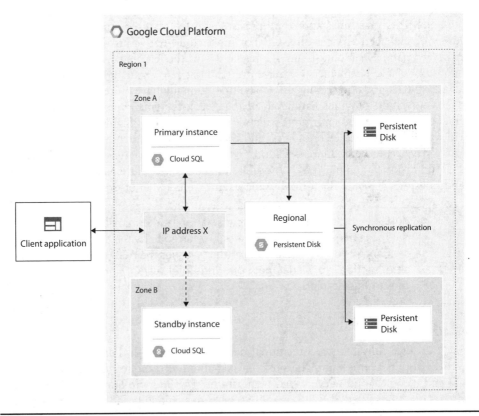

Figure 8-2 High-availability configuration with Cloud SQL

Cloud SQL also supports sharding—it's always a best practice to leverage many smaller Cloud SQL instances rather than one large instance to improve efficiency and scalability.

Cloud Spanner

Cloud Spanner is a fully managed, scalable relational database for regional and globally distributed application data. It combines the benefits of a relational database structure while scaling horizontally like a nonrelational database would. This allows for strong consistency across rows, regions, and contents, with a 99.999 percent availability SLO. Cloud Spanner solved a major issue with traditional databases by eliminating the trade-off between scale and consistency with its horizontally scaling, low latency, and highly consistent characteristics. Cloud Spanner is an online transaction processing database and supports standard SQL queries.

 EXAM TIP Don't forget the term "horizontal scaling." You may see questions about a requirement for a fully managed transactional SQL database that is also horizontally scaling like a traditional nonrelational database would be. Cloud Spanner is the only solution that would meet the criteria.

When databases claim they support standard SQL, that does not mean that they are SQL compatible. Cloud SQL supports MySQL, PostgreSQL, and SQL Server, which all claim to support standard SQL queries. Cloud Spanner also claims to support standard SQL queries. Be aware that you cannot, for example, switch from using MySQL or Microsoft SQL Server to Cloud Spanner just because you want horizontal scaling for your database and then expect that your applications will work. Assume that there will be some level of development needed to refactor your database.

When you create a Cloud Spanner instance, you select your instance configuration and node count. Your instance configuration determines where your database is geographically located and where it is replicated. You can select a regional or multiregional deployment. After choosing your instance configuration, you will be able to choose the node count, which determines the amount of serving and storage resources that are available in that instance. You can modify the node count later if you need to. Each node supports up to 2TB of storage, and its performance is based on the instance configuration, schema design, and your dataset characteristics. As an estimate, each Cloud Spanner node can provide up to 10,000 queries per second of reads and 2000 queries per second of writes. The ability to add nodes is what makes Cloud Spanner horizontally scalable, and that also makes it a much more powerful system than Cloud SQL.

Cloud Bigtable

Cloud Bigtable is a fully managed and scalable NoSQL database for large analytical and operational workloads. It's able to handle millions of requests per second at a consistent sub-10ms latency. Bigtable is ideal for things like personalization engines, ad-tech, digital media, and Internet of Things (IoT), and it connects easily to other database services such as BigQuery and the Apache ecosystem. Bigtable offers a 99.99 percent availability SLO. It can scale to billions of rows and thousands of columns, enabling you to store petabytes of data. It also has an extension to multiple client libraries, including the Apache

HBase library for Java. Bigtable is a great solution for MapReduce operations, stream processing/analytics, and ML applications. By offering low-latency read/write access, high-throughput analytics, and native time series support, it's commonly used to store and query the following workloads:

- Time-series data
- Marketing data, personalization, recommendations
- Financial data
- IoT data, geospatial datasets
- Graph data

Cloud Firestore

Cloud Firestore is a fully managed, fast, serverless, cloud-native NoSQL document database that is designed for mobile, web, and IoT applications at global scale. Firestore is the next generation of Google Cloud Datastore, which was the original highly scalable NoSQL database for mobile and web-based applications. Firestore offers a 99.999 percent availability SLO. Firestore is a great solution for common use cases such as user profiles, product catalogs, and game state.

EXAM TIP If the JencoMart case study is used in the exam, question(s) will outline a requirement to leverage managed services where possible. JencoMart uses an Oracle database for storing 20TB of user profiles. Firestore would be a great solution for this use case. And don't forget that Firestore is the next major version of Datastore and still supports existing Datastore APIs.

Cloud Memorystore

Cloud Memorystore is a scalable, secure, and highly available in-memory service for Redis and Memcached. It enables you to build application caches that provide sub-millisecond data access, and it's entirely compatible with the open source Redis and Memcached. Memorystore provides a 99.9 percent availability SLO.

NOTE Redis and Memcached are open source distributed memory caching systems that are often used to speed up dynamic database–driven applications by caching the data and objects in RAM. You can use these tools to cache the queries for your database backend. To do this effectively, you'll want to get the hashes of your queries and use those to build a key-value store, where your data then gets returned by the caching system rather than your database backend. Google App Engine provides a built-in memcache service by default.

Most organizations use Redis or Memcached, but Cloud Memorystore has an advantage by eliminating the burden of management from the organization. Because it is fully managed, you don't have to worry about managing the deployment, scaling, node configurations, monitoring, and patching. Its compatibility with Redis and Memcached makes it simple for you to migrate your applications without making code changes. Memorystore provides rich metrics that enable you to scale your instances up and down easily, so that you can optimize your cache-hit ratio and your costs.

Data Analytics

Building on the database technology, one of the key value propositions Google Cloud offers over other cloud providers is its powerful data analytics offerings, called Smart Analytics solutions. At the end of the day, Google is a data company, and externalizing its infrastructure as a cloud to customers was a natural business path. Building incredibly powerful analytical tools based on its 20-plus years in the data space is another no-brainer. Forrester Research named Google Cloud a leader in Data Management for Analytics. Google offers unified cloud-native data analytics platforms that provide easy access to streaming and batch processing data at an unmatched scale.

 EXAM TIP   You'll see a lot of questions on the exam that may sound like they are looking for database solutions, but don't forget to distill the requirements down to an online transactional processing (OLTP) or online analytical processing (OLAP) type of data solution. Oftentimes, when the exam refers to analytics, your answers will involve analytical solutions such as BigQuery, Dataproc, Dataflow, and Pub/Sub (covered in the following sections). Don't forget the power of Cloud Bigtable as an underlying database for analytical workloads that integrates with big data tools such as Hadoop, Dataflow, and Dataproc.

BigQuery

BigQuery is a highly scalable, cost-effective, serverless solution for multi-cloud data warehousing. Use it to analyze petabyte-scale data with zero operational overhead. BigQuery is one of Google Cloud's top products and is based on the Google-developed Dremel query engine. It has a 99.99 percent availability SLO. BigQuery is an OLAP database that supports standard SQL queries. It is a great use case for migrating data from Teradata or any of your on-premises legacy data warehouses to increase performance and scalability by an exponential order of magnitude, while decreasing operational burden and cost.

In BigQuery, you can interact with the Cloud Console, the **bq** command-line tool, or directly from the BigQuery REST API. You can also use many third-party tools to interact with BigQuery, such as visualization tools. BigQuery *jobs* are actions that

BigQuery will run on your behalf to load, export, query, or copy data. You can run jobs concurrently so that they can be executed asynchronously, and you can use polling to check the status of the jobs.

BigQuery *datasets* are top-level containers that are used to organize and control access to tables and views. As you can imagine, tables consist of rows and columns of data records. Like other databases, each table is defined by a table schema, which should be created in the most efficient way. *Views* are virtual tables defined by a query. You can create authorized views to share query results with only a particular set of users and groups without giving them access to the tables directly.

Although BigQuery can run massive queries in a fraction of the time that other data solutions can, you should still partition your tables to optimize your database. Think about how this would play out if you had petabyte-size log storage. Rather than storing the log data in a single table partition, you can consider splitting them into partitions to optimize your queries and reduce costs. You can use time-partitioned tables and add rules, such as a rule to delete a partition after 30 days. You can also use table partitioning to manage fine-grained access to a data source between multiple teams.

 EXAM TIP The predefined roles created for BigQuery are important for managing the various tasks involved with standing up, migrating to, managing, and interacting with BigQuery. Get familiar with these roles at a high level for the exam.

Cloud Dataproc

Cloud Dataproc is a fully managed data and analytics processing solution that's based on open source tools. You can build fully managed Apache Spark, Apache Hadoop, Presto, and other open source clusters. It's pay as you go, making it a very cost-effective solution that offers per-second pricing. In Dataproc, you get the benefit of automated cluster management, which handles deployment, logging, and monitoring, so that you can focus on your data.

 EXAM TIP If you see questions about Hadoop or Spark on the exam—don't forget about Dataproc!

When you build your jobs, you can containerize them with Kubernetes (K8s) and deploy them into any GKE cluster. Dataproc is a great use case for migrating Apache Spark jobs and Hadoop Distributed File System (HDFS) data to GCP, as well as for creating a strong data science environment by integrating with ML services and running Jupyter Notebook.

CAUTION When you're interacting with Hadoop and Apache Spark, you'll oftentimes be working with web interfaces that you'll leverage to manage and monitor your cluster resources and facilities. Be very careful not to open the wrong firewall rules to the public and create a Secure Shell (SSH) tunnel to secure the connection to your cluster's master instance. I can't stress how often this happens and organizations get pwned. Dear "you-know-who," if you're reading this book, this paragraph was dedicated to the time you opened 0.0.0.0/0 to the world to access the cluster web UI and your organization got pwned by a cryptominer. It could've been worse. Moral of the story—don't screw with your firewall rules without going through information security.

Cloud Dataflow

Cloud Dataflow is a serverless, cost-effective, unified stream and batch data processing service that is fully managed and is based on the Apache Beam SDK. Dataflow enables incredibly fast streaming data analytics and eliminates the overhead of managing clusters. Dataflow is a great use case for stream analytics, real-time AI solutions such as fraud detection, personalization, predictive analytics, and sensor and log data processing in IoT solutions.

Because Dataflow is based on the Apache Beam open source model, while being a fully serverless solution, your key goals when developing your pipelines are to figure out where your input data is stored, what your data looks like, what you want to do with your data, and where the output data will go. This serves as a great use case for extraction, transformation, and load (ETL) jobs and pure data integration. Dataflow supports batch jobs and streaming jobs.

EXAM TIP You may see questions that involve historical data or real-time data. Historical data is often aligned to batch processing, and real-time data is aligned to streaming solutions.

Cloud Pub/Sub

Cloud Pub/Sub is a global messaging and event ingestion solution that provides a simple and reliable staging location for event-based data before it gets processed, stored, and analyzed. Pub/Sub offers "at-least-once" delivery, with exactly once processing and no provisioning, and is global by default. Pub/Sub offers a 99.95 percent availability SLO. You've probably heard of similar open source tools such as RabbitMQ that offer similar messaging solutions. (In the Dress4Win case study in Chapter 1, the company runs three RabbitMQ servers for messaging, social notifications, and events.)

Messaging tools have strong use cases in an organization. Pub/Sub is short for publish/ subscribe messaging, which is an asynchronous communication method to exchange messages between applications. When you think about all your GCP logs, you'll realize that there is no 1:1 team or 1:1 application mapping between the logs and where they should go. Oftentimes you'll have many consumers of this log data. Let's imagine, for example, that your security team needs to ingest logs into its SIEM, your app team is using Databricks or Datadog and wants to ingest logs into their application, and other teams need the log data for other applications. Rather than designing pipelines to stream your log data across to a variety of applications, you can simply use Pub/Sub as a mechanism that enables any subscriber to consume this data.

There are five key elements in Pub/Sub:

- **Publisher** The client that creates messages and publishes them to a specific topic
- **Message** The data that moves through Pub/Sub
- **Topic** A named resource that represents a feed of messages
- **Subscription** A named resource that receives all specified messages on a topic
- **Subscriber** The client that receives messages from a subscription

Pub/Sub is incredibly powerful, because it's built on a core infrastructure component that Google uses to power all of its messaging across its entire product stack, including Ads, Search, and G-mail. Google uses this infrastructure to send more than 500 million messages per second, or 1Tbps of data. Pub/Sub is also a great use case for streaming IoT data, distributing event notifications, balancing workloads in network clusters, and implementing asynchronous workflows.

Data Security

Protecting your data is one of the pillars of migrating to the cloud. For the longest time, organizations held off migrating to the cloud because of security concerns about cloud providers potentially snooping into or stealing their data and because the attack surface seemed to become larger to the world's malicious actors. The security concerns of cloud providers' default security has been mitigated by now, and most organizations know that the cloud provider isn't at fault when a security incident occurs. In fact, most traditional on-premises security teams know that their organization's technology infrastructure is more like Swiss cheese, and it's only a matter of time till a breach. The focus has become increasingly targeted toward the customers of the cloud making mistakes, because almost all breaches in the cloud happen because a customer fails to follow best practices for the elements of the shared responsibility model that fall under the customer's purview. Every cloud service provider, particularly Google Cloud, has an insane amount of security controls that it attests to and that are continuously audited against to ensure that the provider is not dropping the ball with regard to protecting its customers.

Data Classification

When it comes to data security in the cloud, you should think about how you are classifying and labeling your data; the security controls you're applying to protect it, including access controls, encryption, and data exfiltration prevention; and how you'll monitor your classified data against misconfigurations.

How do you plan on governing your environment if you have no idea where your sensitive data is stored? Data classification is one of the most important elements of protecting your data. Virtually all major organizations use a data classification model, although it may not always be followed. (It's like the annual security course you're forced to take, where your sole purpose is to figure out how fast you can get through the course without actually reading anything...yeah. But let's reserve judgement over the efficacy of mandated security courses for another book.) *Data classification* is the process of classifying your data to its type, sensitivity, and criticality to your organization to secure and govern your data more effectively.

Your organization's information security team will likely have a policy that dictates what type of data falls under which classification tier. You'll commonly see a three- or four-tier model that starts with public data, then confidential data, confidential proprietary data, and optionally a highest sensitivity tier for data. Think about the Internal Revenue Service, which gathers and stores sensitive financial data on all Americans that is quite sensitive in nature and should fall under a high classification tier. It's one thing if my tax records are leaked and the world knows that I have a lot of IOUs, but the problem is quite different if the US president's tax records are leaked. That's the kind of situation where some organizations may include a fourth and highest sensitivity tier to ensure that the highest criticality of data is protected. Truth is, this classification exercise is going to be imposed on your company sooner or later because of either the EU General Data Protection Regulation (GDPR) or the California Consumer Privacy Act (CCPA) regulations.

For each classification category, your information security team likely provides the following security and privacy requirements:

- Data ownership (such as data owner and data custodian)
- Labeling (such as sensitivity and impact)
- Types of data (such as structured and unstructured data)
- Data life cycle (such as generation, retention, and disposal)
- Monitoring requirements
- Data anonymization
- Consent requirements

The reason why this data classification model needs to be sorted out before you start migrating all of your data into data stores in GCP is so that you can properly label and organize the data effectively. When you put labels on the data, your security team will typically use these labels to detect and respond to noncompliance. You can also use Cloud Data Loss Prevention (DLP) to detect, redact, or mask your streaming data or at-rest data automatically to ensure that Social Security numbers and the like don't end up in public buckets. You won't see anything about data classification on the exam, but as a cloud architect, you should strike up this conversation before you migrate your data, because it is a lot easier to architect your data environments accordingly before migration than it is to do it retroactively.

Cloud DLP

Cloud Data Loss Prevention (DLP) is a fully managed service that minimizes the risk of data exfiltration by enabling you to discover, classify, and protect your sensitive data. With Cloud DLP, you are able to perform de-identification on streaming and stored data. You can also continuously scan for environments where data does not meet the classification requirements. Despite its name, Cloud DLP is not like a traditional DLP solution. Cloud DLP does not actually prevent data exfiltration explicitly, as a traditional DLP does, by protecting data from leaving your perimeter.

Encryption

When it comes to encryption, Google Cloud may offer the best premise. Because Google owns its entire infrastructure stack, your cloud environment can take advantage of the same encryption that Google uses in its own corporate environment, which serves billions of users worldwide. Organizations with more stringent encryption needs have a variety of options, each of which has its pros and cons. Let's dive right in.

Default Encryption

By default, Google encrypts all data at rest inside its infrastructure using the AES 256 encryption algorithm. Data gets chunked automatically, and each chunk is encrypted at the storage level with a data encryption key (DEK). These keys are stored near the data to provide ultra-low latency and high availability. The DEK is then wrapped by the key encryption key (KEK) as part of the standard envelope encryption process. When you use default encryption, you don't have to worry about managing any of this because it happens by default. All the operational burden of managing key rings, keys, rotations, and all that jazz is out the door. These keys are managed by a key management service that falls under Google's purview outside the customer's organization. Google has very strict policies for managing these keys, and as mentioned, these are the same exact policies that protect Google's own production services. Default encryption is recommended as the way to go for most organizations.

Cloud KMS

With Cloud Key Management Service (KMS), you can manage your cryptographic keys on Google Cloud. KMS enables you to generate and manage the KEKs that protect sensitive data. KMS supports customer-managed encryption keys (CMEKs), customer-supplied encryption keys (CSEKs), and the external key manager. KMS integrates with Cloud HSM, providing you with the ability to generate a key protected by a FIPS 140-2 Level 3 device.

AWS CloudHSM is a managed, cloud-hosted hardware security module that enables you to protect your cryptographic keys in a FIPS 140-2 Level 3 certified hardware security module (HSM). CloudHSM easily integrates with Cloud KMS, and you pay for only what you use.

Customer-Managed Encryption Keys

With customer-managed encryption keys, customers can generate their own KEKs to protect their data. The benefit of doing this is not so much for customers to own their encryption keys, but to have more control over the management of the keys. At the end of the day, Google is the one generating the keying material. One reason for using CMEK would be if you require more strict key management processes, including faster rotations and revocation, and you need strong audit trails to monitor which users and services access your keys. When you use CMEK, you can also leverage CloudHSM to protect your keys in a cloud-based HSM.

Customer-Supplied Encryption Keys

The customer-supplied encryption key service enables customers to bring their own AES 256 keys so that they can have the most control over the keys to their data. Google Cloud doesn't permanently store CSEKs on its servers, and the keys are purged after every operation, so there is no way that Google or any government agency requesting access to a customer environment could decrypt your data. The issue with CSEK is that it did not get widely adopted among all of the Google services; it's quite a complex engineering feat to roll this out across the entire service list of products. CSEK is supported by only a few services such as GCE, GCS, and BigQuery.

External Key Manager

To counter the lack of CSEK's growth, Google launched a new service, External Key Manager (EKM), a service that enables organizations to supply their own keys through a supported external key management partner to protect their data in the cloud. With EKM, your keys are not stored in Google; they are stored at a third party, and you would typically own and control their location, distribution, access, and management. It's a pretty new service that is going to take some time before it's supported across the spectrum, but EKM is the most promising solution to customers that need to fully own their encryption keys. In my opinion, you should either use default encryption or EKM and nothing in between. But it's going to take some time before the product is fully mature and compatible.

Chapter Review

In this chapter, we discussed all of the storage, database, data analytics, and data security solutions in Google Cloud. You can review the many other products in the Google Cloud ecosystem in more depth than was covered in this chapter if you are going for the Professional Data Engineer certification. On the PCA exam, data-related questions don't get too deep into the weeds.

We started the chapter talking about the storage solutions. Google Cloud Storage is a fully managed, object-based storage solution in GCP. It uses the **gsutil** command-line tool to do all the bucket and object management tasks within the service. Cloud Filestore brings network file systems to your VPC. Persistent disks offer virtually attached block-based storage that can be resized upward, but not downward. Persistent disks also persist after restarting. Local SSD is a physically attached ephemeral block storage disk that is great for temporary storage use cases such as caching or scratch processing space. The Local SSD disappears when you stop an instance.

Cloud SQL is a fully managed RDBMS for MySQL, PostgreSQL, and SQL Server. It does not offer horizontal scaling. With Cloud SQL, you can configure your service for high availability using primary and standby instances, and you can leverage read replicas to offload traffic for read-heavy workloads. Cloud Spanner is a fully managed RDBMS that combines the benefits of a traditional RDBMS with the ability to horizontally scale. Both database solutions support standard SQL queries.

Cloud Bigtable is a NoSQL database designed for large analytical and operational workloads. It makes a great use case for time-series data, marketing data, IoT data, and more. Cloud Firestore is also a fully managed NoSQL database focused on document data, designed for mobile, web, and IoT applications. Cloud Firestore is great for user profiles, product catalogs, and game state. Cloud Memorystore is a solution for providing in-memory service for Redis and Memcached.

BigQuery is a fully managed data warehousing solution that can analyze petabyte-scale data with zero operational overhead. It supports standard SQL queries and is considered an OLAP database. Dataproc is a fully managed data and analytics processing solution geared toward open source Apache Spark and Apache Hadoop workloads. Dataflow is a serverless stream and batch data processing service based on the Apache Beam SDK.

To quickly recap:

- If you need SQL queries via an OLTP system, use Cloud Spanner or Cloud SQL.

- If you need interactive querying via an OLAP system, use BigQuery.

- If you need a strong NoSQL database for analytical workloads such as time-series data and IoT data, use Bigtable.

- If you need to store structured data in a document database with support for ACID transactions and SQL-like queries, use Cloud Firestore.

- If you need in-memory data storage, use Memorystore.

Data security is quite an important aspect of designing a secure cloud environment. Data classification is a mechanism that improves your ability to govern and secure your data by identifying key information and tagging your data accordingly. Cloud DLP offers a data discovery engine that can discover, tag, and de-identify data to minimize the threat of exfiltration. There are a variety of encryption offerings in Google Cloud, but the most important one is that everyone gets encryption at rest by default, a feat that no other cloud provider offers, which is available because Google owns its entire network stack end-to-end.

Additional References

If you'd like more information about the topics discussed in this chapter, check out these sources:

- **gsutil Tool**   https://cloud.google.com/storage/docs/gsutil
- **Using the bq Command-Line Tool**   https://cloud.google.com/bigquery/docs/bq-command-line-tool
- **Platform Overview - Data & Storage**   https://www.youtube.com/watch?v=tc2940Zwvyk

Questions

1. You're an architect for Memegen, a global meme generating company, designing a real-time analytics platform that is intended to stream millions of events per second. Their platform needs to dynamically scale up and down, process incoming data on the fly, and process data that arrives late because of slow mobile networks. They also want to run SQL queries to access 10TB of historical data. They'd like to stick to managed services only. What services would you leverage?

   A. Cloud SQL, Cloud Pub/Sub, Kubernetes

   B. Cloud Functions, Cloud Dataproc, Cloud Bigtable

   C. Cloud Dataflow, Cloud Storage, Cloud Pub/Sub, BigQuery

   D. Cloud Dataproc, BigQuery, Google Compute Engine

2. You need a solution to analyze your data stream and optimize your operations. Your data stream involves both batch and stream processing. Your team wants to leverage a serverless solution. What should you use?

   A. Cloud Dataflow

   B. Cloud Dataproc

   C. Kubernetes with BigQuery

   D. Compute Engine with BigQuery

3. Your team is running many Apache Spark and Hadoop jobs in their on-premises environment and would like to migrate to the cloud with the least amount of change to their tooling. What should they use?

   A. Cloud Dataflow

   B. Compute Engine with a Dataflow Connector

   C. Kubernetes Engine with a Dataflow Connector

   D. Cloud Dataproc

4. You need to develop a solution that will process data from one of your organization's APIs in strict chronological order with no repeated data. How would you build this solution?

   A. Cloud Dataflow

   B. Cloud Pub/Sub to a Cloud SQL backend

   C. Cloud Pub/Sub to a Stackdriver backend

   D. Cloud Pub/Sub

5. Memegen just got breached, and the Security Operations team is kicking off their incident response process. They're investigating a production VM and want to copy the VM as evidence in a secure location so they can conduct their forensics before taking an action. What should they do?

   A. Create a snapshot of the root disk, create a restricted GCS bucket that is accessible only by the forensics team, and create an image file in GCS from the snapshot.

   B. Shut down the VM, create a snapshot, create an image file in GCS, and restrict the GCS bucket.

   C. Use the **gcloud copy** tool to copy the file directory onto an attached Cloud Filestore network file system.

   D. Create a clone of the VM, migrate user traffic onto the new VM, and use the old VM for forensics.

6. You're planning on migrating 5 petabytes of data to your project. This data requires 24/7 availability, and your data analyst team is familiar with SQL. What tool should you use to surface this data to your analyst team for analytical purposes?

   A. Cloud Datastore

   B. Cloud SQL

   C. Cloud Spanner

   D. BigQuery

7. You're consulting for an IoT company that has hundreds of thousands of IoT sensors that capture readings every two seconds. You'd like to optimize the performance of this database, so you're looking to identify a more accurate, time-series database solution. What would you use?

   A. Cloud Bigtable

   B. Cloud Storage

   C. BigQuery

   D. Cloud Filestore

8. You have a customer who wants to store data for at least ten years that will be accessed infrequently, at most once a year. The customer wants to optimize their cost. What solution should they use?

   A. Google Cloud Storage

   B. Google Cloud Storage with a Nearline storage class

   C. Google Cloud Storage with a Coldline storage class

   D. Google Cloud Storage with a Archive storage class

9. BankyBank wants to build an online transactional processing tool that requires a relational database with petabyte-scale data. What tool would you use?

   A. BigQuery

   B. Cloud SQL

   C. Cloud Spanner

   D. Cloud Bigtable

10. Memegen wants to introduce a shopping functionality for their users to connect all of their user purchasing history and activities to their user profiles. They need massive scalability with high performance, atomic transactions, and a highly available document database. What should they use?

   A. Cloud Spanner

   B. BigQuery

   C. Cloud Bigtable

   D. Cloud Firestore

Answers

1. **C.** The requirements for this architecture include dynamic scaling, streaming data on the fly and batch processing data that arrives late, and using SQL to query massive scales of batch data, all through a managed service. Dataflow, GCS, Pub/Sub, and BigQuery are the only solutions that meet all these requirements.

2. **A.** Dataflow is a serverless solution that can be leveraged for both batch and stream processing. Dataproc is not fully serverless.

3. **D.** Dataproc is designed for Spark and Hadoop workloads.

4. **B.** Pub/Sub offers first in, first out (FIFO) ordering of messages, but when the content is stored, it will need to be stored in an ACID-based system such as Cloud SQL.

5. **A.** This is the only valid solution here. They're looking to investigate a production VM, so taking the server down is not a recommended action at this point. They also want to conduct forensics in a secure location to ensure the evidence is not tampered with.

6. D. There are a few indicators here as to why BigQuery is the right answer: large-scale migration, requirement to use SQL, and an analytical use case.

7. A. The dead giveaway here is leveraging a time-series database for IoT sensors. This is where Bigtable shines.

8. D. Using an archival storage class will be sufficient and the most cost-effective here because the use case is infrequently accessing the data, at most once a year.

9. C. Cloud Spanner is the OLTP solution that is relational and offers petabyte scalability. Cloud SQL is not designed for petabyte-scale data.

10. D. Cloud Firestore, formerly known as Datastore, is a great solution for profile storage and purchasing history.

DevOps

In this chapter, we'll cover

- A high-level overview of DevOps
- Infrastructure as code and why it's your best friend
- Various deployment models that you may see on the exam

DevOps is not just a process improvement or a combination of development and operations teams. DevOps is a cult; you know it's a cult because every engineer who follows the DevOps principles has an infinity sticker on their laptop or is waiting to talk about how amazing their philosophy is and why everybody does DevOps wrong. If you put a Jenkins sticker on your laptop because you got it for free at a conference, you open the door to every DevOps follower to stop by your desk and talk about their favorite tools.

I mean, think about it; life before DevOps couldn't have been that bad—all you had to do as a developer when you wanted to build an application was

1. Gather features, enhancements, and bug fixes, and plan your development, testing, and deployment phases around your monthly deployment cycle.

2. Hand off your code to quality assurance (QA) after your development team has done enough coding for the month.

3. Watch the QA team scramble to test everything and send back defects. Then scramble to fix the defects and try to get the code back to QA to retest before the release timeframe.

4. During release, watch as your QA and Operations teams bicker a bit back and forth on the quality of code and whether or not it's ready for deployment.

5. Listen to QA swear they did their job properly, and if there's anything they didn't identify, it's the developers' fault. When they finally agree to deploy the code, the Operations team deploys it.

6. Pray that it doesn't blow up. Otherwise, your Operations team is all hands on deck trying to minimize the impact, your Dev team is trying to fix the bugs, and your QA team is scrambling to retest.

7. Spend a cycle trying to do a postmortem to figure out what went wrong and how to prevent it next time. This, of course, takes time away from your new development cycle.

8. Rinse and repeat this around every monthly release cycle time, and battle to the death with your QA and Ops colleagues about who is to blame for the last month's issues.

9. Deal with Security, who finally musters up the courage to get involved. They're demanding you redesign the entire application from scratch because it violates all of their policies. Uh oh.

Reliability? What reliability? Okay fine. That was awful. What's even more awful is that most companies around the world are still following traditional development models and have yet to adopt a DevOps-centric philosophy. Even companies that try usually don't understand that DevOps is an entire organizational philosophy that requires a massive investment not just financially, but in time and people.

I guess DevOps is not a cult. To be fair, DevOps is a way of life. If you're building consumer-facing applications in 2020, you need to start thinking about who your demographic is going to be throughout your career and how you cater to them. If you want to maintain a strong retention rate with millennials, Gen Zs, and beyond, you can imagine that shipping unreliable software full of bugs and having outages is signing yourself up for failure. Can you imagine if TikTok was full of bugs and unreliable? All those daily active users would be driving their Zuck Trucks down to Instagram.

On the other extreme are organizations that are so fearful of change—because change introduces the potential for new issues—that the cycle time to release new functionality is not measured in days or months, but in years. In those companies, the enemy of good enough is perfection. The idea that nothing should ever go wrong introduces a blame culture, where everyone is doing CYA (cover your "rear") rather than innovating to create business value. As an architect, you need to understand your organization's risk tolerance and look for opportunities that enable your company to be fast and highly available. These are not necessarily mutually incompatible requirements.

In this chapter, we're going to talk a little bit about DevOps at a high level, including why it's so valuable in your organization, what you'll expect to see on the exam around this topic, the importance of codifying your infrastructure, some of the various products and services in Google Cloud that support DevOps processes, and some of the third-party products in the DevOps ecosystem that you'll probably want to be familiar with.

The DevOps Philosophy

The philosophy of DevOps challenges decades of software development, where the people, process, and technology were built on longstanding belief systems based on clearly defined roles for developers, QA, and operations teams, and a rigid structure around the deployment process. Traditional software development uses a factory model of moving work through a conveyor belt of roles (processes), which produces a consistent level of quality as an output. This has frequently proved to be a false axiom, however, as the individuals involved were often the reason why processes either succeeded or failed.

DevOps includes the philosophies, practices, and tools that empower your organization to deliver experiences to its consumers at high velocity and improve service reliability. DevOps is not a role, and it doesn't eliminate the traditional roles of developers, testing, and operations teams. Matter of fact, if you see a job posting for a DevOps engineer, it's antithetical to the idea of DevOps, unless that role is hiring for a DevOps evangelist or someone who can help build the organization's cultural DevOps practice. Instead, DevOps eliminates the rigidity around the development, testing, and production operations teams by including feedback loops across each team and providing more influence over the entire development life cycle, so that team members are no longer siloed by knowing only what goes on in their individual role. In DevOps, the combination of creating feedback loops and shifting left (i.e., shifting tasks as early in the life cycle as possible) enables teams to operate in a more dynamic and fluid fashion. Rather than moving work through people performing steps on a conveyor belt, DevOps development focuses on optimizing the entire end-to-end workflow. As a consequence of the repetitive work of traditional development operations, the work came to be seen as toil, which created an opportunity for automation. But humans should focus instead on continuous improvement or value-creating activities to keep improving efficiencies. Thus, the practice of automating as much of the development, testing, and operational process came to be accepted as the ideal situation so that organizations could focus on building great applications rather than performing repetitive work to create applications that were only good enough.

There are five key pillars of success in the DevOps philosophy:

- Reduce organizational silos
- Accept failure as normal
- Implement gradual changes
- Leverage tooling and automation
- Measure everything

NOTE DevOps does not eliminate the role of a developer, QA, or production support team. Instead, this philosophy is focused on bringing visibility into the entire life cycle and eliminating as many pitfalls as possible so that teams can quickly build, test, deploy, and identify clear, actionable feedback through the entire life cycle to minimize code defects and improve the velocity of development.

Continuous Integration and Continuous Deployment

The two aspects of the DevOps infinity loop are the continuous integration and continuous deployment of code. *Continuous integration/continuous deployment* (CI/CD) is the combined practices of integrating and deploying code that bridges the gap between development and operations activities by enforcing automation, seamless handoffs between teams, and continuous feedback throughout each phase. This concept describes the best practices for delivering code with more velocity, fewer defects, and more business value to your consumers.

To build a CI/CD pipeline of end-to-end workflow, you should do the following:

1. Plan your development cycle.

2. Write and manage your code.

3. Orchestrate the build process.

4. Test your build to identify defects and resolve them.

5. Prepare your release for deployment.

6. Deploy your code.

7. Operate and manage your application.

 EXAM TIP Get familiar with some of the common DevOps tools at a high level and know what they do—Jenkins, Travis CI, GitHub, Chef, Puppet, Ansible, Terraform, and Spinnaker. Because the exam is geared toward seasoned professionals, you're expected to be familiar with a wide variety of technologies that aren't necessarily Google Cloud technologies.

Regardless of your application, whether it is a simple web application or a fully baked customer-facing application, you probably have a massive amount of code that is organized into functions and modules and that is constantly going through updates and iterations based on customer feedback. It's incredibly difficult to manage all of your code if it doesn't follow a central proofing and validation process. The purpose of continuous integration is to integrate code into a shared repository so that developers can collaborate effectively to write code, builds can be automated, tests can be automatically performed, bugs can be fixed, and your release can be prepared for an automated and continuous deployment. Basically, you're optimizing every stage of development up to the point of validating your update in a staging environment and having your release ready to be pushed into production.

You should be aware of two key tenets for agile development:

- Many smaller code changes are better to manage than a few huge changes.
- Following a DevOps model will exercise existing and new code much more, because each small change is put through the whole end-to-end QA process.

In the end, you let the computers do most of the work for you.

Continuous Integration

Building the CI aspect of your pipeline involves centralizing the tools leveraged to plan your development cycles (such as JIRA and Asana) and then providing your team with tools to manage source code (such as Git) and storing code in repositories (such as GitHub, GitLab, or Cloud Source Repositories). Next you orchestrate your build process, compile all of your binaries and packaging into a build with tools such as Maven, and store your binaries in a repository such as Artifactory.

After the build is created, your QA team will likely conduct tests. You should be familiar with the following types of tests:

- **Unit tests**   These tests ensure that the smallest testable aspect of your code works as expected, even in isolation, by running tests against individual units of code without the full environment. External variables are mocked with fake versions—for instance, a database would be mocked during a unit test to ensure that the code does exactly what it's intended to do, even with a fake integration. Unit tests are typically run by developers regularly throughout the development life cycle, often immediately before a code commit or as part of the build process after every commit. As they write new code, they create new tests and/or update existing tests to validate the new code changes. Good developers often develop their tests before they make code changes (but that's a conversation for another time).

- **Integration tests**   These tests ensure that the components and modules of code integrate and work properly with one another and are typically run before major commits that involve many components or the builds for new releases. Integration tests are based on the environment, including all the integrations. For instance, if your application depends on a database and your integration test fails, the test results could identify issues with any of the variables in the environment. Integrations tests are the responsibility of your overall team. QA individuals can develop and build them, but be aware that as developers create and modify code, this can lead to integration tests breaking as a result of improper new code or the need to update your integration tests to incorporate the newly introduced changes. In high-functioning DevOps organizations, developers run published integration tests to ensure that their code changes don't cause problems with other components of the architecture. They don't wait for someone else to uncover an integration bug included in their code changes. Some organizations are able to allocate complete end-to-end testing capability to developers, but this is possible only when everyone works together to focus on operational efficiency!

- **End-to-end tests**   In these tests, an application is run from beginning to end to test the flow of the application and to ensure that the system can be validated for integration and data integrity.

Many other types of tests are often used, triggered by humans or applications automatically throughout this phase. After testing, you can usually do *static code analysis* by running code-scanning applications to scan for security vulnerabilities, resource leaks, null pointer references, and many other areas of code that may have been overlooked. Assuming that all these steps are successful, your build is pushed into a repository, where your automation server will be told that your release is ready to be deployed.

Continuous Deployment

In the continuous deployment phase, your pipeline is designed to get all the changes to your builds into production, including new features, configuration changes, and bug fixes. By the time your code is in this phase, the pipeline will have validated that it is in a deployable state. Although it's possible that mistakes will be missed and a build that shouldn't have been deployed gets deployed, in the DevOps model, the number of defects is minimized well beyond the scope of any other traditional development philosophy.

Organizations that have not embraced DevOps or high-velocity IT often don't realize that properly designed CI/CD frameworks actually "overtest" code. Code is continuously being tested in the background after each little change is introduced. Each developer is responsible for testing and validating their code changes as thoroughly as possible. Pushing out responsibility for testing to people other than developers can slow things down: other people may not share in your priorities and deadlines. The best practice is to automate as much of the end-to-end testing and validation as possible.

TIP   Jenkins and Spinnaker are a great combination for building CI/CD pipelines. Jenkins will handle the continuous integration, and Spinnaker will handle the continuous deployment. Jenkins and Spinnaker go hand-in-hand.

Infrastructure as Code

You've done a great job of conceptually building your pipelines, but before you share your application with the world, you need to create it in an appropriate environment that develops, tests, and sends it to production. Applications require computing power, storage, and databases using Google Cloud products that are either managed or unmanaged. The cloud surely makes it easier to right-size infrastructure and leverage a variety of services, with native integrations, scalability, and near-instant deployments. But you can imagine that all of this infrastructure will get incredibly complex to manage, and a single misconfiguration could jeopardize your entire business. This is where leveraging infrastructure as code (IaC) comes in.

IaC is the practice of writing the elements of your infrastructure in code form, which can be interpreted by tools such as Terraform, Ansible, and Google Deployment Manager. You're basically treating your infrastructure as you would treat your software—with clear code, source code repositories, approved patterns and strong change management, misconfiguration detection and prevention, and rapid deployment.

There are many reasons why you should codify your infrastructure:

- Having the ability to spin up any scale infrastructure by deploying a template speeds up the entire task of deploying infrastructure by an unmatched margin.

- Managing configurations for thousands of servers, services, and beyond can and will always lead to humans making errors and misconfigurations, which could cause a whole slew of issues for your applications, from operational issues to security issues. Using IaC enables you to centrally manage these configurations, scan them for deviances, and govern them centrally.

- Eliminating the need to manually provision new servers and services minimizes the time to deploy your applications. By using IaC, if your application goes through a massive iteration and you need to attach a new database, Pub/Sub sink, or VMs, you can modify your templates rather than having to plan to perform these activities as part of your deployment.

- Freeing up development time for your team to focus on building, testing, and managing your applications, rather than constantly provisioning infrastructure manually, saves money.

- Stop looking at infrastructure as immutable. For high-velocity IT development teams to work as efficiently as possible, give them their own temporary environments to test their new code. Then destroy the environment when they are done. The whole point of public cloud is on-demand infrastructure. This can be achieved only via automation and IaC.

In 2020 and beyond, using IaC tools such as Terraform is a no-brainer. While the benefits of using IaC are incommensurable compared to not using IaC, you will still have risks that need to be managed. Think about it: You use a tool to create templates, you store templates in a repository, and you have a service account that has godlike access to provision the infrastructure across your entire GCP environment. If your templates are improperly modified and you do not have proper prevention and detection controls in place, a template could be deployed that pwns your entire infrastructure. In addition, your repository itself needs to be monitored, tightly access controlled, and ensured that it is not tampered with. Lastly, your service accounts and their service account keys need to be controlled and monitored very rigorously to ensure that they aren't compromised. If a service account with access to the provision infrastructure across your whole stack is compromised, you've given an attacker the keys to the kingdom. Two approaches can be used to limit risk here: First, you could lock down the underlying OS completely that hosts IaC platforms such as Terraform or Ansible, or, better yet, use a GCP-managed service such as Deployment Manager instead. Or you could create multiple service accounts with the least privileged access needed to run the specific playbooks/workflows. Thus, if the service account is compromised, the attacker could, at most, access or modify what the specific workflow job had privileges to. The key here is never to make life easier for a hacker who manages to gain some access to your environment. Godlike account powers should be under the highest level of protection, or just avoided.

 CAUTION Protect your service accounts, templates, and repositories to ensure that every action is deliberately taken and validated before being authorized to commit.

Deployment Strategies

There is no one-size-fits-all approach to deploying applications and changes into production. Oftentimes, based on availability requirements, performance requirements, complexities of your application, and your knowledge and success in deploying applications, you may need to leverage different strategies to deploy code at different times. For the purpose of your exam, you'll need to be familiar with a few of the main deployment strategies.

Blue-Green Deployment

Blue-green deployment involves creating two identical environments—a blue environment and green environment—so that when a release is deployed to one environment, the other environment can be held as a reserve. The idea is that you can deploy the release to one environment and switch all your users over to the new release, while still maintaining your old environment in case you need to fall back to it, without having to do a full rollback. As you can imagine, the infrastructure costs double, and if the application footprint is too large, this is not always a feasible deployment strategy.

 EXAM TIP Blue-green deployments are a very effective way to avoid having to do unplanned rollbacks by having another production environment available in the event things go wrong. Rollbacks take a lot of time and are very disruptive. It's easier to push your users onto your green deployment if the blue one goes bad. On the exam, you'll see scenario-based questions that ask for the recommended deployment strategy, so ensure you have a high-level understanding of these strategies.

Rolling Deployment

In a *rolling deployment*, you maintain one production environment that may consist of many servers with a load balancer in front of them. When you deploy your application, you stagger the deployment across servers, so that some servers run the new application version and others continue to host the old version. This enables you to test real-life traffic and load and potentially identify issues before the application is fully deployed. If you do have an issue, you can just divert all of your users to the servers that do not have the latest release (rather than having to roll back servers entirely). This can be a complicated process, especially around major changes, because the support team managing your application will have to understand how to troubleshoot both users on the older versions as well as users who've been routed to the new version.

Canary Deployment

Canary deployment involves making the new release available to a subset of users before other users. It is similar to a rolling deployment in the sense that some of your users will get access to the new release before others. But in the canary deployment, you're targeting users, not servers. Your infrastructure costs will be higher with this type of deployment because you are maintaining two sets of infrastructure, though your usage on the infrastructure where you target your canary users probably won't be too high if your application is designed to scale on demand.

A/B Deployment

A/B deployment is more focused on testing different changes on end users to understand which they prefer. The idea here is to have half of your users work with version A, while the other half works with version B. It's a way for you to understand how your customers are using your new version and derive insights from their usage patterns to drive customer happiness.

NOTE   In Tesla vehicles, users can opt in to an "advanced" software delivery method, which is similar to A/B deployment. This gives some customers early access to software, ahead of others. This is Tesla's way of offering more risk-tolerant users the ability to get their hands on software sooner than other users, and it helps Tesla ensure that its software is ready before deploying it to everybody.

Deployment Tools

Don't underestimate the power of Google-managed tools within GCP over those you have to self-administer. Many of these are serverless, which makes them operationally and administratively more cost-effective than even open source solutions. There are a few Google-native tools you can leverage for various aspects of the CI/CD process, all of which have their pros and cons.

Google Cloud Deployment Manager

Cloud Deployment Manager enables you to create and manage cloud resources using deployment templates by treating your infrastructure as code and simplifying the deployment process. It's similar to AWS CloudFormation Templates or Terraform templates. Cloud Deployment Manager is Google's homegrown tool to help you do IaC provisioning and management in GCP. This tool isn't that popular, however. Most organizations opt to use Terraform because of their multi-cloud nature, and the idea of using an open source tool makes it easier for developers to code and prevent vendor lock-in. Cloud Deployment Manager does not integrate across multi-cloud environments (nor does AWS CloudFormation). Cloud Deployment Manager uses YAML (Yet Another Markup Language) to orchestrate a deployment, similar to Ansible and Kubernetes (K8s) deployments. YAML inherently allows for jinja2 extensions along with custom Python code integration into your deployments, making it very flexible and powerful.

TIP   You can leverage Kubernetes deployment files as a way to create a declarative template to provision your Pod infrastructure using **gcloud** to provision your clusters and **kubectl** to run your deployment template.

Cloud Build

Cloud Build is a serverless CI/CD platform that has curated the steps to build, test, and deploy code into GCP. You can build software using all programming languages, have complete control over the CI/CD workflow, and deploy across multiple environments, whether they are VMs, K8s, or managed services. Cloud Build integrates with many third parties across the workflow, from build tools such as Apache Maven, to continuous delivery platforms such as Spinnaker, as well as across multiple cloud service providers. Although most organizations have not yet hit the point of using cloud-native CI/CD tools, Cloud Build is a simple and cutting-edge product that should certainly be explored by organizations as an easy way to manage their pipelines.

TIP   Spinnaker is an open source continuous delivery platform originally developed by Netflix and then picked up by Google. It has been validated by thousands of teams with millions of deployments, and it has consistently proved its worth in improving velocity and deployment confidence. Spinnaker supports multiple cloud providers.

Cloud Source Repositories

Cloud Source Repositories is a private Git repository that you can use to design, develop, and securely manage your code. It enables you to extend your Git workflow by connecting to other tools such as Pub/Sub, Cloud Monitoring/Logging, and more. You can mirror code from GitHub or BitBucket to get powerful code search, browsing, and diagnostic capabilities. You can also use regular expressions to refine your search across the directories.

TIP   For those security-conscious architects out there, please don't underestimate the value of mirroring repositories from public repositories. You can create an effective air-gapped, change management–controlled architecture. This can prevent unauthorized access and the use of dangerous and untested code that often lives in these public repositories, and it's an effective way to prevent the exfiltration of data out of your environment to these repositories.

Container Registry

Container Registry is a private Docker repository in which you can store, manage, and secure your Docker container images. You can also perform vulnerability analysis and manage access control to the container images. With Container Registry, you can integrate your CI/CD pipelines to design fully automated Docker pipelines. When you're using the Container Registry, you can automatically build and push images to your private registries immediately upon committing code to your source code repository tools such as Cloud Source Repositories, GitHub, or BitBucket.

Chapter Review

In this chapter, we discussed the benefits of DevOps and how the DevOps philosophy has changed the technology world for good. DevOps is not a technology or a tool; it is a philosophy focused on creating a highly automated development, test, and release pipeline that brings full visibility across the stack to every role that interfaces with the full life cycle so that you can improve the velocity of code and minimize the number of defects. This is the core characteristic of high-velocity IT. Organizations that follow DevOps philosophies need to engrain these philosophies across the entire technology organization. Oftentimes, they're able to ship high-quality code with greater customer satisfaction, all while optimizing their development hours and resources. Continuous integration and continuous delivery, also known as CI/CD, is the idea of creating development pipelines that integrate code development activities and deployment activities across one pipeline, automating as many of the elements of this pipeline as possible. Remember that small, incremental changes are much easier and faster to integrate into a code base than large, massive changes. So if you can get good at making many small changes continuously, your organization is able to move and adapt much faster.

There are a variety of different deployment methods available to organizations, and they should be leveraged based on the needs of their application. Rolling deployments push your release to individual servers and stagger their deployment so that your users can gradually onboard new releases. Canary deployments push a subset of your users to the new release so that you can test with just a small sample of users before migrating everyone over. Blue-green deployments involve creating two identical production environments and pushing your release to one of them, so that you can switch to another deployment if things go wrong and you need to roll back.

While having a strong CI/CD process in place helps your team build and ship high-quality code, what is all your code without an environment to deploy to? To do all of this work and operate your applications, you need development, testing, and production environments that consist of infrastructure and services that power your applications. Manually provisioning this infrastructure is cumbersome, inefficient, and oftentimes insecure. Infrastructure as code (IaC) is the practice of codifying all of your infrastructure deployments into deployment templates, where you can simply design what the infrastructure looks like as declarative code, manage these templates in repositories, and have deployment servers automatically attach these templates as part of their deployment process. With sufficient automation, you can give your developers their own on-demand temporary environments using IaC to self-test their unit tests, integration tests, and even end-to-end tests, reducing unnecessary operations delays involving other people in the development cycle for testing small code changes. Protect your service accounts! Don't forget about those when you're using IaC tools, because these accounts often have god-like access.

Google Cloud Deployment Manager is a tool, similar to Terraform, that is designed to accept codified infrastructure templates and deploy them accordingly. Cloud Build is a serverless end-to-end CI/CD product on GCP that enables developers to do most of their build, test, and deployment processes natively in GCP. Cloud Source Repositories is a source control management tool that enables you to store your code in repositories, similar to GitHub and BitBucket, so that your developers have one central process and area in which to manage their code. Container Registry is a tool that is designed to store your container image builds so that you can control your golden and trusted images, integrate into your CI/CD pipelines with ease, and scan your images for vulnerabilities and misconfigurations. Don't underestimate the power of Google-managed tools within GCP over those you have to self-administer. Many of these are serverless, which makes them operationally and administratively more cost-effective than even open source solutions for which you will need to spin up a GCE VM. DevOps is no cult. DevOps is life!

Additional References

If you'd like more information about the topics discussed in this chapter, check out this source:

- **Software Delivery for Beginners Series Intro**   https://medium.com/@gwright_60924/software-delivery-for-beginners-series-intro-751b90fbe078

Questions

1. Your application has a high failure rate and a high mean-time-to-resolve, and it is running on Google Compute Engine. The application performs a variety of functions, and when one function goes down, it triggers an entire malfunction. What should you do?

    A. Leverage a green-blue deployment model.

    B. Use a canary release in the QA environment.

    C. Migrate the applications database onto a managed service in GCP.

    D. Fragment the application into microservices.

2. Your solution is producing performance bugs in production that you did not see in staging and test environments. You want to adjust your test and deployment procedures to avoid this problem in the future. What should you do?

    A. Minimize the number of times you're making code changes.

    B. Minimize the size of your code changes.

    C. Do more testing to avoid this issue.

    D. Deploy your changes to a canary cluster of users to test them adequately.

3. You want to automate the creation of several configurations of your GCE environment, especially by adding autoscaling managed instance groups and other VM configuration templates. What should you do?

    A. Use Terraform to codify and deploy your infrastructure.

    B. Create a golden VM image for your deployment.

    C. Build your managed instance group templates in the Cloud Console and then automate the deployment of those.

    D. Use the Container Registry to store your images.

4. Which of the following is *not* a benefit of infrastructure as code?

    A. It simplifies the management of your infrastructure.

    B. It minimizes the number of misconfiguration issues.

    C. It prevents potential security configuration issues from arising.

    D. It increases the time to deploy code.

5. A canary deployment

    A. Deploys a release to a subset of users

    B. Deploys a release to a subset of servers

    C. Deploys a release to a cloned production environment

    D. Deploys a release to a percentage of your nonproduction traffic

6. A rolling deployment

    A. Deploys a release to a subset of users

    B. Deploys a release to a subset of servers

    C. Deploys a release to a cloned production environment

    D. Deploys a release to a percentage of your nonproduction traffic

7. A green-blue deployment

    A. Deploys a release to a subset of users

    B. Deploys a release to a subset of servers

    C. Deploys a release to a cloned production environment

    D. Deploys a release to a percentage of your nonproduction traffic

8. Which of the following is *not* a benefit of DevOps?

    A. Improves development velocity

    B. Minimizes the number of bug defects

    C. Increases the number of hours during the testing cycle

    D. Automates much of the development workflow

9. What are unit tests?

    A. The smallest microservice to test in your application

    B. The smallest testable aspect of your code, tested independently of other elements of code

    C. The smallest test in your environment

    D. The smallest test of your environmental variables to ensure that they work with one another

10. What are integration tests?

    A. Tests conducted to ensure that code and modules work independently of one another

    B. Tests conducted to ensure that code and modules work with one another

    C. A form of testing to analyze your static code

    D. A form of testing to analyze your dynamic code

Answers

    1. **D.** Break up your code so that you aren't running one giant monolith in GCP. The whole point of adopting a microservices-based model is to prevent one function of your application from breaking the entire application. Can you imagine what would happen if Facebook's story feature broke and the entire website went down?

    2. **D.** Use a canary deployment method so that you can test these changes to a smaller set of users and extend your testing phases to capture items that you wouldn't have captured without dealing with a real load.

    3. **A.** Terraform is a great solution to turn your infrastructure into code, and you can manage all of the configurations via the Terraform templates you create.

    4. **D.** IaC does not increase the time to deploy code. In fact, it does the opposite.

    5. **A.** A canary release deploys your releases to a subset of users so that you can test the deployment with these users before pushing the changes to everyone.

    6. **B.** A rolling deployment deploys your release to a subset of your servers and enables you to stagger the deployment so that it is a gradual change.

    7. **C.** A green-blue deployment deploys your release to a secondary, or cloned, production environment so that you can maintain your old release in production in case you need to divert traffic back.

    8. **C.** DevOps does not increase the number of hours spent on any cycle; it focuses on optimizing every aspect of the development life cycle.

    9. **B.** Unit tests are tests performed on the smallest aspects of your code to ensure that they work independently of other elements of your code.

    10. **B.** Integration tests are designed to ensure that your code and modules work with one another in your environment.

CHAPTER 10

Cloud Operations

In this chapter, we'll cover
- Setting up your logging infrastructure in GCP
- Creating metrics and alerts
- Monitoring your applications for performance, uptime, and overall health

Reliability is the best metric for retaining customers. Knowing this, Google spun up Site Reliability Engineering (SRE), a philosophy similar to DevOps (and oftentimes referred to as a subset or sibling of DevOps), that focuses on leveraging aspects of software engineering and applying them to infrastructure and operations problems.

Even today in most traditional on-premises environments, operations management is typically handled by an IT operations team in charge of infrastructure provisioning, capacity management, cost control, performance, and security for all of the organization's assets. If you've ever worked in traditional IT roles or you've worked as a developer alongside IT ops team members, you know how difficult it can be to partner with another team to manage an application's operations. IT ops usually doesn't have full context of the applications they support since they are traditionally focused solely on ops and not development. Typically, the way they'd understand the relative importance and value of an application is by how it's classified in the asset database. Typically, there are availability requirements for each application service tier, and IT ops folks do their best to ensure that they meet those service level objectives (SLOs).

When it comes to issues, it's a total blame game, with teams deflecting responsibility as much as possible. The development team opens a ticket, IT ops investigates and blames it on a bug, and development blames it on IT ops; as a result, the infrastructure is not equipped to provide full visibility of an issue to arrive at a quick solution, and work is often very reactionary in nature and not proactive. Siloed teams often cause rifts in the organization. It's similar to what occurred at the beginning of the COVID-19 outbreak in 2020, as we watched state and federal governments bicker back and forth about who was to blame for the lack of masks, ventilators, and other medical equipment, all while tens of thousands of people were dying. That may be a brutal analogy, but bickering about responsibility is a distinct possibility in the tech space as well and as you can imagine, this may affect your service level metrics. CYA (cover your "gluteus maximus") is alive and well in many IT organizations. In fact, some organizations have turned office politics into an art form.

Hopefully, your applications, or lack thereof, are designed to avoid causing any deaths if outages occur. For some software teams, however, their applications are literally keeping people alive. Imagine, for example, that your software is designed for a real-time blood glucose monitoring device. What happens if you have a major outage and you are not equipped to resolve reliability issues quickly? What happens to all the millions of users who depend on your device for understanding and responding to their blood sugar levels? Reliability is important, and it may actually mean life or death for some software teams and their users.

 TIP Word of wisdom for everyone—creating an inclusive environment is your job, no matter where you work. Working in silos only elevates a team's feeling of self worth, as team members start to believe that they "do everything" themselves; in reality, of course, this is not the case. So when you're engaging with people who need your help, or when you need help from other people, think about how you can create bridges between your teams and not elevate yourself or your team as a KIA (know-it-all). Build bridges, and don't blow them up!

DevOps and SRE exist to avoid silos. DevOps is the bridge that brings together everyone across the development life cycle by sharing a set of principles, including development, testing, and operations roles. SRE is a dedicated engineering role that is often viewed as an implementation of DevOps with some idiosyncratic extensions. SRE focuses on the "what" and "how" of improving reliability. Site reliability engineers spend half of their time doing operations-related work, working on issues, on-call situations, and manual investigations. The other half of a site reliability engineer's role is dedicated to developing new features, scaling, or automation that will improve availability and performance requirements for an application's architecture. DevOps-oriented software teams typically are expected to be highly automatic and able to self-heal, and this includes the partnership between the developers, testers, and operations folks. This enables site reliability engineers to perform day-to-day activities and innovate to improve performance and reliability.

A fundamental tenet of SRE is the concept of *error budgets*. Unlike traditional operation models, where the objective is to keep failures as close to zero as possible, a site reliability engineer actually has a error budget. Basically, if your objective is to provide 99.9 percent uptime, then technically you have 0.1 percent budget to deal with risks. If you are actually running at 100 percent uptime, this tells senior management that you are not taking enough risks to improve IT velocity. That error budget is meant to be spent! So when your development teams complain about having to deploy all these releases and your error budget is not spent, then you, as a good site reliability engineer, encourage and help developers to push the releases through into production. If these changes cause problems and consume your error budget, you can put the breaks on further changes so that as a team, you stay within your SLOs within the timeframe in question. If everyone in the organization is aligned to meeting these common objectives, then everyone will look for ways to stay within the allocated error budget while trying to rapidly innovate new business value from their applications.

NOTE Benjamin Treynor Sloss, the senior VP overseeing technical operations at Google, came up with Site Reliability Engineering. Check out his book to read up about SRE best practices at https://sre.google/sre-book/part-I-introduction/ if you're interested in diving into this world. Only the most advanced organizations are thinking about this ever-growing function, and eventually it will become a standard for all enterprise organizations.

Now how does the cloud fit into this discussion? The cloud enables teams to bring visibility into their work by building bridges between their roles to integrate while still being decoupled, to automate where they could not automate before, and to innovate in ways that could never have happened on-premises. For all that to be measurable and actionable, you need to have telemetry data that you can leverage to improve your key performance indicators and overall application reliability. This is commonly referred to as *instrumentation*.

In this chapter, we discuss Google's *Cloud Operations Suite*, a platform that enables organizations to log, monitor, troubleshoot, and improve their application performance in GCP. We'll talk about how to set up your logging architecture; some of the key types of logs in GCP; and how to monitor your applications' health, build metrics, and create alerts.

EXAM TIP Cloud Operations was formerly known as the Stackdriver suite. When you take the exam, it's possible that the product name may appear as Stackdriver instead of Cloud Operations Suite. For example, you may see references to Stackdriver Logging, Stackdriver Monitoring, Stackdriver Trace, and so on.

Cloud Logging

The first element of the Cloud Operations stack is Cloud Logging, a real-time log management and analysis tool that enables you to store, search, analyze, monitor, and alert on log data and events. It allows for ingestion of any custom log data from any source and is a fully managed service. Cloud Logging also natively integrates into Cloud Monitoring (discussed in the next section), so that you can define alerts based on certain metrics you select. Cloud Logging also natively integrates with Amazon Web Services (AWS) and supports a logging agent that is based on the Fluentd data collector and that can run on your virtual machine (VM) instances.

NOTE The Cloud Logging agent, based on the Fluentd log data collector, collects logs from user applications and sends them to the Cloud Logging API using Fluentd configuration files. There are many preconfigured Linux and Windows logs, and you can customize your own. Cloud Logging supports many common third-party solutions such as Apache, Chef, Jenkins, Mongodb, Cassandra, MySQL, and more.

In Cloud Logging, you typically store your logs in a user interface known as the Logs Viewer, and you use an API to manage your logs programmatically. You can read and write log entries, query your logs, control how your logs are routed, and create exporting sinks and log-based metrics. *Log entries* are recorded events that are captured from products, services, third-party applications, or even your own applications. The messages that your log entries carry is known as a payload, and the collection of your log entries makes up a log; without log entries, there is no log. The *Logs Viewer* is a user interface that enables you to view and analyze your log data. In the Logs Viewer, you can build queries by using the GUI or by using its query builder language, and it saves your queries so that you can refer to them in the future.

EXAM TIP You don't have to know everything about the Logs Viewer for the exam, but it's a good idea to have a very high-level understanding of using it. Log into the Cloud Console and take a look at some sample logs through the Logs Viewer. Get familiar with some very basic navigation and syntax. Where would you search for network logs? For network interface configuration changes to your GCE instances?

In Cloud Logging, your logs are stored in a logging project by default and can have a 400-day or 30-day retention period based on the log type. Some logs are customizable up to a 3650-day retention period within a logging project. Most organizations, however, use logs in Cloud Storage for long-term retention and use BigQuery for analysis. You can also route your logs to a Cloud Pub/Sub topic, where they can be ingested by any third-party application. A typical use case for Pub/Sub forwarding is integration with a third-party security information and event management (SIEM) platform such as Splunk. Many DevOps teams like to use their own set of tools to analyze and monitor their logs; others use the native Cloud Operations tools. Either way, you must set up your log architecture accordingly.

If your logs are routed to any other log storage, whether GCS, BigQuery, or Pub/Sub, the logs are automatically passed through the Cloud Logging API, where they pass through the Logs Router. The *Logs Router* then looks at each log entry and the rules you've set to determine which logs to ingest, which logs to export, and which log entries to discard to save money and ensure efficiency. You can configure your logs to be exported into an appropriate *log sink* storage destination. For every project, a default log sink routes all your logs into a default log bucket. You can leverage exclusions to create filters and exclude certain types of logs from being stored in Cloud Logging by default to reduce costs and minimize the number of logs you're storing. Aggregated sinks can be set up at the organization, folder, or project level.

Figure 10-1 shows an illustration of the Cloud Logging architecture.

The Cloud Logging API also enables ingestion of any custom log data from any data source. Being a fully managed service, it performs at scale and can support massive environments at a phenomenal price-to-performance ratio. All this while still being able to analyze your logs in real time! You can also export data with one click to BigQuery for advanced analytics, and SQL-like querying is incredibly powerful, enabling organizations to run massive queries in little time.

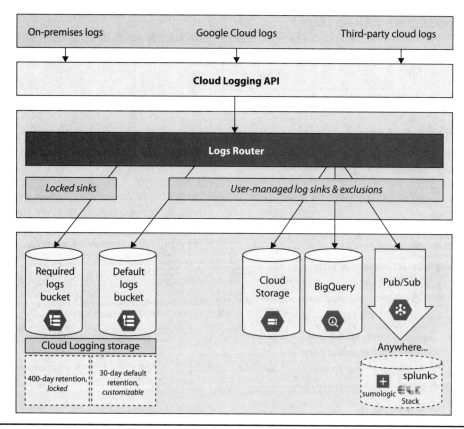

Figure 10-1 Cloud Logging architecture

 TIP Many compliance frameworks, such as the Health Insurance Portability and Accountability Act (HIPAA) and the Payment Card Industry (PCI) Data Security Standard, require long-term archival requirements for your logs. If these logs don't need to be analyzed, think about how you can leverage various storage classes in GCS to store your logs and save money.

Log Types

Many categories of logs are available in Cloud Logging, which receives, indexes, and stores log entries from services, instances running the Cloud Logging agent, other cloud providers, and custom log sources. Logs can be captured at every layer of the resource hierarchy, whether that's at the organization level, folder level, or project level. Although there are many logging sources, there are a few key ones you should know about at a high level.

Admin Activity Audit Logs

Admin activity audit logs come from Cloud Identity, which operates from admin.google .com rather than from the GCP. These contain administrative activity and user activity in the Cloud Identity platform and include things like account creation, deletion, authentication, configuration modifications to your identity provider (IdP), password changes, and so on.

Cloud Audit Logs

Cloud audit logs consist of administrative activity audit logs, data access audit logs, and system event audit logs.

- **Administrative activity audit logs** These logs contain log entries for API calls or any other user administrative modifications to configurations or resource metadata. For example, these logs may record when an administrator makes modifications to roles and permissions inside of GCP or spins up a VM.
- **Data access audit logs** These logs contain log entries for API calls that read resource configurations, metadata, or read/write user-based API calls. These logs are disabled by default, and they do not log publicly shared resources. Log entries could include reading data within a service or writing data to a service.
- **System event audit logs** These logs contain log entries for administrative activity that modifies resource configurations based on activity generated by Google systems and not user-based activity. For example, log entries could indicate that a transparent maintenance event occurred.

Network Logs

Network logs consist of Virtual Private Cloud (VPC) flow logs, Domain Name System (DNS) logs, Cloud network address translation (NAT) logs, and firewall logs.

- **VPC flow logs** These logs provide visibility into VPC traffic and capture TCP and UDP traffic to and from internal traffic, network attachments, servers to Internet endpoints, and servers to Google APIs.
- **DNS logs** These logs record every DNS query received from VM instances and inbound forwarding flows within your networks.
- **Cloud NAT logs** These logs provide context into NAT connections and errors.
- **Firewall logs** These logs provide connection records for TCP and UDP traffic only. These records contain things like source and destination IPs, protocols, ports, times, and so on.

Access Transparency Logs

These logs provide insight behind the scenes when a Google Cloud Support engineer had accessed parts of your infrastructure and for what purpose. Access Transparency is actually a critical feature in the modern day, increasing trust in Google Cloud by giving organizations the ability to know what exactly is going on behind the scenes of their Cloud Platform and having an audit trail to do so. Google Cloud has consistently held the position that no customer data is ever accessed for any reason aside from fulfilling contractual obligations. With this level of transparency, Google Cloud can provide customers the evidence behind that commitment.

 EXAM TIP Don't worry about memorizing the details of every single log type. Just know that they exist. If you see a question about troubleshooting a DNS issue, your answer probably won't be to review the admin audit logs.

Create Your Own Logs

You can also create your own logs using supported client libraries. To create your own logs, you just need to write the log entries. There is no separate Create operation in Cloud Logging. However, don't mix this up with identifying Create syntax in your actual logs. These could be referring to the point at which a certain resource was created. For instance, if you provision a network attachment to your GCE instance, you can look through the network logs to find the origin of this activity via a Create or Insert log entry.

Cloud Trace, Cloud Profiler, and Cloud Debugger

The application performance management tools included in Cloud Operations combine the capabilities of Cloud Logging and Cloud Monitoring, along with Cloud Trace, Cloud Debugger, and Cloud Profiler to help you reduce latency and cost and run more efficient applications.

Cloud Trace is a distributed tracing service that you can use to collect latency from your applications and track how requests propagate through your applications. It can provide in-depth latency reports to surface performance issues and works across VMs, containers, or App Engine projects. *Tracing* refers to latency analysis between your applications or on incoming requests. In App Engine, traces are automatically submitted to Cloud Trace. For other applications, you can leverage the Cloud Trace SDK or API to send latency data for analysis. Think about scenarios where you deploy a new release and you're getting feedback from your users about longer load times. You can use Cloud Trace to trace exactly where your request latency is higher than normal.

Cloud Profiler is a continuous CPU and heap profiling tool that is used to analyze the performance of CPU or memory-intensive functions you run across an application. While Cloud Trace is focused on latency analysis, Cloud Profiler is able to determine which aspect of your code is causing higher CPU and memory consumption.

Cloud Debugger is a real-time application debugging tool you can use to inspect your running applications and identify the behavior of your code, continuously searching for bugs in a live environment without incurring any performance impacts to your users. It integrates into your existing developer workflows, enabling developers to take snapshots directly from any area of your application and even add new logging statements on demand when you're doing deep bug identification work.

Cloud Monitoring

Cloud Monitoring is a full-stack, fully managed monitoring solution that gives you visibility into the performance, uptime, and overall health of your applications. You can define and gather metrics, events, and metadata from your GCP environment and non-GCP environments through agents, APIs, and partnerships with other third parties. Cloud Monitoring provides rich visualizations and customizable dashboards that help you analyze your data. Because it's a managed service, you don't have to worry about managing any infrastructure for the service. You can leverage a plethora of monitoring tools to do a variety of tasks such as gathering metrics, dashboarding, uptime monitoring, and building alerts, but Cloud Monitoring provides all of this functionality with a strong integration into many third-party products, making it a strong contender in the operational monitoring space.

Cloud Monitoring offers both white-box and black-box monitoring techniques. *Black-box monitoring* enables you to monitor your application as if you were an end user, without having any underlying knowledge of the internal configuration of the service. It provides this via uptime checks. *White-box monitoring* enables you to monitor all aspects of your service with full underlying knowledge of the internal infrastructure. You can build custom metrics based on certain indicators by using the API or using an open source library like OpenCensus. You can also build log-based metrics from the logs you collect in your Cloud Logging architecture.

When it comes to monitoring your application and environment in the cloud, some of your key goals may be to understand your application health, the load on your application, uptime, and performance of your applications. This requires collecting metrics from various sources, making them easy to view and digest, and generating alerts when metrics don't meet your desired criteria.

Workspaces

Workspaces are created to organize and manage key monitoring data across projects. Workspaces can manage the monitoring data for one or many projects, but a project cannot be assigned to multiple workspaces. The workspace is created for a host project, which is used as the basis for the workspace that stores all of the configuration items for dashboards, alerting policies, uptime checks, notification channels, and more. If you delete the host project, you delete the workspace along with it.

 NOTE You can monitor up to 100 projects inside a workspace. Workspaces are not a great solution if you need to build a centralized, organization-wide monitoring and alerting system. The main team that will typically need an organization-wide monitoring solution with centralized metrics will be your security operations teams. That is where a SIEM third-party solution comes into play.

Cloud Monitoring is designed for software teams, not security teams, and is similar to New Relic, Datadog, and Splunk. When you create a workspace, you should think about how you can group together applications that share similar metrics and even organize them within teams.

Monitoring Agent

The *Cloud Monitoring agent* is a collectd-based daemon that gathers system and application metrics from your VMs. The Monitoring agent collects disk, CPU, network, and process metrics by default. You can also configure it to monitor third-party applications. The agent is optional, but it's recommended that you install it on your instances, because the insights you can gain from having it on your VM instances will enable you to gather a much richer source of data than what's provided by VMs by default. Also, having the ability to monitor third-party applications eliminates the need to install other third-party tools that do the same thing, making your deployments and configuration management quite a bit simpler.

Uptime Checks

Uptime checks are pings that are sent to a resource to see if they respond. You'd want to leverage uptime checks to monitor the availability of VM instances, App Engine services, public websites, and even AWS load balancers. Similar to a load balancer health check, an uptime check is simply a request that says, "Hey service. Are you alive?" A response may be business as usual, but the event generated when there is a lack of a response can be leveraged to kick off an incident analysis workflow. You might set an alerting policy to trigger an alert if there are three consecutive failures on the uptime check, for example. That may trigger a slew of events, including paging your on-call, automatically generating a ticket with prefilled diagnostic details, failing over to another server or environment, and more.

 TIP   Configuring uptime checks is pretty simple, but it's common to forget to open your firewall rules when doing so. You need to ensure that your firewalls are set up to permit incoming traffic from the uptime-check servers to avoid issues.

Metrics and Alerts

Metrics are a collection of measurements that help you understand how your application and services are performing. More than 1500 types of metrics are available by default in Cloud Monitoring, including metrics for Google Cloud, AWS, and third-party software. Metrics could include things like latency of requests to a service, amount of disk space on a machine, and number of tables in your SQL database. Metric metadata will typically contain details about the source of the measurement, timestamps, and details about the exact values of the measurement.

This is a pretty simple concept, so we don't need to spend too much time on it, but the "TLDR" (too long, didn't read) is that you have many predefined metrics and the ability to generate your own custom metrics at the platform, application, and service levels. You use these metrics to gather key performance indicators for things you're looking to measure. Think about availability requirements for your application, performance requirements, using metrics to track bottlenecks in your application and optimize the performance of code, and so on. When you're trying to figure out how to break these down into actionable metrics, start with defining your SLOs and what your requirements are. If your SLA has an availability SLO of 99.95 percent, what metrics will help you understand your system's availability? What are the service level indicators (SLIs) telling you? Is your system is at risk? In summary, the key here is to capture a number of SMART (Specific, Measurable, Attainable, Relevant, Timed) metrics that map to service indicators that demonstrate operational success or failure. These indicators then validate that you are meeting the business objectives of your organization.

 TIP   Don't forget about SLOs, SLIs, and SLA. You measure your SLOs, service level objectives, with your SLIs, service level indicators. Your SLA, service level agreement, is the performance level you've contractually guaranteed to provide to your customers. A breach of these agreements could cost you!

The SLIs that are clear indicators of system degradation (failures) should be used to create an alerting policy. *Alerting policies* define the conditions in which one or multiple resources are in a state that requires you to take action and what actions to take upon meeting those conditions. Alerting policies consist of conditions, the indicators based on the breach of a metric threshold; notifications; and documentation that can be provided to help your support team resolve the issue. When an alert policy triggers, Cloud Monitoring will show an incident notification in the console, and it will also kick off any notifications to people or services that you've defined in the policy.

Dashboards

One of the other powerful abilities that Cloud Monitoring is equipped to handle natively is the ability to provide predefined and custom dashboards to view and analyze your most important metric data. The predefined dashboards don't require any effort to set up or configure. Custom dashboards can be configured using the Cloud Monitoring API. There is a lot of flexibility here on what you can do, from building custom charts and visualizations, to exporting that data, to sharing data with Grafana.

The Importance of Resilience

Paul Revere was a famous American patriot during the American Revolution, known for his famous midnight ride, when he rode his horse through the night to warn the colonial militia that the British forces were arriving for battle. Thanks to Revere and his early warning, the colonial militia was able to prepare for the impending battle. Actually, scratch that. In history, we think of Paul Revere's acts as heroic. In modern day, in many organizations, we're more than likely to ignore Revere and his warning because of timelines, budgets, and other political issues within an organization. Then we deal with the battle and are demolished as a consequence. Then we fire Revere for warning us. Go home, Paul Revere!

The moral of the story is that I'm sure many of you can relate to this situation in the modern day: You noticed a big flaw in a system design. You stepped up and analyzed the flaw. A peer reviewed it with a colleague. You finally mustered up the courage to raise the alarm with leadership, expecting them to take a strong decisive action toward remediating the vulnerability. Next thing you know, you get shot down. Budget issues, people issues, and "This is a significant risk but we have deadlines to meet in this quarter. We can visit this in a few sprint cycles." Maybe you could've done a better job assessing and presenting the risk to your leadership team. But more often than not, poor leadership allows these incidents to occur in the first place. Most incidents occur because of pre-existing conditions of an architecture that are already known to the hands-on technical teams working in the environment. Poor leadership is rampant in the world.

NOTE   PSA to all current and future technology leaders: It costs significantly less to design your system to be resilient both from operational and security concerns today than it does to pay huge sums of money and time to recover, while demolishing your team's morale throughout the process. *Technical debt* is a term cloud architects need to wrap their minds around. There is no free lunch. The act of cutting corners here or there, choosing less optimal solutions, reinventing your own wheel, just because you can, all have long-term consequences.

Business continuity. Disaster recovery. Resilience. What do all these things mean? They all sound so similar, yet they're all focused on different scenarios. The end result of these is the same: to get your business back to baseline, and, for the most part, in the cloud, the technical solutions you implement are going to be similar.

- **Business continuity planning (BCP)**   A plan of action for getting the business back to full functionality after a crisis
- **Disaster recovery planning (DRP)**   A plan for getting the technology infrastructure and operations back in order after an outage
- **Resilience**   Your infrastructure's ability to withstand faults and failures and continue running with little to no downtime

In short, these three planning efforts are intended to answer these questions: How do you restore your technical infrastructure back to full baseline after an outage? How can you still serve your customers during an outage? How can you design your infrastructure to absorb failures and still operate without having an outage?

Let's forget about BCP and DRP for a minute. We know that failure will happen and it is accepted as part of the principles of DevOps. But this is where SRE comes into play. The sole purpose of SRE is to help find opportunities to improve your infrastructure's ability to handle fault and failure while continuing to serve your customers, and to do this, ideally, in a way that doesn't require you to trigger your disaster recovery plan or your business continuity plan. Resilience is the Number 1 goal. But it is imperative you have plans B and C in place to kick off BCP and DRP if a full outage were to occur (which is more common than not).

How do you know that your system is resilient? You can do all the testing in the world when it comes to your applications and your environments, but you never know how an application will handle real live data and real live users in production without experimenting with your application in production!

Chaos Engineering is an SRE discipline focused on experimenting with your systems in production by injecting real faults, ranging from small experiments to massive experiments, to see how your application can truly handle them. The goal is to validate your hypotheses of how your system will perform based on the design iterations you implement to improve resilience. Let's say, for example, that your application was hosted in a US-east region, and if that US-east region goes down, your application goes down. You decide to replicate your application and run multiregional resiliency. In design, your team did a great job of replicating your application stack and planning all of their dependencies to be redundant across the regions. But, in reality, you still have no idea how this will work when you have 50 million daily active users and an entire region goes down. You still need to provide service to all those users. You won't know the answer unless you actually test and validate your architecture.

 NOTE Netflix is behind the Chaos Engineering discipline. It started with a 2011 tool built to test resilience, called Chaos Monkey. Chaos Monkey intentionally disabled computers inside the Netflix production network, and then engineers assessed how many systems would respond to this type of outage. The name explains itself. Just imagine a bunch of monkeys, *Planet of the Apes* style, rolling into your data center and "going ham." Racks flying everywhere, NICs ripped out, cables flung around, monkeying around. That's a Chaos Monkey. It's one thing to test such resiliency in testing environments. It's another thing to do this in your production environment when it is providing services to paying customers.

Chapter Review

In this chapter, we started out discussing some of the changes in how traditional IT operations and software teams used to work together and how the DevOps philosophy was the best thing to happen to software development and infrastructure operations. Although this philosophy significantly improved the ability of operations teams to deploy and operate code and improve availability, a new discipline has spun out to provide a force multiplier to reliability objectives—Site Reliability Engineering. SREs are strictly focused on improving reliability by innovating, tackling key architectural design constraints, and running the day-to-day operations as part of their job.

We then dove into the logging architecture in Google Cloud. Cloud Logging is a real-time log management and analysis tool that lets you store, search, analyze, monitor, and alert on log data through its tight integrations with Cloud Monitoring. Your logs are stored in a log storage, typically a GCS bucket, BigQuery environment, or Pub/Sub topic, where they can be ingested by third-party tools. The Logs Viewer is a user interface to view and analyze your logs directly from the console. You can build queries in the console as well. There are a variety of logs, but some of the key logs include admin audit logs from Cloud Identity, cloud audit logs, logs derived from the Cloud Logging agent, network logs, and access transparency logs.

Cloud Trace is a distributed tracing service you can leverage to collect latency from your application based on how requests propagate. Cloud Profiler is a continuous CPU and heap profiling tool that is used to analyze the performance of CPU or memory-intensive functions across an application. Cloud Debugger is a real-time application debugging tool used to inspect your applications in runtime and in a live environment.

Cloud Monitoring enables you to monitor and alert on metrics derived from various layers of your stack in GCP. These metrics can be derived directly from logs, they can be default metrics provided by all of your applications and services, or they can be custom metrics that you build based on indicators using the API or an open source library like OpenCensus. Workspaces enable you to organize and manage key monitoring data across projects, where you can monitor multiple projects on one workspace but not one project on multiple workspaces. The monitoring agent is a collectd-based daemon that gathers deeper system and application metrics from your VMs. Uptime checks are leveraged to ping your resources to determine if they're available or not, similar to load balancer health checks. Don't forget to ensure that your firewall is set up to enable the uptime check service.

Metrics are measurements that help you understand how your application and services are performing; there are more than 1500 types of metrics available in GCP by default, as well as the ability to build custom metrics. Alerting policies are a set of conditions that are required to be met before a notification is triggered across your notification channels requiring you to take action. An alert will show up as an incident in the console. Dashboards enable you to do strong, custom visualizations and dashboards to monitor the most important data points to your team.

Business continuity planning is a set of plans created to get your business operations back in full functionality to serve your customers after a crisis. Disaster recovery planning is a set of plans created to get your technology infrastructure and operations back in full order after an outage. Resilience means designing your infrastructure so that it can withstand faults and failures and continue running with little to no downtime. Resilience is king.

Through Chaos Engineering, you can inject faults and flaws into your system to determine how it will perform. The goal is to test your hypotheses of how your system will perform in the event of a fault or failure and to determine how it will perform in real time with all the real dependencies an application has in production. Site Reliability Engineering is a discipline focused on resilience. Think SRE, and hire SRE!

We're almost there! If you've made it this far, I applaud your perseverance. Reading technical books is probably not what I would want to be doing on my time off. I'm more of a gamer—I'd much rather be playing *Call of Duty*. But that's alright.

The next chapter on security is going to be a big one, and although it won't be a huge aspect of the exam, it's one area that needs to be embedded into every single focus area of a cloud technologist. Take a break, get some rest, and come back to the next chapter when you're ready to absorb!

Additional References

If you'd like more information about the topics discussed in this chapter, check out these sources:

- **Principles of Chaos Engineering**   https://principlesofchaos.org/
- **Site Reliability Engineering**   https://landing.google.com/sre/
- **Patterns for Scalable and Resilient Apps**   https://cloud.google.com/solutions/scalable-and-resilient-apps

Questions

1. When it comes to designing resilience in your architecture, which of the statements is true?

   A. Business continuity planning, disaster recovery planning, and resilience are all the same in the cloud.

   B. Chaos Engineering is a form of testing the resilience of your systems.

   C. The goal of resilient architectures is to recover from a major outage.

   D. Resilience is the idea of continuing your business operations when there is an outage.

2. You're the architect for AntiSocialGram, a social media application in which users are incentivized to share only the negative aspects of their lives, rather than the positive, in hopes of building strong community-based support networks. The application runs out of a regional managed instance group and has a backend Cloud Spanner database that stores petabytes of user data. You'd like to do some resilience testing on your application stack to see how your application behaves. What should you do?

   A. Deploy an IaC template that terminates your Cloud Spanner service and analyze your system afterward.

   B. Contact Google Cloud Support and schedule a support-driven termination procedure, where you have Support shut down aspects of your application.

   C. Increase the load on your production environment.

   D. Turn off all your GCE instances in one of your zones and analyze your system afterward.

3. Security mandates that your data access logs must be tamper-resistant and tamper-evident. What should you do to protect these logs?

   A. Store your logs in an archival GCS bucket where they're not supposed to be accessed more than once a year to ensure that your logs are both protected and tamper-evident.

   B. Store your logs in GCS, enable object versioning, restrict IAM access only to authorized individuals, and leverage digital signatures to ensure that your logs are both protected and tamper-evident.

C. Take a hash of your logs upon posting them to GCS and provide that hash to your security team to validate it every time they access a log.

D. Upload your logs to BigQuery and protect them using authorized views.

4. Your DevOps team has been leveraging the default metrics from your GCE environment to do their operations work. They're at a point where the data provided from the VMs is not rich enough. What would be a logical step to assess?

A. Install the Cloud Logging agent on their VMs and assess the new data that is derived from that agent.

B. Install the Cloud Monitoring agent on their VMs and assess the new monitoring capabilities from that agent.

C. Build custom metrics based on key indicators that they need to assess.

D. Use as many of the 1500 predefined metrics as you can to build a better story around the operational needs of your business.

5. Your software team for Blinding, an internal community designed for tech individuals to communicate anonymously, deployed a new release. Your users are complaining that they can't stand how long it takes to post updates and vent their frustrations about their employers. What should you do to diagnose where your application is getting held up?

A. Leverage Cloud Profiler to assess the CPU and memory performance of the functions of your application.

B. Leverage Cloud Trace to track how user requests propagate through your application to determine where the latency may be the highest.

C. Leverage Cloud Debugger to do real-time application debugging in the live environment.

D. Create a clone of the VM and migrate user traffic onto the new VM, and then use your old VM to do a rollback.

6. You work for a healthcare company that falls under the purview of the HIPAA compliance regulations. They've mandated that all logs need to be retained for six years. Your organization has required that these logs should be stored in the most cost-effective manner. What should you do?

A. Store these logs in BigQuery so that they can be readily available if a compliance auditor needs to analyze the logs.

B. Store these logs in Cloud Storage in a coldline storage class bucket.

C. Store these logs in Cloud Storage in a nearline storage class bucket.

D. Store these logs in Cloud Storage in an archival storage class bucket.

7. All of the following are metrics except which one?

   A. Average CPU utilization

   B. Average memory utilization

   C. HTTP load balancer requests per second

   D. Average time to rehydrate AMIs

8. Google Cloud Operations was formerly known as what?

   A. Piledriver

   B. Cloud Piledriver

   C. Cloud IT Operations suite

   D. Stackdriver

9. What is Stackdriver Profiler?

   A. A continuous CPU and heap profiling tool used to analyze the performance of CPU or memory-intensive functions you run across an application

   B. A distributed tracing service that you can use to collect latency from your applications

   C. A real-time application debugging tool used to inspect and identify the behavior of your code

   D. A full-stack, fully managed monitoring solution that gives you visibility into performance, uptime, and overall health of your applications

10. What is Stackdriver Debugger?

    A. A continuous CPU and heap profiling tool used to analyze the performance of CPU or memory-intensive functions you run across an application

    B. A distributed tracing service that you can use to collect latency from your applications

    C. A real-time application debugging tool used to inspect and identify the behavior of your code

    D. A full-stack, fully managed monitoring solution that gives you visibility into performance, uptime, and overall health of your applications

Answers

1. **B.** Chaos Engineering is the discipline within SRE of hypothesizing how your system will react to faults and then testing your hypothesis by inducing faults in your system in production and seeing how it reacts.

2. **D.** Because you're running regionally managed instance groups, your application should be balanced across multiple zones. If you shut down an entire zone's VMs, you can see how this architecture would react with your traffic. Shutting down your Cloud Spanner service will do you no good in testing your system resilience.

Google Cloud Support does not have a process to terminate your environment on demand. Increasing the load on your production environment sounds okay to see how scalable your architecture is, but not for testing its resiliency.

3. **B.** Storing your logs in GCS and restricting IAM access only to authorized individuals can ensure that your logs are being protected and to minimize the risk of tampering. Enabling object versioning ensures that your objects don't get deleted or overwritten. To show that logs have been tampered with, digitally sign your log entries.

4. **A.** The Cloud Logging agent will provide deeper and more granular logging information around the VM environment and should be the next step to assess whether it provides the most sufficient information for the team.

5. **B.** Cloud Trace can be leveraged to track how a user request propagates through your application. Using this tool, you can determine which aspect of your application has higher-than-usual latency.

6. **D.** The requirement does not ask for the logs to be analyzed or monitored. The most cost-effective way to store the logs in case they need to be accessed is by storing them in GCS in an Archival storage class.

7. **D.** AMI rehydration is not a metric, and AMIs do not exist in Google Cloud Platform—AMIs are from AWS!

8. **D.** Google Cloud Operations used to be called Stackdriver. If you see a question that mentions Stackdriver on the exam, just remember that it's referring to the Cloud Operations suite of tools. The Piledriver is a famous wrestling move, and dangerous one, that was notably performed by a wrestler known as The Undertaker.

9. **A.** Stackdriver Profiler, now known as Cloud Profiler, is leveraged for analyzing the performance of CPU or memory-intensive functions in your application.

10. **C.** Stackdriver Debugger, now known as Cloud Debugger, is a real-time application debugging tool that you can use to gather more information about how your code is performing in live environments.

CHAPTER 11

Security

In this chapter, we'll cover

- The fundamental security knowledge that every cloud architect should possess
- A recap of all of the infrastructure security best practices discussed so far
- Detection and response activities in the cloud

In earlier chapters, you read about some fundamental technology concepts and how you can relate these digital concepts to biological commonalities that have existed since the beginning of human evolution. Networking enabled humans to use one another's resources to innovate and drive society toward today's advanced state. These resources form a force multiplier and are similar to computing power, because when they are combined, they can perform calculations at scale to solve complex problems. After all, two brains are better than one. And a million brains? *Planet of the Apes* wasn't based on the wits of one monkey! The actual insights that humans have captured, stored, and analyzed, along with the resources within their networks, have provided what we need to innovate and solve problems.

The one thing we haven't mentioned yet is human opportunism. Opportunism is often seen as a paradigm of natural selection, or survival of the fittest, as a biological mechanism to facilitate evolutionary development in the animal kingdom. The idea is that our evolutionary state requires us to find opportunities to survive without thinking of the consequences, even if our actions are selfish in nature and at the expense of others. This form of survival is not responsible for the most revolutionary developments in human biology but is more of a reflexive mechanism to improve survival. As the human mind evolved through the years, our opportunism took natural selection beyond biological survival, pairing it with our intellect to find more clever and innovative ways to gain advantages over other humans or the environment around us. Humans use opportunism to gain advantage over others—in business, finance, sports, relationships, and beyond.

Inherent within opportunity is the concept of risk. Your intention is to achieve a reward, but if you haven't fully thought through the consequences, you don't understand the consequences, or you've accepted the consequences, you face more risk. If you take no risks, you'll never win, and if you take too much risk, you'll lose.

A core focus of security is to manage the risk you face when you take advantage of new opportunities. How can you minimize your risk while maximizing your reward? In cloud architecture, when you're designing a system, your reward is not the security of your system. Instead, your reward is the success of the business outcome you're trying to achieve. Take a look at your threat landscape. How can you maximize the reward while protecting your assets to prevent loss?

It would be great for productivity if your employees could access your network environment any time, anywhere, and from any machine—but when you factor in the likelihood of IP theft and other malicious activity, you realize that you have to sacrifice some of your employee productivity for a more secure system. Unfortunately, companies are oftentimes reluctant to invest in security solutions until they face a breach and make the front page of the *Wall Street Journal*, which results in a few key executives being fired. Then, suddenly, security budgets miraculously become available. As with any investment, however, it is often less costly to reduce your risks early on than to try to retrofit and patch up security following a breach.

Let's discuss the risks in the cloud. As you and/or your enterprise move toward building innovative and morally positive solutions that will hopefully drive opportunism, you need to realize that others will see your investment as an opportunity for their own benefit. You competitors may want to steal your ideas to remove any "first mover advantage" you may have. Your employees may see an opportunity to make money by stealing your data or your customer's data and selling it to your competition. Others may just want to steal your data for bragging rights! The point is that every time you make an investment, there are people out there who will try to abuse the opportunity to take advantage of you. So what do you do when the world around you is so dangerous? Well, you look to reduce the risks in your environment. I mean, if you went skydiving, would you carry one parachute or two? Best practice is to have a backup parachute because of the obvious consequence of the first parachute failing. A similar thing happens within cloud architectures: things will fail; it's just a matter of when, not if.

If you think about it, our minds are wired to think about security every minute of the day. You are threat modeling, whether you know it or not, everywhere you go. As you walk out of your house, you lock the door behind you; you get in the car and buckle your seatbelt; and as you drive, you constantly scan the road for dangerous activities, even the most miniscule hazardous lane change. You eat healthy and exercise to prevent disease. You communicate clearly to protect your wants and needs but not share your secrets. You call your significant other frequently to ensure that they're safe. Our minds are literally threat modeling and running countless scenarios every second in the background, unbeknownst to our prefrontal cortex. The same approach has to be taken when we talk about the cloud. For many of us, the landscape is both foreign and evolving, which introduces new risks. Solutions that used to keep us safe stop being effective as new threats and vulnerabilities present themselves. The role of a cloud architect is to be well versed in the threats involved in our designs and to work hard at protecting and securing our assets against those threats.

The most advanced and morally positive human beings have applied risk management by using their knowledge, rationality, and logic to enable opportunism while minimizing the risks and the consequences of their outcomes. Focusing on being morally positive is important, because even in the most developed countries, where we are equipped to understand the consequences of opportunities, people will prey on others for their own benefit. So how do we create a future that is inherently more secure and susceptible to less risk?

What we really need is a world more like the one in *Star Trek*, where civilization is united. On the *Starship Enterprise*, genders, ethnicities, races, species, and sexual orientations are no longer concerns, because all of these sentient creatures have come together to solve intergalactic problems. As we deal with the turmoil in the world today, we may doubt the possibility of such a utopian future. Creating a safe and secure future for our children includes managing our human and environmental risks and building solutions that are morally positive, inclusive, and equitable to everyone. This is critical; unfortunately, as technologists, we've blindly built systems without any historical data since the rise of the Internet, and we've suffered in various ways from the consequences of risks we took knowingly or unknowingly. As a cloud architect, you should never discount the power you hold for shaping the future of our world.

NOTE *The Social Dilemma* is a phenomenal documentary that outlines some of the unintended consequences of opportunism in the tech industry. Although this documentary focuses on tech companies, the same theme applies to every single industry. Understanding the intended and unintended impacts of your work is your moral responsibility. I recommend giving this documentary a watch.

In this chapter, we're going to build upon the security elements discussed in previous chapters, spend some time talking about more generalized security concepts, and dive into the ways we build in detection and response on Google Cloud—and what that even means. You won't see much of this content on the Professional Cloud Architect exam, but in the real world, you are absolutely required to possess this knowledge to protect our ever-growing digital society.

Security Fundamentals

I often hear the term "security" thrown around like it's a simple solution for anything. "Let's just add some security to it." "Sprinkle in some security." "We need to talk to Security." What most people don't know is that security has traditionally been a massive practice that consists of multiple domains, where each domain depends on very different people with very different objectives. Governance and risk management, compliance, architecture, engineering, policy, operations, disaster recovery, legal, marketing—in all of these domains, security is not merely a technical aspect; in fact, security involves many roles and responsibilities.

NOTE Security as a philosophy still hasn't gone through a full DevOps-like revolution. Security professionals are often like the organization's boogeymen. There seems to be an overarching fear of them: they have traditionally been viewed as people who don't approve anything and who don't understand anything about your business application. They also do extremely technical work involving scary things and have the power to shut down your sprint cycle and give you busy work that you'll never finish patching. You know, this sounds like the old Development, Testing, and IT Ops teams that were in place prior to DevOps. But these siloes crush the souls of people who want to do good work.

Before we dive into the details of modernizing security in the cloud, let's get some quick fundamentals out the way to clarify the security lingo.

CIA Triad

We touched on the CIA triad in Chapter 6. To reiterate, the CIA triad is the most foundational information security model that provides three principles of strong security: confidentiality, integrity, and availability (CIA). Together, these principles form the basis of any security infrastructure and should be the guiding rubric on achieving security goals and objectives for an architecture.

Confidentiality is a protection mechanism that ensures that your data has not been improperly accessed by the wrong people. Before someone can access your data, they need to be granted specific access to it. Encryption, which has been an important consideration for a very long time, is one way that you can ensure confidentiality. Julius Caesar created a form of encryption (today known as the Caesar Cipher) that essentially substituted characters to form a message that was unreadable to anyone who did not know the cipher. Given that this encryption simply involved shifting characters forward by three places, it wasn't much of a difficult code to crack—but hey, life was simpler then. These days, we store a lot of intellectual property, sensitive customer data, and algorithms, and all of these things need to be protected from opportunistic individuals. Confidentiality is the principle of protecting them.

Integrity ensures that your data can be protected against unauthorized modifications. Suppose, for example, you put your drink down at the bar, and when you next lift the glass, the taste is funky—you know you should stop drinking it. It would be nice if there were a way to detect whether it had been modified before you started drinking it again. That's basically what hashing does for data—it tells you whether your data has been tampered with. Hashing calculates a set of numbers, known as a message digest or hash, and appends it to your data file so that you can validate that the hash is the same one used the last time the file was opened. If your data has been tampered with, that original hash value (assuming you're using a hashing algorithm that is not outdated) will not be present and another will be used. If the hash value has changed, you know that your data has probably been compromised.

Availability ensures that your product or service is available to its consumer as needed. Imagine calling 911 only to get a busy signal. Sorry buddy. Try again next time! Availability is typically dictated by a service level agreement (SLA) that defines clear service level objectives (SLOs) and service level indicators (SLIs) that you will be providing to the consumer of your service. The availability aspect of the triad is commonly associated with network architectures, performance of systems, and outages. Distributed Denial of Service (DDoS) attacks, geographical redundancy, application bottlenecks, and suboptimal network designs are all things that can impact your availability. If a hacker is trying to attack you, stealing your data may be only part of what they're after. What if your data doesn't matter and they just want to cause you financial harm by rendering your business unavailable?

Control Categories

When it comes to controls, there are three categories: administrative controls, technical controls, and physical controls.

Administrative controls describe the policies, procedures, and guidelines for humans to follow in accordance to the organization's security controls. Think of your organization's documented security policies, security training, incident response procedures, security principles, and so on.

Technical controls are logical mechanisms you implement to protect your assets. Think of your firewall, identity and access management (IAM) configuration, network restrictions, and antivirus software. These are essentially the things you've configured and deployed in the cloud to ensure that bad things can't happen.

Physical controls are physical mechanisms used to secure your environment. These include badges for access to the facility, surveillance cameras, two-factor hardware tokens, the twisty road and gates at your data center that keep people from driving a car into your server racks, and so on. Can you imagine that? Car smashes into a data center: "We're holding all your racks hostage. We own your data. Wait, how do you use this thing? Do these boxes need a password or something?!"

Control Functions

Aside from the category of controls, the controls themselves can perform three different types of security functions: they can be preventive, detective, or corrective in nature.

Preventive controls are security controls designed to stop unauthorized activity from materializing. Think of how you design your IAM policies and bindings to prevent unauthorized access, your firewall and network patterns, data security controls, virtual machine (VM) configuration and image hardening, and so on. When it comes to designing your cloud infrastructure, you can imagine that you're designing the infrastructure to prevent most security threats from materializing by minimizing the attack surface. An *attack surface* is the sum of all your possible security risk exposures. Typically, preventive controls may be documented by security architecture and policy teams, but they're implemented by the development or operations team.

Detective controls are security controls designed to detect unauthorized activity that has materialized. In this case, your security operations detection team is usually doing the work, looking for indicators of compromise in your environment, automating detection capabilities, building signatures, and receiving alerts on malicious activity. An *indicator of compromise* is an artifact or piece of data that gives your security team high confidence that a user or machine is compromised. If an intern is performing a privileged action, that could be an indicator of compromise. If your antivirus software detected malware on a VM, that's a detective control doing its job.

Corrective controls are security measures to correct unauthorized activity or resolve detected threats and vulnerabilities. Patching your VMs after a critical security flaw, responding to an incident, and rolling back or getting back to a known good state of your system—these are all examples of corrective controls.

TIP Preventive controls are usually a joint effort by the information security and architecture teams, but the development teams are usually required to implement them. Detective and corrective controls are usually handled by the security operations detection and response teams.

Asset × Threat × Vulnerability = Risk

What is the difference between a risk, a threat, and a vulnerability? People use these terms interchangeably so often that it makes me want to punch the air out of the sky and then repent to Mother Nature for the failed attempt. When it comes to security, our goal is to protect our assets. *Assets* are people, property, and data—tangible or intangible. A *threat* is anything that can exploit a vulnerability, whether it be intentionally or unintentionally, to obtain, damage, or destroy an asset. *Vulnerabilities* are weaknesses or gaps in a system that can be exploited by a threat to gain unauthorized access to an asset.

The next factor, which tends to be forgotten, is understanding the risk probability and impact. *Risk probability* is the likelihood of a risk materializing. The *risk impact* is the effects and consequences of that risk event. Going back to the skydiving use case, let's say that the probability of a parachute malfunction when you pack your own chute is 1 in 100. We know that the impact of a parachute malfunction is near certain death. Not many die-hard skydivers would still be around if 1 in 100 jumps ends in death, so obviously that is not happening. It is generally best practice to jump with two parachutes—a main chute and a backup. So when you use two self-packed chutes, your risk probability goes from 1 in 100 to 1 in 10,000. Using a professionally packed chute substantially increases your odds, and this is why most skydivers use a professionally packed backup parachute, which they hope never needs to be deployed. The second chute is a *risk mitigation*—a mechanism to reduce the probability or likelihood of a risk materializing.

You can't eliminate all risks. All you can do is reduce their probability and/or their impact. In Figure 11-1, you can see this idea. A threat can't materialize against an asset without a vulnerability. A vulnerability is meaningless without an asset to attack. An asset with a vulnerability has no risk if there is no threat. The idea is this: you need all three, and that intersection is the risk. In other words, if I'm in a boxing ring with nobody else, there's no risk. If I'm in a ring with Mike Tyson (a threat) and no protection (a vulnerability), that's a huge risk. If I'm in a ring with Tyson and I'm wearing a full metal suit,

Figure 11-1
The intersection of an asset, a thread, and a vulnerability creates a risk.

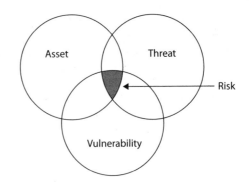

I've mitigated the risk. (That said, knowing the power of Tyson's brute-force attacks, I probably still wouldn't be safe and would need more security to mitigate the risk!)

Security Modernization

Traditionally, and in most organizations, there are a variety of security teams: security architecture, infrastructure security, data security, application security, security operations, risk management, compliance, and so on. Usually these represent very distinct roles, and oftentimes security gates are in place to require development teams to go through these individuals to get their applications risk assessed and approved. I use the term "gates" loosely. A security gate is like a baby gate you use to prevent your baby from going into the kitchen, but it falls over within seconds when that two-year-old hulk-smashes into it. Like babies, most development teams smash right through them—commonly referred to as Shadow IT. It's really difficult to get someone in a distinct role to be proactive in approving your design and managing your application when the person doesn't know the full context of your business application or doesn't even know what type of work you do aside from security requirements and best practices. On the flip side, you can't trust developers who just got out of college to ship code that hosts your most critical IP to the world and expect it to be secure. This exact issue leaves security operations teams (your firefighters) consistently under water, stressed out and burnt out, constantly trying to respond to threats and incidents. There is no time for automation, because they still haven't figured out how to build manual detection for all of their stack, and they're too busy getting hacked by 14-year-olds in Russia all day to have downtime. This model simply does not work. The human element is the weakest element.

With the cloud, however, the shared responsibility matrix removes a massive burden from organizations, as they no longer own their entire security portfolio end-to-end. Depending on what element of the Infrastructure as a Service (IaaS), Platform as a Service (PaaS), or Software as a Service (SaaS) stack you're looking at, Google will own a varying level of security for a variety of administrative, technical, and physical controls that traditionally were managed by the organization itself. The controls assumed could be preventive, detective, or corrective in nature. Your organization still has a significant responsibility here owning the residual security controls—and that is the responsibility of everyone in your organization, not just the security professionals. Basically, it's your responsibility to understand the shared responsibility matrix!

NOTE Most incidents that happen in the cloud are the result of a cloud customer not following their responsibilities in the shared responsibility matrix. Even with a massive burden of the security elements of a tech stack offloaded from an organization, still organizations can't get security right. That just proves that security breaches are not always your organization's fault. A massive shift needs to occur in the mindset of every single technologist! If everyone thought about security, we wouldn't have security people kicking and screaming for budgetary consideration; security would be included into every budgetary decision made at every level of an organization.

Organizations that migrate to the cloud are often strong believers of DevOps and automation, and this plays a major role in their overall security posture. In DevOps-oriented organizations, much of the security work related to the infrastructure and application stack is added into the pipeline, automated where possible, and shifted left (moved to the earliest possible point in the development process) when possible. People use the term DevSecOps often; regardless of your lingo, security should be seen as a fundamental requirement for everything.

There is still a never-ending and always-growing need for dedicated security professionals and a dedicated security organization. We can envision most world-class security teams operating in the same way DevOps teams are augmented with site reliability engineering (SRE). Security teams should spend 50 percent of their time supporting the work that other people are already doing and the other 50 percent of the time automating and innovating. When you think about modernizing the security of your organization, think about how you can continue driving toward automation. Balance out the security responsibilities across your organization and minimize your threat surface by providing built-in security specifications in the architectures that you design and implement.

There's so much more to unpack about how we can improve the various domains and functions of your security organization, but that's for another book. Just remember that the only way we'll get to a well-managed state is if we all take the responsibility, along with the security team, to build in the necessary security controls across our technology stack.

Security Automation in Practice

Nick Reva, a senior technical security manager at Snap, has spent his career focused on developing engineering tools and solutions to continue shifting security left. Understanding the fine balance between developer freedom and security is a challenge to increasing automation. While working with his team to design a firewall rule management solution that could've inhibited developer freedom, Nick found success in driving change by homing in on principles of kindness and empathy to build automation that assumes good intentions by the developers, hence minimizing anxiety and providing guardrails to catch mistakes.

The solution—a tool that assigns risk scores to firewall rule changes, automating the approval of low–moderate risk changes, flagging security to review high-risk patterns, and automating the closure of clear high-risk mistakes. By automating the bulk of firewall rule changes and removing security from being directly involved in every change, this solution sped up the time to deploy firewall changes and increased developer productivity throughout the organization. Key takeaway: think about how you can lead with kindness and assume the best intentions from your developers to shift security monitoring left without slowing down the pace of innovation.

Compliance

Compliance is every security engineer's least favorite word and every security risk manager's favorite word. No need to feel offended; I've been on both sides of this. Risk management folks, we need to do a better job understanding the actual risk beyond our compliance requirements. If we don't understand how the system works but we keep repeating the same policy, we won't keep friends on the other side. There are risks with 0 percent probability because of architectural constraints, or risks with almost no impact. Security engineers, we need to do a better job understanding how risk management works and why these folks are saving our rears. Risk management is preventing us from fines, punishments, and jail. You may not be the best person to digest and understand policies, but you're a brilliant nerd. Remember the bridge? Build that bridge. Figure out how you can prove that your risk is mitigated by the way your system is architected, even if it doesn't meet the requirements of the compliance mandate in English. Compliance regulators can understand that system design is incredibly complex. If you can demonstrate that a risk is mitigated to your own teams, you're making it easier for them to work with the actual regulators and protect the business.

In Google Cloud, a variety of compliance offerings are offered by GCP and G Suite. We'll discuss a few of them. For some of these compliance offerings, Google may self-attest to the controls required. For others, Google has independent third parties, such as EY and Coalfire, which will audit their environment to ensure that it meets the criteria to be certified compliant or to provide the ability for customers to build a compliant environment.

The *Payment Card Industry Data Security Standard* (PCI-DSS) provides companies that interact with credit card data the minimum security requirements they must meet to store, process, and transmit cardholder data. One common mechanism companies employ to descope all of these controls is by tokenizing credit card data. *Tokenization* is the process of substituting nonsensitive data, referred to as a token, for sensitive data. In the context of credit cards, imagine substituting your credit card numbers with a theoretical, nonreversible string of characters. If that credit card database gets exposed, that's too bad for the hacker, because they can't do anything with the tokens.

Credit card breaches are very common and very costly, and they can cause massive amounts of damage to individuals whose cards are exposed. It's often easier simply to reframe your thought process to assume a 100 percent probability that you will be breached or something will fail. If that happens, how can you prevent the impact of that risk? Rather than just think, "no way will my parachute not deploy," it's easier to go at your problem with, "I know for a fact that in the next six months of skydiving, this parachute will not deploy. What can I do to avoid meeting the Grim Reaper and enjoy my exciting hobby of jumping out of perfectly good airplanes?" In the credit card case, just assume that your database will be accessed or copied via some unauthorized path, because there are just too many people who have access. What will you do to secure it? Easy—take the sensitive data out of the picture. Then ask yourself, "What is the impact of the credit card database being breached if there is nothing left in the data that can provide an opportunity to a bad actor?"

Capital One's Industry-Leading Breach Response

The 2019 Capital One data breach exposed millions of credit card numbers, and this was incredibly costly for the organization. It's never about *if* a security incident will occur; it's about being prepared *when* an incident occurs. From the point at which the incident was discovered, Capital One led one of the fastest breach responses in technology history. Media research company CyberScoop called this "Light Speed" recognition (for more, see the "Additional References" section at the end of the chapter). In 2019, the average time to discover a breach was 297 days; Capital One discovered the breach and an arrest was made by the FBI within 12 days. This was a major organizational response, but in particular, it demonstrated a massive effort by the incident response team at Capital One. The company was not only able to assist the FBI in making an arrest quickly, but the response also came in fast enough time to prevent the millions of exposed data records from being routed across the Internet. This resulted in an $80 million civil penalty, which is relatively small compared to the $700 million penalty levied for the 2017 Equifax breach. If I had to guess, I'd say that the lower fine resulted from Capital One's ability to minimize the data exposure.

I'd love to give major recognition to my brother, Iraj Ghanizada, who ran the incident response program at Capital One at the time of the breach. Big shout out to his team for leading a historic breach response.

The moral of the story is that your organization will get pwned one day. Prepare; push your executives to provide budgets to minimize the impact; and ensure that your security operations teams have adequate funding to be able to detect, respond, and recover from incidents as effectively as possible.

To read more about the Capital One breach, see the link in the "Additional References" section at the end of the chapter.

The *Health Insurance Portability and Accountability Act* (HIPAA) was enacted in 1996 by former President Bill Clinton and mandates how the flow of protected health information (PHI) should be managed. If you break HIPAA laws, you can go to jail. Protecting patient records is incredibly important. Healthcare companies typically align to a compliance framework known as HITRUST, a combination of more than 40 different compliance frameworks that provides a very thorough set of security requirements across all security domains for an organization to adhere to.

 TIP HIPAA and other compliance frameworks may set a mandatory retention period for logs. For HIPAA, it's six years. How would you design a cost-effective solution to long-term, archival-based storage that needs to retain six years' worth of logs?

General Data Protection Regulation (GDPR) is a regulation in the European Union that describes how to protect user data and ensure user privacy for any data residing in the European Union or the European Economic Area. It describes how to manage user consent, minimize data collection, provide users the right to erase their data, and more. For organizations in the United States that think GDPR does not apply to them, think again. You are not allowed to store European citizen data outside of the European Union unless you follow GDPR rules. Furthermore, the great state of California requires personal information management in the United States as well, as described in the California Consumer Privacy Act (CCPA) of 2018. If you store a California resident's private data anywhere, you need to follow most of the GDPR compliance rules, even within the United States. Failure to do so is a criminal violation—not just a slap on the wrists and a big fine. Executives could end up in jail for knowingly not playing by the rules.

Let's face it. Many enterprises have done a poor job of protecting our private data over the years. With the speed and growth of big data today, self regulation just didn't work. Hopefully, when a CISO or CIO realizes that they could go to jail for not doing their due diligence and due care in protecting their clients' sensitive data, they may come up with the budgets needed to safeguard their customers' personal data properly.

 EXAM TIP Oftentimes, when you see a compliance-related question on the exam, you won't need deep subject matter expertise in the compliance framework itself. Instead, a question will present a requirement that you need to fulfill, and you'll need to define how to architect that requirement.

Infrastructure Security Highlights

This section is going to be very straightforward—no fluff. It highlights some of the key security principles of each layer of the infrastructure. There are probably five more layers of depth when you're doing actual engineering and implementation work beyond these line items. But keep these as guiding principles for building out your GCP infrastructure.

Identity Security

Cloud Identity handles your user authentication. This can include directory synchronization from Lightweight Directory Access Protocol (LDAP) or Active Directory (AD), as well as single sign-on (SSO) and integration with any of your third-party identity providers. Some of the best practices to follow for protecting your user authentication are as follows:

- Use fully managed Google accounts tied to your corporate domain name.
- Employ SSO and directory synchronization to simplify the end-user experience and prevent misuse of credentials by end users.
- Consider using reputable identity management solutions such as Okta.
- Apply strong password policies. Leverage two-step verification by using hardware or software tokens to validate that a user is who they say they are before being approved to access your GCP resources.
- Migrate unmanaged accounts (or conflict accounts) so they can be managed through Cloud Identity.

Resource Management Security

Google Cloud Resource Manager provides resource containers such as organizations, folders, and projects and enables you to group and hierarchically organize GCP resources into those containers to simplify governance, manage billing, and manage your organization effectively. Some of the best practices to follow for managing your resource hierarchy are as follows:

- Automate your project creation and the naming convention associated with your resource containers.

- Leverage a many-projects approach with clear organization through the use of a folder hierarchy to separate and organize your projects based on the structure of your organization.

- Factor in how your organization wants to manage billing across the various teams and functions, and leverage labels to ensure that you can govern your organization and manage your costs effectively,

- Use the Organization Policy Service to define restrictions on certain resources at various layers of the resource hierarchy.

IAM Security

Cloud Identity and Access Management (Cloud IAM) handles your IAM policies, including your role bindings. This is managed in GCP. Role-based access control enables you to define roles that your users can fit into, providing a simplified and scalable solution to manage users and teams en masse. Further, attribute-based access control enables you to define context-aware conditions in which your users can access an environment. Some of the best practices to follow for managing access to your environment are as follows:

- Follow the principle of least privilege to ensure that your roles are privileged with only the minimum set of permissions that allow a user to do their job if they fill that role.

- Follow the principle of separation of duties to ensure that your users don't play many different roles, preventing insider threat, minimizing the attack surface, and minimizing the likelihood of collusion.

- Don't directly assign permissions; assign roles.

- Leverage groups and service accounts to delegate responsibilities in an efficient manner.

- Do not download service account keys; use short-lived tokens. If you need to download a service account key, use a key management solution such as HashiCorp Vault.

- Protect your application secret keys by using a key management solution such as HashiCorp Vault or Google Secrets Manager to protect, rotate, revoke, and manage your secret keys.

EXAM TIP   Understand the predefined role naming convention. It's pretty self-explanatory, but some questions on the exam may ask you which role is appropriate for a certain set of permissions. Knowing the general role naming convention of Viewer, Browser, Admin, and Owner will help you be successful here. Also, remember that predefined roles should be leveraged where they can; use custom roles only if necessary.

Network Security

The design of your network is a fundamental element that protects you against compromised users and insider threats. Opening your network to billions of people across the globe is very dangerous. Even if you don't open your network to the world, small configuration mistakes can trigger massive compromises. Some of the best practices to follow for protecting your network are as follows:

- Google traffic is encrypted in transit by default, as the Google Front End (GFE) employs authentication and Transport Layer Security (TLS) to all traffic that hits the reverse proxy. After traffic is proxied, you're trusting Google to route your traffic on its fully owned private network. Google provides many assurances to protect your traffic's confidentiality, integrity, and availability.

- Leverage firewalls to monitor and control incoming and outgoing network traffic. Store documented and risk-assessed network patterns in a central policy repository, and use automation to deploy firewall patterns across your stack.

- Avoid using public IPs as much as possible.

- Protect your public endpoints with Cloud Armor and other web application firewall (WAF) solutions to defend against common attacks such as cross-site forgery (CSRF), cross-site-scripting (XSS), SQL injections, and so on.

- Use VPC firewall rules to allow or deny traffic to and from your VMs.

- Leverage Private Google Access to minimize the need for external IP addresses on services that need to reach out to public Google endpoints.

- Put your VMs behind external load balancers when you need to expose them to the outside to mitigate and minimize availability attacks and avoid exposing your VMs directly.

- Use VPC Service Controls to constrain public Google endpoints to your Virtual Private Clouds (VPCs) to avoid data exfiltration from malicious insiders or compromised users. That way, any data in a Google endpoint falls under the same enforcement boundaries that you use to protect your VPCs.

- Use the Identity-Aware Proxy (IAP) to control user access to your applications and eliminate the need for a VPN, as contextually aware solutions provide stronger security and simplify the end-user experience.

- Ensure that all of your network logs are being monitored by your security teams to detect malicious activity within your VPC.

- Do resilience testing by introducing faults in your environment and determining how they affect your architecture.

- Document all network patterns and assess risk via your enterprise architecture team so that your developers cannot build their own network patterns on the fly and are required to build around existing patterns, or they get their patterns approved by your architects before they are deployed in the organization.

Application Layer Security

The various IaaS, PaaS, and SaaS computing offerings are associated with varying best practices based on your responsibilities in the shared responsibility model. Some of these offerings don't fit exactly into a category and may be hybrids (think Kubernetes, for example). Some of the best practices to follow for protecting your application layer are as follows:

- Follow IAM best practices to protect access to your resources.

- Avoid using unencrypted communication traffic between application services. Use TLS or Secure Shell (SSH) to ensure that traffic never flows in cleartext. Yes, this means likely managing internal certificates and certificate authorities. But there are practices that can simplify this operational overhead.

- Follow networking best practices to ensure that only approved traffic flows between resources.

- Harden the configuration of your computing resources to minimize unnecessary services and configuration items being enabled on such resources.

- Centralize the configuration and monitor your resources against deviances from this configuration.

- Leverage an image repository, approved images, and a trusted deployment process.

- Leverage managed services where possible. If this meets your needs, it should strengthen your security, minimize the operations needed, and simplify the end-user experience.

- Use OS Login to simplify SSH access management to VMs, linking them to their Google identities to ensure that you can monitor and govern privileged access.

- Leverage automatic upgrades where possible and follow a strong patch management process.

- Use templates whenever possible to programmatically manage your infrastructure.

- Manage your APIs through an API management platform such as Apigee or Cloud Endpoints to protect access to your application interfaces.

Data Security

Your data is the most critical asset to your organization. Protecting your data is protecting your business. A data exposure could cause serious harm to your business—fines, customer churn, imprisonment, and a complete loss of your business. Exposure does not necessarily mean a hacker stole your data; data may be exposed accidentally, it may be stolen, it may be mistakenly revealed by an insider, or it may involve a loss of availability. In the 21st century, data is our most valuable asset. Some of the best practices to follow for protecting your data are as follows:

- Data in GCP is encrypted in the server side at rest by default using AES 256. Default encryption is the most secure solution for server-side encryption, depending on your perspective, if you think about minimizing the operational burden and mismanaging your own encryption keys.

- Use an external key manager if you must fully own the keys to your data.

- For organizational requirements, use Cloud Key Management Service (KMS) and CloudHSM to manage and protect your key-encrypting keys.

- Consider using client-side encryption if you really want the added layer of protection.

- Follow IAM best practices to protect against unauthorized access to data.

- When transferring data to storage solutions to or within GCP, you must have appropriate security measures in place based on your transfer mechanism to ensure confidentiality and the validation of integrity upon completion.

- Leverage managed services where possible to minimize the operational overhead for your teams.

- Label your data environments and data according to their classification model to ensure that you can properly govern and monitor your data.

- Leverage Cloud Data Loss Prevention (DLP) to discover, classify, and protect your sensitive data either on ingestion or at rest.

- Consider tokenizing personally identifiable information (PII) data and limiting access and unnecessary copies of this data. Each copy is an increase to your threat surface.

- Leverage additional database security features where applicable and properly design your table schemas.

DevOps Security

Continuous integration and deployment is the most effective way to build, ship, and manage code. The continued emphasis on automation enables organizations to focus on building great products rather than managing complex processes. There are many opportunities for adding security gates through this automation process, and organizations should strive to automate everything they can. Some of the best practices to follow for protecting your pipelines are as follows:

- Ensure that security considerations are integrated through the entire product life cycle, from design to development, delivery, operations, and all over again.

- Do threat modeling during your planning phases to identify threat vectors that need to be protected against.

- Perform code reviews/peer reviews during code development.

- Track and remediate vulnerabilities at various stages of the life cycle through static code analysis, dynamic code analysis, and penetration testing.

- Use infrastructure as code (IaC) to deploy your infrastructure.

- Eliminate embedded credentials in code by using secret key management solutions.

- Control, monitor, and audit access to privileged accounts.

- Protect your service accounts that require highly privileged access to deploy IaC.

Security Operations

I always like to say there are two separate focus tracks handled by two different teams or functions: security of the infrastructure and security operations. Security of the infrastructure is typically handled by architects, developers, operations, and engineers. These are all mostly preventive security items such as designing your networks properly, ensuring that your secrets are managed properly, designing your data ingestion pipelines and storage, and so on. Think about it: all the best practices described in the previous chapters focused on designing your overall infrastructure to prevent bad activity from occurring in the first place. Usually these requirements are driven by your central security team. But the actual work is federated to the development side of the house, depending on how your organization operates.

Now what happens when bad activity has occurred? Who is best equipped to detect and respond to this activity? The answer is not always black-and-white and usually depends on the size of your organization. The more mature an organization, the more likely it will have a security operations center (SOC) or a detection and response (D&R) team—whatever you want to call it—that handles all of this type of work. For some smaller or less-equipped organizations, this may be federated to the actual developers (which is a bad practice because developers don't have the skills that a dedicated security operations team would have) or federated to a managed security services provider (MSSP), which has its own pros and cons. Yes, having an MSSP is better than not having a security monitoring and response capability. But, as you can imagine, it is so challenging having folks who are not employees of the business integrate with the folks on the development side of the house to drive change. They are contractors after all, and they don't really have much stake in the game.

Whether the organization uses an SOC or a D&R team, the end goal is the same: to detect bad activity, respond to bad activity, and provide feedback to the business to mitigate and prevent this activity from occurring again. The skillset for this type of work is very technical, but it is not the skillset of a typical software engineer. For that reason, it never makes sense to have your development teams owning this function. Because you're looking to become an architect and the purpose of this book is to help you get ready to take the PCA exam, I won't dive too deep into this because it is its own practice. At a high level, however, here's the 10,000-foot view of security operations:

- The logging architecture must be able to provide all relevant security logs to this team. Typically this will be ingested in a security information and event management (SIEM) tool, such as Splunk, which enables security teams to analyze, enrich, alert, and respond to potential incidents.

- Security operations teams will usually include an engineer who handles tooling and works with the cloud architecture team to build the logging architecture. The team will also identify all of the relevant log sources.

- The log architecture is built, the logs are aggregated, and the logs are ingested in the SIEM.

- The detection team, usually a team of analysts of varying levels, will look to correlate data and identify signatures (or patterns) of bad behavior that they will want to generate alerts on.

- Structured alerts are created to trigger based on these indicators. Throughout this time, the team is continually seeking ways to enrich the data to provide better analytical insight so that they can minimize false positives and improve the detection capabilities.

- When an alert triggers, it gets analyzed first. Upon analysis, it goes through handoffs to investigate any indicators of compromise. Then it may be formally determined that an incident is occurring or has occurred. This triggers the incident response team to take over the case.

- When the incident response team takes over, a formal incident response workflow is kicked off. Through this workflow, a team is identified to take on varying roles depending on the size and scope of the incident. These roles can include communications lead, incident manager, subject matter expertise, and many more.

- The goals of the incident response activities are to contain, eradicate, and recover from the incident.

- Finally, the teams will join together for a postmortem, where they can create the lessons learned and share them back through the feedback loop to prevent this type of incident from occurring again.

In Figure 11-2, you can the standard incident response life cycle.

Various tools can automate different tasks throughout the workflow, and automation should always be the goal. But as of 2020, most of this work is still heavily manual, and hackers are incredibly elusive. So it's not always easy to automate mitigations for their behaviors. This gap will be closed through the use of machine learning and some of

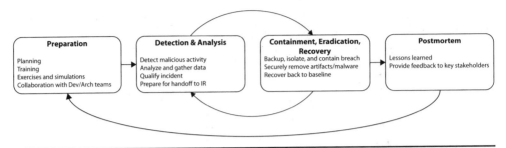

Figure 11-2 Incident response life cycle

the latest great security companies out there. The industry is headed toward a state of automation, similar to the DevOps-like transformation, but that is many years out. In order to get there, we really need to focus on training security operations teams on doing automation and pushing leadership to allocate the budgets to hire headcount. In turn, that will minimize their utilization, giving them time to focus on creating automation and getting closer to the DevOps teams.

As I said, this won't be on the exam, but within security operations is a massive, technical practice, and it's important that you understand what your peers do so that you can build a better bridge between your teams. You also have to remember that being the firefighters of your organization, they are consistently under heavy stress loads. It's hard for them to focus on automation and the like, because they are usually understaffed and overallocated, consistently responding to incidents. Be patient when working with your security operations partners.

Cloud Asset Inventory

Cloud Asset Inventory (CAI) is the metadata inventory service that enables users to keep track of all of their assets in Google Cloud. CAI is incredibly important for doing governance. Think about the purpose of an asset management system. You don't know what you don't have visibility of, but if you have visibility of your entire infrastructure and things are properly tagged, it becomes easy to manage and deploy changes across the entire infrastructure. Oftentimes you would want to leverage asset inventory systems to scan your infrastructure for changes, to deploy certain policies across the stack, or to audit for compliance. Imagine, for example, that a security incident occurs and you notice that one of your firewall rules is open. You can analyze the asset history in the CAI to understand when the firewall rule change was made and then investigate that exact event to determine who made it, and then you can dial down to a root cause. Let's say you want to deploy an organizational policy that prevents VMs from having external IP addresses. Your CAI knows where all your VMs are when that organization policy is deployed at a layer of its hierarchy and will update to reflect the new policy changes. Asset management is super important for many teams outside of security, and oftentimes when you ask people in on-premises environments what their biggest challenges are, you'll most likely hear asset management as one of the top issues they face.

Security Command Center

Security Command Center (SCC) is a security and risk management platform that provides visibility into various security elements of your organization. It does this by being connected directly to the CAI service and continuously analyzing for changes. Those changes are analyzed by various tools that make up the SCC suite of tools—namely, Cloud Threat Detection, Security Health Analytics, Web Security Scanner, and more. When a flaw is identified, it's reported as a *finding*. These findings provide insight into who, what, where, and when the change was triggered. Security professionals can work directly out of the SCC interface or can have these findings exported to a SIEM of their choice, where they can analyze it in their native security tools. SCC is the start of a journey toward security modernization, and it is very quickly becoming a powerhouse tool in Google Cloud.

Cloud Threat Detection

One of the logic engines within SCC is the Cloud Threat Detection (CTD) tool, which provides automated detection of certain threats in GCP through a few of its subtools. Within CTD are a few tools that focus on different threats.

Event Threat Detection (ETD) and Container Threat Detection (KTD) are currently the main tools included in CTD. ETD focuses on log-based threats, and KTD focuses on threats in the container runtime.

Remember the difference between threats and vulnerabilities? Most security teams build threat signatures in their SIEM so that they can easily identify where there may be a compromise in the organization. Building these threat signatures manually is cumbersome, takes a ton of time, and needs to be continually iterated to be effective. The idea with CTD is that Google is doing the work for you, using their threat analysis data and all of their engineers to create various detections. This enables your team to free up some time to focus on other detections. As you can imagine, when the prebuilt detection list continues to grow, automation improves, and security operations teams can focus more of their time on innovation and automating other areas of their jobs, while spending the rest of their time focusing on their day-to-day job. The result of these detectors, or findings, can be exported to the SIEM. This enables your SOC or D&R teams to manage all threats using a single tool, such as Splunk. For smaller organizations that may not have a budget for Splunk or other SIEMs, using only the SCC user interface may be sufficient.

 NOTE You probably won't find any information about Cloud Threat Detection, per se, in the public documentation. You can look up Event Threat Detection and Container Threat Detection separately. These likely won't be on the PCA exam.

Security Health Analytics

The Security Health Analytics (SHA) tool is focused on vulnerabilities within GCP. SHA looks for vulnerabilities in the GCP, not host-based vulnerabilities such as those that Rapid7 or Qualys would look for within VMs. SHA will scan the CAI every 12 hours looking for things like open firewall rules or open GCS buckets. It's based on a system of scanners: the tool leverages its prebuilt scanners to detect certain vulnerabilities. The findings can be exported to a SIEM. Usually, the SOC team does not focus on vulnerabilities, and instead a dedicated vulnerability management team focuses on remediating vulnerabilities at most organizations. It is possible that the vulnerability management team may be colocated alongside the SOC or D&R teams, but their job functions are very different.

Web Security Scanner

Web Security Scanner (WSS) is focused on scanning your public GCP endpoints for web-based vulnerabilities. For example, if you have a public IP address on one of your Google Compute Engine (GCE), Google Kubernetes Engine (GKE), or Google App Engine (GAE) instances hosting a web server, WSS will look for things like XSS vulnerabilities or cleartext password fields, based on the OWASP Top Ten Web Application Security Lists.

NOTE OWASP, the Open Web Application Security Project, is a highly trusted community that determines the top web-based security issues that organizations need to protect against. For more information, see the "Additional References" section at the end of the chapter.

Chapter Review

Congratulations! By sticking with this chapter, even though some of this information isn't on the exam, you've built a decent foundational understanding of some of the security responsibilities of development teams and security operations teams. There are many more organizational security teams that weren't covered; reach out to your security peers to learn more. This knowledge will serve you and help you become a better architect and a better leader.

In this chapter, we started talking about some of the security fundamentals, starting with the CIA triad—the confidentiality, integrity, and availability of your data. Confidentiality ensures that your data has not been improperly accessed by inappropriate people. Inappropriate access can often be prevented by using access controls and encryption. Integrity ensures that your data has not been tampered with, often by employing some method of hashing. Availability ensures that your data is available when necessary. This can be achieved by network attack mitigation, geographical redundancy, system design, and network design. Availability closely aligns to the most important principle of running a business—reliability. Site reliability engineers play a major role in system availability. The three CIA principles dictate all of the areas of security that you need to focus on when designing a system.

Within your control categories are administrative controls that are focused on policies, procedures, and guidelines for humans to follow. Technical controls are logical mechanisms used to protect your assets—think of the technical security controls you implement in GCP such as firewall rules. Physical controls are physical mechanisms to secure your environment, such as locks, access codes, hardware tokens, and so on.

Your controls have functions as well. They can be preventive, detective, or corrective in nature. Preventive controls are implemented to prevent a bad activity from occurring. These are typically aligned with the way you design your infrastructure. You can use strong, role-based access controls to prevent the wrong people from having access to data. Detective controls will detect malicious activity when or after it occurs. But just because you put strong role-based access controls in place doesn't mean you can't get compromised. If your platform triggers an alert that an unauthorized person has privileged access to a top-secret data lake, when he should only have unprivileged access to the monopoly money database, it's quite possible that your users and your environment were compromised because a privilege escalation took place. Corrective controls are the measures you take to correct this unauthorized activity and get back to baseline. You could isolate the unauthorized user's access and monitor to gather some more intelligence on the hacker behind it before you kill all user access, and then patch the vulnerability to prevent it from occurring again.

A threat is anything that can exploit a vulnerability; a vulnerability is a weakness or gap in a system that can be exploited by a threat. Your risk probability is the likelihood of a risk materializing. The risk impact is the effects of that risk materializing. Risk mitigation is focused on employing mechanisms to reduce the probability of a risk. Security is all about risk management at the end of the day. The most advanced organizations are continually finding ways to bring automation into the security space so that security professionals can focus on playing more SRE-like roles, spending half of their time doing their day-to-day work and the other half focused on automation and innovation.

Google Cloud Platform and Google Workspace meet dozens of compliance needs, from GDPR to HITRUST, HIPAA, PCI-DSS, and more. GDPR is a data-privacy regulation in the European Union that focuses on protecting user data and ensuring the privacy of data of citizens residing in the European Union or European Economic Area. PCI-DSS is focused on the security of credit card data and provides the controls required to store, transmit, and process credit cards securely. HITRUST and HIPAA are healthcare-related compliance mandates that provide information on how to secure protected health information (PHI). GCP and Google Workspace meet many more compliance frameworks, regulations, and self-certifications, which are all listed on the GCP compliance page.

The way you design your infrastructure is very important. All of the best practices you employ when designing your infrastructure are mostly preventive security controls that will prevent breaches from occurring in your environment. It is best to align these to your security policies, and when you identify a gap, support your security teams by identifying improvements that they can use to readjust their policies to capture. The public cloud is very new for many organizations, and not all policies translate equally to traditional on-premises best practices. So a bit of learning and teaching needs to occur between teams.

Security operations is a function within a greater security team that focuses on detecting and responding to security breaches in the cloud. While the development teams implement preventive measures, the security operations folks will continually seek out ways to detect when bad activity happens and then contain, eradicate, and recover from it. GCP includes various tools that support security operations teams in different ways.

The last chapter is coming up, and it's an easy one—how exciting!

Additional References

If you'd like more information about the topics discussed in this chapter, check out these sources:

- **What Capital One's Cybersecurity Team Did (and Did Not) Get Right**   https://www.cyberscoop.com/capital-one-cybersecurity-data-breach-what-went-wrong/
- **OWASP Top Ten**   https://owasp.org/www-project-top-ten/

Questions

1. You are deploying an application that needs to integrate with an on-premises database, but you don't want to expose your on-premises database to the Internet. The performance requirements are not important. What's the quickest, most secure, and most cost-effective approach?

    A. Use firewall rules to limit access to the on-premises database.

    B. Use Cloud VPN to limit access to the on-premises database.

    C. Use Partner Interconnect to limit access to the on-premises database.

    D. Use Dedicated Interconnect to limit access to the on-premises database.

2. You've been asked to lead the compliance aspect of your application design. To meet PCI-DSS requirements, what is the best approach to take?

    A. Google already meets PCI-DSS by default, so most best practices are already implemented.

    B. Turn on the compliance baseline API and determine whether there are any outstanding compliance issues for your application.

    C. Gather the PCI-DSS requirements and then begin designing the application around the requirements your application needs.

    D. Hire a contractor who has the PCI-DSS certification under his belt.

3. What is the GDPR?

    A. A compliance mandate in Asia that describes how to handle sensitive user information

    B. A compliance mandate in the European Union that describes how to protect user data and privacy

    C. A healthcare compliance regulation that describes how to secure protected health information

    D. A California-based privacy mandate that describes how to protect California user information

4. What is a secret?

    A. A piece of data, typically a key of some sort, that is typically used for the purpose of authentication

    B. One factor of authentication

    C. A password

    D. A passphrase

5. All of these are best practices around role-based access control *except* which one?

    A. Leverage primitive roles over predefined roles.

    B. Ensure the users have the least amount of privileges necessary to do their jobs.

    C. Assign roles to groups rather than individuals where possible.

    D. Separate duties between users to minimize the chance of collusion and insider threat.

6. All of the following are ways to add security to your CI/CD process *except* which one?

    A. Perform penetration tests.

    B. Integrate static code analysis scanning.

    C. Implement dynamic code analysis.

    D. Manually append information security requirements to your JIRA tickets.

7. You are designing a complex architecture that connects many services to a central database. How should you store the credentials securely?

    A. Store the keys in the source code.

    B. Leverage a secret management system.

    C. Store it in a configuration file.

    D. Memorize them.

8. What is a vulnerability?

    A. Anything that can exploit a threat to gain unauthorized permission over an asset

    B. A mechanism that exploits a weakness to gain unauthorized permission over an asset

    C. A weakness or gap in a system that may allow authorized permission over an asset

    D. A weakness or gap in a system that may allow unauthorized permission over an asset

9. All of the following are encryption options on Google Cloud Platform *except* which one?

   A. Default encryption

   B. External key manager

   C. Customer-managed encryption keys

   D. Customer-sampled encryption keys

10. What is a threat?

   A. Anything that can exploit a vulnerability to gain unauthorized permission over an asset

   B. A mechanism that exploits a weakness to gain unauthorized permission over an asset

   C. A weakness or gap in a system that may allow authorized permission over an asset

   D. A weakness or gap in a system that may allow unauthorized permission over an asset

Answers

1. **B.** The fastest, most secure, and most cost-effective approach, since the performance requirements are not important, would be to leverage Cloud VPN to set up a private tunnel between the on-premises database and the application.

2. **C.** Gathering requirements is always fundamental to designing any secure or regulation-compliant system.

3. **B.** The GDPR is a compliance mandate in the European Union that specifically discusses user privacy and data protection.

4. **A.** A secret could be a password, passphrase, a token, or any value that is agreed upon to be the method of authentication for a system.

5. **A.** Do not use primitive roles unless you absolutely need to. These are the old, archaic roles that were created in the early days of the cloud.

6. **D.** The whole purpose of CI/CD is automation. Manually appending anything, even if it's beneficial, does not meet the bill of being a continuously integrated and deployed model.

7. **B.** Leverage a secrets manager if you need to store and manage your secret keys. Too often, developers run shortcuts and store their secrets in code during development, and then they forget to remove the secrets when they go to production—which are then gained by hackers scanning GitHub for the noobs who don't secure their secrets! It's one of the biggest attack vectors in the modern day!

8. D. A vulnerability is an identified weakness or gap in a system that will allow someone to get unwanted access to your system.

9. D. Customer-sampled encryption keys do not exist.

10. A. A threat can be anything that can exploit a vulnerability to take advantage of a system. Threats can be intentional or unintentional—from a hacker to an earthquake—and can trigger a massive outage of a system.

CHAPTER 12

Billing, Migration, and Support

In this chapter, we'll cover

- How to optimize your costs using Cloud Billing
- How to plan a migration to GCP
- How to use Google Cloud Support to support your journey

Well. There's not much philosophy here. We live in a free-market society and the best of us optimize our costs every step of the way as we grow our net wealth. In other words, we can't forget about saving bread on our quests to make more bread. In this chapter, you'll learn about different billing models. You'll also learn how migration can be a costly endeavor. And, finally, we'll talk about how you can maximize your experience with Google Cloud with the help of Google Support.

Let's start by talking about why billing is important. Billing can be incredibly complicated. Every organization follows a different cost model. If you're running a startup with ten people, you're probably charging everything to your CEO's credit card. If you're running a large enterprise with one source of business, one division probably funnels all the money your way. If you're working for a company like Disney, which is a massive conglomerate and where each business takes its cloud migration journey in its own way, you probably want each business to pay for its own venture. Within the topmost billing aspect, your finance team probably needs to find a way to do accounting in a way that lets them understand who is spending all of the cloud money. This is where you need to have proper organization and labeling of your GCP account. The shift to operating expenses in the cloud can definitely be incredibly less expensive than all of the capital expenses and operating expenses required to manage everything in your on-premises environment. But when you get one massive bill versus many smaller bills, it can feel like shell shock.

Migrations are also an incredibly complex and costly event. Planning a migration will take dozens of individuals directly working on the effort to shift the organization-wide philosophy toward the cloud. While each organization has its own approach to migrating to the cloud, we'll cover migration at a high level here, including some things you may see on your test.

Lastly, support is going to be your best friend in your journey to Google Cloud and beyond. You cannot run a multimillion-dollar business in the cloud without having a proper support team behind it. Issues and challenges come up every day in unexplainable ways—from the cloud service provider undergoing outages, upgrades, and maintenance, to issues that your own developers cause by wreaking havoc in your environment and beyond. Having a strong support team can be the X factor in improving your overall reliability and in building applications in the cloud according to best practices.

Billing Fundamentals

When it comes to billing in the cloud, your costs are determined by resource usage. In the Google Cloud Platform (GCP), you know that a resource can refer to many things, including virtual machines, databases, storage buckets, projects, folders, and so on. As you can imagine, with this level of cost granularity, it can be really difficult to understand your costs if you are not organized properly and do not have a strong labeling strategy. It's also important that you understand your overall costs so that you can better budget and forecast across your teams and organization, and so that you can take advantage of the variety of discounts available to you as a GCP customer. Lastly, time is of the essence. Being unorganized in how you've structured your billing setup costs more in labor hours for teams working on cost-related issues.

In GCP, you can set up a single billing account or multiple accounts. For most organizations, having a single billing account is ideal, and it's the easiest of the options to manage. Support contracts can attach themselves only to one billing account. So if you pay for enterprise support, you'll need to buy one enterprise support contract for each billing account if you're running more than one account. Multiple billing accounts are necessary for large multinational companies. Think of the Disney example: This massive conglomerate consists of many different companies, with each having its own business models and objectives, and some of which seemingly even compete against others. It doesn't make sense to have one entity footing the bill for such an enormous organization.

A billing account defines who pays for a given set of resources, including Google Cloud resources and use of the Google Maps platform APIs. You can control access to the billing account by Cloud IAM. You'll get a single invoice per billing account, and it operates in a single currency. So, in this instance, if you need to pay with multiple currencies, you'd probably want to have multiple billing accounts.

All projects should be linked to a billing account. If a project is not linked to a billing account, it won't be able to use anything outside of the free services available. An online account enables you to manage your payments online, using credit, debit, or ACH Direct Debit. If you use an offline account, invoices are sent and payment is collected by check or wire transfer.

The key roles in Cloud Billing are as follows:

- **Billing account admin**   Managed inside of Cloud IAM, this user can enable Billing Export, view cost/spend, set budgets and alerts, and link/unlink projects. Typically someone on your finance team.

- **Billing user**   Managed inside of Cloud IAM, this user can link projects to billing accounts but cannot unlink them. It's usually linked to project creators in your organization so they can ensure their projects are linked to a billing account.

- **Payment profiles admin**   Managed outside of GCP in the Google Payments Center, this is where you can manage how you pay for all Google products and services, including cloud, ads, and more.

Cost Control

When it comes to managing your costs, you should follow a strong naming convention so that you can query your costs effectively. This should not be manual work. If you follow infrastructure as code (IaC) best practices, your templates should be inclusive of these labels so that you don't have to worry about discovering any rogue projects that are missing labels. Oftentimes, teams will be tracking their budget in Cloud Billing. When more fine-grained analysis is required, you can set up billing exports to BigQuery and run custom queries to find more granular billing-related data. Doing this is as simple as a one-click export in the Cloud Billing console, and your billing data will be set up as a BigQuery dataset.

Having awareness of your costs is very important, and managing the company wallet is everyone's responsibility. Like security, you can't just pass off cost control to the finance team alone. With tools like BigQuery, you can run petabyte-size queries. Imagine if an inexperienced data scientist runs enormous queries without realizing how much money they're racking up for the organization. Someone's going to be really mad! If their queries end up costing the organization ten times their salary, who knows how their management team is going to react! There are ways to ensure that this sort of activity doesn't happen, and the most important one is to set up proper cost alerts. When you set up alerts, you can trigger budget alerts based on a threshold.

 TIP   Budget alerts aren't just useful for your cost purposes. They can also be a detective security control. Here's an example: One of my customers had a Dataproc cluster that used up more than $100,000 of usage in two days, when it normally uses less than $1000 a day. This was the result of an attacker taking advantage of an open firewall port, attacking a vulnerable Hadoop cluster, and injecting crypto-mining malware. Had budget alerts been set up, this activity could've been detected and mitigated much sooner. Granted, the open firewall rule should've been the first misconfiguration detected.

You can view console reports, invoices, and BigQuery exports, and you can set up Google Data Studio to your BigQuery dataset to create a custom dashboard for interpreting your costs any way you want. Data Studio is an incredibly powerful visualization tool, and many online templates are available to help you create a predefined dashboard for common billing use cases.

Taking advantage of the available discounts is helpful for organizations of all sizes. There are two main types of discounts available for customers: committed use discounts and sustained use discounts. For *committed use discounts* (CUDs), you've purchased committed use contracts in exchange for deeply discounted prices. For example, let's say you've forecasted your consumer demand for the next three years on GCE. Rather than paying on-demand, you decide to buy a committed use contract so that you'll have significant discounts on your resources since you're committing to X resources for Y years. *Sustained use discounts* (SUDs) are discounts that everyone will automatically get based on how long they've been running a resource per month. An example of this is on GCE: If you've run your VMs for 90 percent of the month, you may get up to 30 percent off based on the machine type you're running. This is Google's way of saying thank you for using its products. You can also get discounts by using preemptible VMs, and lastly, you can get contractual discounts when you're negotiating a deal with Google Cloud Sales. Pretty much every cloud customer on every cloud provider will negotiate some type of contractual discounts based on its commitment deals.

 TIP If you can forecast your usage, why not save money? In GCP, discounts apply to the aggregate number of virtual CPUs, memory, graphics processing units (GPUs), and local solid-state drives (SSDs) within a region, so they are not affected by changes to your instance's machine setup. Plan and forecast your spending where you can, and you can take advantage of the great savings that come with CUDs.

Migration Planning

Planning a migration to GCP is no easy feat. It can take dozens, or hundreds of employees working on this initiative, and it will involve your entire organization undergoing a cultural adoption of cloud-first. You can imagine the people that are involved at every stage of the organization: the board of directors, C suite executives, executive sponsors, senior leaders, architects, engineers, program managers, project managers, and more. For most enterprises, migrating to Google Cloud or any cloud is a first, so they may even hire contractors and new employees who are directly focused on the effort. On Google's side, sales teams are working on building the foundation for your enterprise transformation. And Google Cloud's Professional Services Organization team focuses on mobilizing your migration efforts from the time the sales cycle wraps up to the processes required in planning, coordinating, executing, and managing the migration end to end.

Google Cloud's methodology focuses on migrations in four stages: assess, plan, migrate, and optimize:

- Assess and evaluate your IT landscape and workloads.
- Plan what can move, what should move, and in what order.
- Migrate by picking a path, and get started.
- Optimize your operations and save on costs.

Resource Quotas vs. Capacity

In your migration planning efforts, you'll need to forecast all sorts of things: what services you'll be using, which business applications will be getting migrated, your usage, your spending, and beyond. When it comes to usage, you must understand the difference between a resource quota and capacity. *Resource quotas* are usage-based restrictions to prevent abuse and accidental usage of resources. Everyone gets a default resource quota. *Capacity* is the total amount of the actual resource that is available to you to be provisioned in your environment.

Imagine, for example, that you have requested to increase your quota to a total of 2 petabytes of SSD storage in the us-east-1 region. By doing this, you're preventing your development team from intentionally or unintentionally going above this 2PB limit. Now you can imagine that there are thousands of GCP customers operating in a single region, and this is where capacity comes in. Even though you set that limit on your environment, it doesn't mean that 2PB is actually available for you to use. There's only so much SSD storage that one region can handle (until additional data centers open and they expand existing centers' storage sizes). So it's entirely possible that even if you set a resource quota, the region may run out of capacity sooner than your team hits that quota. That's the intention behind *reserving capacity*. By reserving capacity, you are paying for resources, whether you currently use them or not, that will be reserved for your organization so that you don't run into resource constraints at any time. Marketers talk about "infinite scalability" in the cloud, but that is factually incorrect. Only so many sticks of memory, disk, CPU, GPU, and networking can exist in one physical location. If you're planning a massive deployment, work with your Google Cloud support team to understand the resource availability and forecast of a region. Then you can accurately predict your resource usage and align your resource quotas and capacity to it.

 CAUTION   Remember that you can have all the resource quotas in the world, but if you don't have reserved capacity, another cloud customer could be eating up any of the remaining capacity in resource-constrained regions. Plan, forecast, and work with your Google Cloud support team to ensure that you're preparing for the quarter, half, and year ahead.

Transferring Applications and Data

So, you have an existing on-premises data center with 220 applications on VMs and 25PB of data. How do you plan on migrating all of this to GCP? When you're doing a migration, there are always thousands of time, money, security, and resource variables that affect your planning strategy. What if it's going to take two months before your dedicated interconnect pipe is set up from your ISP to Google Cloud and you need to get data over to it immediately? Do you do this over the Web? Do you attach a USB drive to a pigeon and fly it over?

For migrating applications, here are three things to note:

- **Rehosting** This is the concept of "lift and shift," migrating any of your existing applications into GCP without making changes to the platform or applications. For example, you can use GCP VMware Engine to run your existing VMware workloads on GCP without having to make any changes.

- **Replatforming** This is the concept of "lift and optimize," migrating your applications and workloads without rewriting them, but running them on a GCP cloud-native platform. For example, you can use Migrate for Compute Engine to move VM-based workloads to GCE.

- **Refactoring** This is the concept of "move and improve," converting any of your existing applications and workloads to run on modern form factors without modifying code. For example, you can use Migrate for Anthos to convert applications that run on VMs into container-based applications on Google Kubernetes Engine (GKE).

You also need to consider how fast you want to transfer all of your data. For anything using your existing network, having a proper interconnect setup between your data centers and GCP can expedite this greatly. Consider the following:

- **Online transfer** Use the GUI, **gsutil**, or JSON API to transfer files to GCS using your existing network.

- **Storage transfer service** Perform large-scale online data transfers from your on-premises environment or from other cloud providers to GCS using your existing network, taking advantage of the logic the tool provides to optimize for the size and performance of the transfer.

- **Transfer appliance** Securely store, ship, and upload your data to GCS using one or multiple physical 100TB or 480TB disk drives. If you need to securely migrate terabytes of volume without disrupting your business operations, this is your best bet.

 EXAM TIP If you need to transfer less than 1TB from on-premises, use **gsutil**. If you need to transfer data between clouds, use the Storage Transfer Service. If your data size is over 10TB, use a transfer appliance. Expect to see a question around the optimal mechanism to transfer a certain size of data.

Training and Enablement

Some of the most overlooked and underestimated elements of a successful cloud transformation are training and enablement. It's like buying a Lamborghini without a warranty, without understanding how to drive it properly, and without having supercar experience. It's great that you've got the money to buy the car, but if you don't know how to drive it, and you aren't prepared to maintain it to optimize its lifespan and efficiency, you're going to have trouble.

When it comes to GCP, the extra money that you spend on training your organization should not be an afterthought. When you invest in your team, you're investing in the following:

- Increasing productivity
- Improving confidence and morale for users interacting with GCP
- Increasing the speed of innovation
- Saving costs and labor hours on users who need to invest the extra time trying to figure things out on their own
- Building stronger relationships with your employees by showing your unconditional commitment to their learning and growth
- Creating a faster journey to the cloud

If you didn't value training, why else would you be reading this book? There are so many resources available for training—certifications, self-paced courses like Coursera and QwikLabs, books (like this one!), professional training courses offered by instructors both virtually and in person, and more. If you're working in a large organization and a technical account manager is assigned to your support plan, that individual will typically be curating a learning plan tailored to your organization's needs and will recommend targeted training. It's not rocket science. An untrained team will operate poorly, will make an unacceptable number of mistakes, and will bring a ton of risk to your organization if the deployment and operations in GCP are not carefully managed.

I think we all know that having a certification does not magically make you a black-belt guru. There's no such thing as someone who knows it all. Technology is an ever-evolving practice, and the landscape is ever-changing, so learning and practical experience go hand in hand. Having certifications helps drive individuals and teams toward a higher level of maturity, and it is a well-known fact that the more certified Professional Cloud Architects there are in the world, the faster the speed of innovation at GCP and maturity of the solutions will grow. The beauty of our industry is that what drives growth and change in the world isn't the works of the nerds at Google or AWS; it's the works of the entire community. So I highly recommend setting goals for your teams to become certified while they're also in the field working with the technology. This will foster a strong culture of learning and enablement. I cannot emphasize this point enough!

Google Cloud Support

Google Cloud offers two support offerings that typically align to the size and budget of your organization. If you're working in a large enterprise that spends millions of dollars on GCP, you'd certainly want to have the best support possible. In smaller organizations, you'd need a more cost-effective solution that could provide the support you need in critical times. Role-based support and Premium support are the two key support offerings by Google Cloud. We won't dive into the details of all the differences, but you can take a look at the Google Cloud Support site to get an idea. Key things to note include whether the offerings vary in terms of 24/5 or 24/7 support; whether the response times are guaranteed on high-priority tickets; whether support includes case, phone, or chat support; and how escalations are handled. With Premium support, you also get a technical account manager—essentially a dedicated Googler who helps bridge the gap between your organization's strategic and tactical goals and all things inside Google.

 NOTE A technical account manager is an incredibly valuable resource for large enterprises. This is essentially like getting a dedicated Googler to be your company's eyes and ears. Account managers focus on helping you plan, create strategies with leadership, and unblock major hurdles, and they advocate and drive your organization's success at Google Cloud. Most features that exist in Google Cloud today were built around customers, and those who have technical account managers get direct access to feature requests and a multitude of ways to make the cloud fulfill their needs.

Chapter Review

In this chapter, we discussed the importance of being organized across your organization for billing purposes. Organization enables governance at large, so billing aside, everything becomes easier, including deployments, security, monitoring, billing—you name it. Working in the cloud can be much more cost advantageous than working on-premises. Still, it's possible to run up the usage bills to crazy levels if you're not careful about how you utilize services and monitor and control costs and whether you build alerts where necessary. Managing your company's wallet is the responsibility of everyone working on the platform, not just the finance team. You can develop many reports to bring awareness of your cost expenditures to your team through the console, invoices, exporting your billing data to BigQuery, using Data Studio, and much more.

Sustained use discounts are applied when you're sustaining use of a resource, such as a Compute Engine VM. Committed use discounts are contractual discounts you will get if you commit to using a resource based on a certain set of guidelines, such as committing to use X amount of vCPUs, memory, GPUs, and SSD over a period of time.

Migrating to the cloud is a daunting and major feat. It involves the work of an entire organization, but in particular the extreme effort of a dedicated cloud migration team. This team can consist of executive leaders, technology leaders, architects, engineers, project managers, program managers, and so on. It's important to assess and evaluate your IT landscape and workloads, plan what will move in what order, migrate by picking a path and getting started, and optimize your operations to save on costs. When it comes to migrating your applications, there are a variety of ways to work. You can rehost, replatform, and refactor your applications during your migration planning. The goal of moving to the cloud should always be to simplify your life and consider moving toward managed services where you can. But oftentimes you may not be able to achieve operational simplicity because of timeline constraints and other variables. So you may just want to lift and shift your applications and reassess at a later time.

You have a variety of options for migrating data to the cloud. You can use a regular online transfer, uploading content to GCS. You can use a transfer appliance to copy content onto your appliance and ship it back to Google Cloud. Or you can use the Storage Transfer Service to use your existing Cloud Platforms to perform large-scale optimized transfers to GCS.

When it comes to support, Google Cloud offers role-based support and Premium support options that are based on your organization's size. The varying support options offer differing service level agreements (SLAs), communications media, costs, and more. With Premium support, you get access to a technical account manager, who essentially is an internal advocate for your organization who will track and own your success internally at Google. Support is an incredibly important function for every customer running critical businesses in the cloud. So don't discount the importance of having a strong support model.

Questions

1. You're the cloud architect who oversees the GCP implementation, and you need to design a system that can provide cost visibility to your finance department so that they can track expenditures. What should you do?

   A. Apply labels on your resources and set up the BigQuery Billing Export.

   B. Configure Data Studio.

   C. Consolidate all of the invoices into a structured format.

   D. Use the Cloud Billing Export feature.

2. What is a committed use discount?

   A. An automatic discount for a consistent amount of usage of a resource over a period of time

   B. A discount for a cloud commitment

   C. A discount for purchasing a commitment-based contract based on forecasted amounts of usage

   D. A discount for being a good sport

3. What is a sustained use discount?

   A. An automatic discount for a consistent amount of usage of a resource over a period of time

   B. A discount for a cloud commitment

   C. A discount for purchasing a commitment-based contract based on forecasted amounts of usage

   D. A discount for being a good sport

4. How can you leverage billing alerts for non-billing–related operations?

A. You can use billing alerts for detecting security incidents.

B. You can use billing alerts to identify nuances in between teams.

C. You can use billing alerts to understand when you need to increase your capacity.

D. You can use billing alerts to understand when you need to increase your resource quota.

5. You want to migrate your entire VM infrastructure to VMware Engine on Google Cloud. What sort of migration is this?

A. Replatforming

B. Rehosting

C. Refactoring

D. Rephasing

6. What are the four phases of migrating to Google, in order?

A. Plan, assess, migrate, optimize

B. Plan, assess, deploy, optimize

C. Assess, plan, migrate, optimize

D. Assess, plan, deploy, optimize

7. You need to transfer 40TB of data to Google Cloud in the most secure and operationally effective way. You have a 1 Gbps uplink to GCP. What should you do?

A. Use a transfer appliance.

B. Use the storage transfer service.

C. Directly upload the data to GCS.

D. Provision a better uplink.

8. Refactoring means

A. Lifting and shifting your existing applications into GCP without making any changes to the platform or applications

B. Lifting and optimizing your applications and workloads without rewriting them, but running them on GCP cloud-native platforms

C. Moving and improving your existing applications and workloads to run on modern form factors without modifying code

D. Completely redesigning your entire application from scratch on GCP

9. Rehosting means

A. Lifting and shifting your existing applications into GCP without making any changes to the platform or applications

B. Lifting and optimizing your applications and workloads without rewriting them, but running them on GCP cloud-native platforms

    C. Moving and improving your existing applications and workloads to run on modern form factors without modifying code

    D. Completely redesigning your entire application from scratch on GCP

10. Replatforming means

    A. Lifting and shifting your existing applications into GCP without making any changes to the platform or applications

    B. Lifting and optimizing your applications and workloads without rewriting them, but running them on GCP cloud-native platforms

    C. Moving and improving your existing applications and workloads to run on modern form factors without modifying code

    D. Completely redesigning your entire application from scratch on GCP

Answers

1. **A.** Following a strong labeling naming convention is important to ensure that you're able to track costs accurately based on various things such as departments, teams, organizations, and so on. By using the BigQuery Billing Export, you can see the expenditures in BigQuery, where you can analyze them.

2. **C.** A committed use discount is based on a commitment contract. You typically will have an idea of what your forecasted usage will look like before signing the contract, because you'll have to spend the money whether you use the resources or not!

3. **A.** Sustained use discounts are automatically applied based on sustained usage of resources.

4. **A.** Billing alerts can be helpful to identify security incidents such as cryptomining incidents or other usage-based malware incidents.

5. **B.** By rehosting your platform on GCP, you can retain the use of your existing platform but move it over to Google Cloud. VMware Engine on GCP enables you to migrate your existing VM-based architecture on-premises to GCP.

6. **C.** Assess your landscape and your workloads, plan which ones are going into the cloud and in which order, migrate them, and then optimize for spend.

7. **A.** The key thing here is that you're transferring a significant amount of data to GCP, and using a 1 Gbps uplink may not be the fastest way to do this. It's recommended that you use a transfer appliance when terabytes of data need to go to GCP.

8. **C.** Refactoring consists of moving and improving your existing applications. Think about running a large MySQL database on-premises and then deciding you want to move to a managed CloudSQL database where you no longer have to manage the database infrastructure and you can strictly focus on the data.

9. A. Rehosting is the concept of lifting and shifting so that you can get your applications and data into GCP and not have to do any engineering to redesign any of the functionality. This may be an easy approach for customers who need to get into the cloud and then focus on iterating and improving from there, or for noncritical applications that don't need to be prioritized for a redesign or refactor just yet.

10. B. Replatforming is basically lifting your applications from your existing platform and onto a new platform and then optimizing them without needing to rewrite them. If you have a bunch of VMs in VMware on-premises, you can just run them on GCE and reap the benefits of using the Google GCE platform.

Closing Thoughts

Dear Cloud Architect,

You now carry a wealth of knowledge. The sheer fact of you reaching this point in the book demonstrates your willingness to learn and grow and your desire to drive change in the world. None of us would have made it this far without the communal efforts of technologists all over the world, from all walks of life and all backgrounds. With great power comes great responsibility. Whether you've automated a portion of your job and are able to browse Reddit for half of your day, or you're consistently under water but trying to stay afloat, I can promise you that your role in this world is of utmost value. You may be contributing to the projects you're working on, contributing to your profession, contributing to the well-being of your peers—every action you take on this planet can positively impact you and those around you. Even if you didn't work on the headlining project at work, or you didn't meet your performance review goals, or you made a huge blunder and looked like a fool in a meeting (we have all been there), the most impactful thing happens in the way you approach people and problems in your everyday life. Find opportunities to mentor one another and to seek mentorship. Reach out and learn from your colleagues—the challenges they've faced in their lives and what they did to get to this point in their careers. Ask where you have blind spots and where you can improve, and don't make demands on others. And speak up when things sound off—even if you're not confident in your own thoughts. You don't know what you don't know, and you won't know unless you take the initiative!

As you prepare for your exam, don't overtax yourself. It costs $200 US to take the exam, and you may save $200 in time and stress by taking it a little earlier than you anticipated. If the outcome isn't favorable, you will know exactly what you need to work on before you take it again. Some of my closest friends and family (you know who you are, I'm calling you out!) have taken years out of their lives to prepare for an exam, going through the stress of uncertainty and a lack of confidence for an unnecessary duration of time, only to end up forgetting all of the knowledge and failing the exam when they finally took it! Failing is okay. I've failed many exams, I've failed on projects, and I've failed with people. I failed the Professional Cloud Architect exam the first time I took it. I could tell of so many embarrassing stories that this could end up being a novel. Failing is what it takes to learn and be successful. But taking this exam should not consume your mental well-being. It's surely a tough exam, but if you paid attention throughout the book and you do a decent job on the practice questions in the book and in the accompanying online test engine (see Appendix B), you'll do just fine! Though I highly recommend learning how to navigate GCP while studying, I passed my first GCP certification without even opening the console. Lastly, I have created TheCertsGuy.com as a blog site for me to share some additional test-taking tips and wisdom to prepare you for this exam and beyond—follow my website and subscribe to my blogs for insights on passing certifications, building your resume, and growing in your career!

When I started writing this book, I stared at the word "the" for the first few weeks, terrified of what I'd signed myself up for and questioning whether I was up for it. Baby steps led to bigger steps, bigger steps led to tripping and falling over again. Yet here we are at a completion, several hundred pages deep.

I really hope that you got the value you needed from this material. I really want to emphasize the importance of sharing feedback and increasing visibility. If you have any feedback (good or bad) to share, please head to Amazon, Google Books, or Goodreads and offer your opinions so that I can continue to iterate and improve. If you want to share more direct feedback or ask for advice, feel free to reach out to me on LinkedIn, Twitter, or Instagram—you can find my social links at TheCertsGuy.com. Tell me how your certification went, tag me in your posts about the book, and please share this book on your networks and with peers you think would benefit from it. Every time you tag me in something, I'll be sure to reshare it where it best fits. Remember that you can be the greatest engineer in the world, but if you aren't bringing visibility into your success, hard work, and achievements, it could go unnoticed! Think about how you can bring awareness and visibility into the power of you.

My goal is to get thousands of people certified in GCP, in the hope that thousands of people can grow in their careers, create better lives for themselves and family members, share their knowledge with thousands of others to help them grow, and build technology that can positively impact the billions of inhabitants of this planet. This is the beauty of the world we live in: if we put our minds together, we all have the power to grow together and help everyone around us.

Thank you for taking time out of your life to read this book, and I look forward to engaging with the growing community of GCP Architects! Lastly, I will leave you with a few words from the bestselling novel, *The Alchemist*:

When you want something, all the universe conspires in helping you to achieve it.
–Paulo Coelho

Objective Map

Google Cloud Professional Cloud Architect Exam

Official Exam Objective	All-in-One Exam Guide Coverage Chapter
1.0 Designing and planning a cloud solution architecture	
1.1 Designing a solution infrastructure that meets business requirements	2
1.2 Designing a solution infrastructure that meets technical requirements	2
1.3 Designing network, storage, and compute resources	4, 6, 7, 8
1.4 Creating a migration plan (i.e., documents and architectural diagrams)	12
1.5 Envisioning future solution improvements	10
2.0 Managing and provisioning a solution infrastructure	
2.1 Configuring network topologies	4, 6
2.2 Configuring individual storage systems	8
2.3 Configuring compute systems	7
3.0 Designing for security and compliance	
3.1 Designing for security	3, 5, 6, 11
3.2 Designing for compliance	11
4.0 Analyzing and optimizing technical and business processes	
4.1 Analyzing and defining technical processes	2
4.2 Analyzing and defining business processes	2
4.3 Developing procedures to ensure reliability of solutions in production (e.g., chaos engineering, penetration testing)	10
5.0 Managing implementation	
5.1 Advising development/operations team(s) to ensure successful deployment of the solution	9
5.2 Interacting with Google Cloud programmatically	2

Official Exam Objective	All-in-One Exam Guide Coverage Chapter
6.0 Ensuring solution and operations reliability	
6.1 Monitoring/logging/profiling/alerting solution	10
6.2 Deployment and release management	9
6.3 Assisting with the support of the deployed solutions	10
6.4 Evaluating quality control measures	10

About the Online Content

This book comes complete with TotalTester Online customizable practice exam software with 100 practice exam questions.

System Requirements

The current and previous major versions of the following desktop browsers are recommended and supported: Chrome, Microsoft Edge, Firefox, and Safari. These browsers update frequently, and sometimes an update may cause compatibility issues with the TotalTester Online or other content hosted on the Training Hub. If you run into a problem using one of these browsers, please try using another until the problem is resolved.

Your Total Seminars Training Hub Account

To get access to the online content you will need to create an account on the Total Seminars Training Hub. Registration is free, and you will be able to track all your online content using your account. You may also opt in if you wish to receive marketing information from McGraw Hill or Total Seminars, but this is not required for you to gain access to the online content.

Privacy Notice

McGraw Hill values your privacy. Please be sure to read the Privacy Notice available during registration to see how the information you have provided will be used. You may view our Corporate Customer Privacy Policy by visiting the McGraw Hill Privacy Center. Visit the **mheducation.com** site and click **Privacy** at the bottom of the page.

Single User License Terms and Conditions

Online access to the digital content included with this book is governed by the McGraw Hill License Agreement outlined next. By using this digital content you agree to the terms of that license.

Access   To register and activate your Total Seminars Training Hub account, simply follow these easy steps.

1. Go to this URL: **hub.totalsem.com/mheclaim**

2. To register and create a new Training Hub account, enter your e-mail address, name, and password on the **Register** tab. No further personal information (such as credit card number) is required to create an account.

   If you already have a Total Seminars Training Hub account, enter your e-mail address and password on the **Log in** tab.

3. Enter your Product Key: **fzr5-5qjq-9zc6**

4. Click to accept the user license terms.

5. For new users, click the **Register and Claim** button to create your account. For existing users, click the **Log in and Claim** button.

   You will be taken to the Training Hub and have access to the content for this book.

Duration of License   Access to your online content through the Total Seminars Training Hub will expire one year from the date the publisher declares the book out of print.

Your purchase of this McGraw Hill product, including its access code, through a retail store is subject to the refund policy of that store.

The Content is a copyrighted work of McGraw Hill, and McGraw Hill reserves all rights in and to the Content. The Work is © 2021 by McGraw Hill.

Restrictions on Transfer   The user is receiving only a limited right to use the Content for the user's own internal and personal use, dependent on purchase and continued ownership of this book. The user may not reproduce, forward, modify, create derivative works based upon, transmit, distribute, disseminate, sell, publish, or sublicense the Content or in any way commingle the Content with other third-party content without McGraw Hill's consent.

Limited Warranty   The McGraw Hill Content is provided on an "as is" basis. Neither McGraw Hill nor its licensors make any guarantees or warranties of any kind, either express or implied, including, but not limited to, implied warranties of merchantability or fitness for a particular purpose or use as to any McGraw Hill Content or the information therein or any warranties as to the accuracy, completeness, correctness, or results to be obtained from, accessing or using the McGraw Hill Content, or any material referenced in such Content or any information entered into licensee's product by users or other persons and/or any material available on or that can be accessed through the licensee's product (including via any hyperlink or otherwise) or as to non-infringement of third-party rights. Any warranties of any kind, whether express or implied, are disclaimed. Any material or data obtained through use of the McGraw Hill Content is at your own discretion and risk and user understands that it will be solely responsible for any resulting damage to its computer system or loss of data.

Neither McGraw Hill nor its licensors shall be liable to any subscriber or to any user or anyone else for any inaccuracy, delay, interruption in service, error or omission, regardless of cause, or for any damage resulting therefrom.

In no event will McGraw Hill or its licensors be liable for any indirect, special or consequential damages, including but not limited to, lost time, lost money, lost profits or good will, whether in contract, tort, strict liability or otherwise, and whether or not such damages are foreseen or unforeseen with respect to any use of the McGraw Hill Content.

TotalTester Online

TotalTester Online provides you with a simulation of the Google Cloud Certified Professional Cloud Architect exam. Exams can be taken in Practice Mode or Exam Mode. Practice Mode provides an assistance window with hints, references to the book, explanations of the correct and incorrect answers, and the option to check your answer as you take the test. Exam Mode provides a simulation of the actual exam. The number of questions, the types of questions, and the time allowed are intended to be an accurate representation of the exam environment. The option to customize your quiz allows you to create custom exams from selected domains or chapters, and you can further customize the number of questions and time allowed.

To take a test, follow the instructions provided in the previous section to register and activate your Total Seminars Training Hub account. When you register you will be taken to the Total Seminars Training Hub. From the Training Hub Home page, select **Google Cloud Certified Professional Cloud Architect TotalTester** from the Study drop-down menu at the top of the page, or from the list of Your Topics on the Home page. You can then select the option to customize your quiz and begin testing yourself in Practice Mode or Exam Mode. All exams provide an overall grade and a grade broken down by domain.

Technical Support

For questions regarding the TotalTester or operation of the Training Hub, visit **www.totalsem.com** or e-mail **support@totalsem.com**.

For questions regarding book content, visit **www.mheducation.com/customerservice**.

2-Step Verification (2SV)   Google Cloud uses this term instead of multifactor authentication or two-factor authentication to refer to the process that involves two authentication methods being used one after the other to verify that someone or something is who or what they declare to be before they are allowed to log into systems across an enterprise.

AAA security model   One of the core principles of security. The three A's refer to authentication, authorization, and auditing. Authentication refers to the act of proving an identity; this is often referred to as a form of an assertion. Authorization is a set of privileges (typically known as permissions in GCP) that gives a user access to certain resources. This is referred to as access management in this book. Accounting (typically referred to as auditing in GCP) ensures that the digital ledger includes accounts for every user's access and that these logs are immutable, or unable to be tampered with.

Access Transparency logs   Logs that provide insight behind the scenes into when a Google Cloud support engineer had accessed parts of your infrastructure and for what purpose.

admin activity   Audit logs that contain entries for API calls and other administrative actions that can modify configurations or metadata of resources.

admin audit logs   Logs that come from Cloud Identity.

administrative activity audit logs   Log entries for API calls or any other user administrative modifications to configurations or resource metadata.

administrative controls   The policies, procedures, and guidelines for humans to follow in accordance with the organization's security controls.

Andromeda   Google's Software Defined Networking (SDN)–based stack that provides an abstraction on top of all of the underlying networking and data center hardware for Google and its cloud tenants to conduct business securely, privately, and efficiently.

Apigee   A full end-to-end API management platform that enables customers to manage the full API life cycle in any cloud, including multi- and hybrid-cloud environments.

attack surface   The sum of all possible security risk exposures.

auto mode VPC network   The default network that is created when you create a project. In this configuration, a default /20 subnet is created in each region automatically.

availability   The assurance that authorized users are able to access a service or data when needed.

BeyondCorp   Google's internal implementation of the zero trust security model, including all of Google's internal best practices regarding how they authenticate and authorize employees.

BigQuery   A highly scalable, cost-effective serverless solution for multi-cloud data warehousing.

BigQuery datasets   Top-level containers that are used to organize and control access to tables and views.

BigQuery jobs   Actions that BigQuery will run on your behalf to load, export, query, or copy data.

black-box monitoring   The ability to monitor your application as if you were an end user, without having any underlying knowledge of the internal configuration of the service.

block storage   A data system in which the data is broken up into blocks and then stored across a distributed system to maximize efficiency.

blue-green deployment   A deployment strategy that involves having two identical environments, called a blue and a green environment, so that when a release is deployed to either environment, the other environment will be held as a reserve.

Border Gateway Protocol (BGP)   A very complex exterior gateway path-vector routing protocol that advertises routing and reachability information among autonomous systems on the Internet.

canary deployment   A deployment strategy that involves making a new release available to a subset of users before all users have access.

capacity   The total amount of an actual resource that is available to be provisioned in an environment.

capital expenditures (CapEx)   The capital spent up-front to purchase servers and equipment intended to be used for years and years to come.

CIA triad   The most foundational information security model. CIA stands for confidentiality, integrity, and availability.

Classless Inter-Domain Routing (CIDR)   The guiding standard for Internet Protocol (IP) that determines the unique IP addresses for networks and devices. These IP ranges are typically referred to as CIDR blocks.

click-through agreements   Legally enforceable contracts that collect user consent. You've likely encountered thousands of these, such as every time you sign up for a new service or agree to an updated privacy policy.

Cloud Armor   A managed web application firewall that integrates directly with external HTTP(S) load balancers for any applications that are exposed to the world through an external IP.

Cloud Asset Inventory (CAI) The metadata inventory service that enables users to keep track of all of their assets in Google Cloud.

Cloud audit logs A category of logs that consist of administrative activity audit logs, data access audit logs, and system event audit logs. They provide the necessary authentication and access information for each cloud project, folder, and organization.

Cloud Bigtable A fully managed and scalable NoSQL database for large analytical and operational workloads.

Cloud Build A serverless continuous integration/continuous delivery (CI/CD) platform that has curated the steps to build, test, and deploy code into GCP.

cloud computing The on-demand availability of computing services over the Internet that offer faster innovation, flexible resources, and economies of scale.

Cloud Data Loss Prevention (Cloud DLP) A fully managed service that minimizes the risk of data exfiltration by enabling you to discover, classify, and protect your sensitive data.

Cloud Dataflow A serverless, cost-effective, unified stream and batch data processing service that is fully managed and is based on the Apache Beam SDK.

Cloud Debugger A real-time application debugging tool available in Google Cloud that is used to inspect running applications and identify the behavior of code, continuously searching for bugs in a live environment without resulting in performance issues that could affect users.

Cloud Endpoints An API management platform that enables you to secure, manage, and monitor your APIs on Google Cloud.

Cloud Filestore A high-performance managed file storage for applications that require a file system.

Cloud Firestore A fully managed, fast, serverless, cloud-native NoSQL document database that is designed for mobile, Web, and Internet of Things (IoT) applications at global scale.

Cloud Functions A Function as a Service (FaaS) offering that consists of an event-driven serverless execution environment.

Cloud HSM A managed, cloud-hosted hardware security module that enables you to protect cryptographic keys in a FIPS 140-2 Level 3 certified hardware security model (HSM).

Cloud Identity An Identity as a Service (IDaaS) solution that provides a unified identity, access, application, and endpoint management platform and a variety of avenues to enable the various users consuming Google Cloud Platform to connect and access resources.

Cloud Identity and Access Management (Cloud IAM)   An enterprise-grade access control service that enables administrators to authorize who can take actions on certain resources and the conditions in which they can take action.

Cloud Key Management Service (KMS)   A platform used to manage cryptographic keys on Google Cloud. KMS offers the ability to generate and manage the key encryption keys (KEKs) that protect sensitive data.

Cloud Load Balancing   A fully distributed, high performance, software-defined, managed load balancing service that dynamically distributes user traffic across the infrastructure to reduce performance and availability issues.

Cloud Logging   A real-time log management and analysis tool that enables you to store, search, analyze, monitor, and alert on log data and events.

Cloud NAT   A managed network address translation (NAT) service that enables virtual machines (VMs) and Google Kubernetes Engine (GKE) clusters to connect to the Internet without having external IP addresses. Cloud NAT logging provides context into NAT connections and errors.

Cloud Operations Suite   A suite of tools that enable organizations to log, monitor, troubleshoot, and improve their application performance in GCP.

Cloud Profiler   A continuous CPU and heap profiling tool that is used to analyze the performance of CPU or memory-intensive functions that you run across an application.

Cloud Router   A managed service that dynamically exchanges routes between your VPC and on-premises network using Border Gateway Protocol (BGP) via a dedicated Interconnect or cloud virtual private network (VPN).

Cloud Run   A serverless compute platform that enables you to run stateless containers, abstracting away all of the infrastructure management. It is built on an open source Knative framework.

Cloud Source Repositories   Private Git repositories that enable you to design, develop, and securely manage your code.

Cloud Spanner   A fully managed, scalable, relational database for regional and globally distributed application data.

Cloud SQL   A fully managed relational database for MySQL, PostgreSQL, and SQL Server that offers a simple integration with just about any Google applications, including Google Compute Engine (GCE), Google Kubernetes Engine (GKE), and Google App Engine (GAE).

Cloud Threat Detection (CTD)   A service that provides automated detection of certain threats in GCP.

Cloud Trace   A distributed tracing service used to collect latency from applications and to track how requests propagate through an application.

Cloud VPN   A transitive IPSec VPN tunnel.

cluster   The foundation of GKE. All Kubernetes (K8s) objects run on top of the GKE cluster.

cluster master   A Google-managed control plane that runs all of the K8s control plane processes, including the API server, scheduler, and resource controllers.

cold potato routing   A form of network traffic routing in which Google holds onto all network packets through their entire life cycle until they reach their destination.

committed use discounts (CUDs)   Deep discounts a customer receives when it commits, by contract, to use a particular level of resources for a specific amount of time.

community cloud   A collaborative effort in which infrastructure is shared among several customers from a specific community with common concerns; it may be managed internally or by a third party, and it is hosted internally or externally.

compute-optimized machine types   Optimized for compute-intensive workloads, these offer more performance per core than other machine types.

Confidential VMs   A breakthrough technology that Google Cloud developed to enable customers to encrypt data that is in use.

confidentiality   Refers to protecting an organization's sensitive and private data from unauthorized access.

conflicting accounts   What occurs when a user creates a personal Google Account with the same domain name as the existing organization.

Container Registry   A private Docker repository where a team can store, manage, and secure its Docker container images.

continuous integration/continuous delivery (CI/CD)   The combined practices of integrating and deploying code that bridges the gap between development and operations activities by enforcing automation, seamless handoffs between teams, and continuous feedback throughout each phase.

corrective controls   Security measures taken to correct unauthorized activity or resolve detected threats and vulnerabilities.

custom images   Boot disk images that you create, own, and control access to.

custom mode VPC network   A network that does not come with any subnets, which gives the network administrator full control to define the subnets and IP ranges before the network is usable.

custom roles   An IAM role you create with a set of permissions that are tailored to the needs of your organization when a predefined role does not meet your criteria.

custom service accounts   User-created service accounts that can be used for various applications, including applications running on-premises or from another cloud.

customer-managed encryption key (CMEK) A mechanism used by customers to generate their own key-encrypting key to protect their data.

customer-supplied encryption key (CSEK) A service that enables customers to bring their own AES-256 key so that they can have the most control over the keys to their data.

data access logs Audit logs that contain log entries for API calls that read resource configurations, that access metadata, or that read/write user-based API calls.

data classification The process of classifying data according to its type, sensitivity, and criticality to your organization with the intention of securing and governing this data more effectively.

Dataproc A fully managed data and analytics processing solution based on open source tools.

Dedicated Interconnect A Google offering that provides a direct, dedicated physical connection between an on-premises network and GCP.

default route A system-generated route that defines a path for traffic that meets Internet access criteria to leave the VPC.

default service accounts Service accounts that are automatically generated for Compute Engine instances upon project creation.

detective controls Security controls designed to detect unauthorized activity that has materialized.

DevOps The philosophies, practices, and tools that empower an organization to deliver experiences to its consumers at high velocity and improve service reliability by unifying software development (Dev) and software operation (Ops).

DNS logs Logs that record every Domain Name System (DNS) query received from VM instances and inbound forwarding flows within your networks.

edge node Also known as content delivery network points of presence (CDN PoPs), edge nodes are PoPs where content can be cached and served locally to end users.

Edge point of presence (Edge POP) A location where Google connects its network to the rest of the Internet via peering.

egress traffic Packets that originate inside a network boundary but have a destination outside the network boundary.

end-to-end tests The process of running an application from start to finish to test the flow of the application and ensure that the system can be validated for integration and data integrity.

entitlements The process of granting users privileges and the scope of the privileges that are granted.

external IPs IP addresses that are accessible to the public Internet.

External Key Manager (EKM) A service that enables organizations to supply their own keys through a supported external key management partner to protect their data in the cloud.

external load balancers A load balancer that balances the load of external users who reach your applications from the Internet.

FIDO U2F (Fast Identity Online Universal 2nd Factor) A protocol that was defined by the FIDO Alliance, which was founded by PayPal and other industry leaders to eliminate the world's reliance on passwords and to promote strong authentication mechanisms.

file storage A data system in which data is stored in files and those files are organized in a folder hierarchy, providing a simple user interface to organize and sort data and the ability to leverage metadata within files.

Filestore A service that provides high-performance, network-attached file storage, like a traditional network file system, that can be attached to your instances.

firewall logs Audit logs that provide connection records for TCP and UDP traffic only. These logs include source and destination IP, protocols, ports, times, and so on.

firewall rules Rules leveraged to allow or deny traffic to and from VPC networks.

folder Another logical container that is intended to group similar projects or data.

General Data Protection Regulation (GDPR) A regulation in EU law that describes how to protect user data and ensure user privacy for any data about citizens residing in the European Union or in the European Economic Area.

general-purpose machine types Machines that offer the best price-to-performance ratio for various workloads.

Google accounts Accounts of human users authenticated from an identity provider that can be entitled to perform certain roles or actions in GCP.

Google App Engine (GAE) A Platform as a Service (PaaS) solution that offers a fully managed, serverless application platform on which users can build and deploy applications without having to manage the underlying infrastructure.

Google Cloud Deployment Manager A tool used to create and manage cloud resources using deployment templates, which treats your infrastructure as code and simplifies the deployment process.

Google Cloud Directory Sync (GCDS) A tool that provides a one-way directory sync from Microsoft Active Directory or an LDAP server.

Google Cloud Resource Manager A mechanism that provides resource containers such as organizations, folders, and projects and enables you to group and hierarchically organize GCP resources into those containers.

Google Cloud Storage (GCS) A globally unified, scalable, and highly durable object storage offering from Google.

Google Compute Engine (GCE)   Google Cloud's Infrastructure as a Service (IaaS) solution that enables users to launch virtual machines on demand. With GCE, users have to manage all the underlying infrastructure associated with the VM instances, including the machine types.

Google Front End (GFE)   A reverse proxy that protects the backend Google services and the point where Transport Layer Security (TLS) connections are terminated.

Google identities   Identities that can be consumed by Cloud IAM for role/permission management in the GCP console.

Google Kubernetes Engine (GKE)   A managed Kubernetes solution for deploying, managing, and scaling containerized applications on GCP.

groups   Logical containers or groupings of one or more accounts to define clear roles and ensure ease of manageability of a cloud access model.

Health Insurance Portability and Accountability Act (HIPAA)   A US law that was enacted in 1996 by former president Bill Clinton and mandates how to manage the information flow of protected health information (PHI).

hot potato routing   A form of routing by which Google will offload network traffic as fast as possible and hand it off to the public Internet to save a customer money on GCP.

hybrid cloud   A mix of public cloud and private cloud used to create a more diverse environment.

IAM Conditions   An attribute-based access control feature that lets you define the conditions in which a user is able to be authorized to access a resource.

IAM policy   A configuration that binds together one or more members and roles for the purpose of enforcing only approved access patterns through a collection of statements.

IAM role   A collection of permissions that determine what operations are allowed on a resource.

Identity-Aware Proxy (IAP)   A mechanism used to control access to cloud-based and on-premises applications and VMs on GCP that uses identity and context to determine whether a user should be granted access.

indicator of compromise   An artifact or piece of data that gives a security team high confidence that a user or machine is compromised.

Infrastructure as a Service (IaaS)   A cloud operating model in which a customer leases infrastructure in the cloud; it provides the most control over the customer's infrastructure compared to other operating models.

infrastructure as code (IaC)   The practice of writing the elements of an infrastructure in code form, which can be interpreted by tools such as Terraform and Google Deployment Manager.

ingress traffic   Packets that have a destination inside a network boundary.

instance groups   A collection of VM instances that can be managed as a single entity. There are two kinds of instance groups: managed and unmanaged.

integration tests   Tests intended to ensure that components and modules of code integrate and work properly with one another.

integrity   The protection of data against modification from an unauthorized party.

internal load balancer   A load balancer that distributes traffic to instances inside of GCP.

Jupiter network fabric   Google's system of networking hardware represented as a fabric. It provides Google with a tremendous amount of bandwidth and scale, delivering more than 1 Petabit/sec of total bisection bandwidth.

Kubernetes (K8s)   An open source container orchestration system intended for automating application deployment, scaling, and management.

Kubernetes API server   The endpoint for your cluster, where you can interact with the cluster via HTTP/Google Remote Procedure Calls (gRPC) API calls through the K8s command-line client **kubectl**.

Lightweight Directory Access Protocol (LDAP)   An open cross-platform protocol that is commonly used for directory services authentication, such as Active Directory.

local solid-state drive (SSD)   A high-performance, ephemeral block storage disk that is physically attached to the server that hosts your VM instances. A local SSD offers the highest performance, transient, local block storage.

log entries   Recorded events that are captured from products, services, third-party applications, or even your own applications.

log sinks   A mechanism to configure logs to be exported into an appropriate storage destination.

Logs Router   In Cloud Logging, the Logs Router looks at each log entry and the rules you set to determine which logs to ingest, which logs to export, and which log entries to discard to save money and ensure efficiency.

machine type   A set of virtualized hardware resources that include system memory size, virtual CPU (vCPU) count, and persistent disk limits for VM instances.

managed instance group (MIG)   A service that enables you to operate multiple identical virtual machines to make your workloads scalable and highly available.

member   An entity that may be a Google account (human user), a service account (programmatic account for applications and VMs), a Google group, or a Google Workspace or Cloud Identity domain that can access a resource.

memory-optimized machine types   Optimized for memory-intensive workloads, these machine types offer more memory per core than other types (up to 12TB RAM).

Memorystore   A scalable, secure, and highly available in-memory service for Redis and Memcached.

multi-cloud   The use of several cloud computing and storage services in a single heterogeneous architecture.

network logs   A category of logs that consist of VPC flow logs, DNS logs, Cloud NAT logs, and firewall logs.

network tags   Strings that are used to make firewall rules and routes applicable to specific VM instances. They are added to the tags field in any resource, such as a compute engine instance or instance templates.

node   The worker machine that runs containerized applications and other workloads.

nonrepudiation   The assurance that someone cannot deny something.

Object Lifecycle Management   A feature that enables you to apply a configuration policy to buckets to determine what actions to take automatically based on a condition that objects meet.

object storage   A data system with a flat structure that contains objects, and within the objects are data, metadata, and a unique identifier.

object versioning   A feature that maintains old versions of files in your bucket when they are overwritten or deleted, based on parameters you set.

operational expenditure (OpEx)   Day-to-day costs for services as they're consumed.

organization   The root node and top-level element of the Google Cloud resource hierarchy.

organization policies   A configuration of constraints that are set on a resource hierarchy node (that is, at the project, folder, or organization level).

OS login   A mechanism to simplify Secure Shell (SSH) access management by linking your SSH users in Linux to their respective Google identities in Cloud Identity.

Partner Interconnect   A process that provides a connection between on-premises and VPC networks through a supported service provider.

Payment Card Industry Data Security Standard (PCI-DSS)   A group of PCI Security Council standards that apply to companies that interact with credit card data. PCI-DSS establishes minimum security requirements for these companies with regard to storing, processing, and transmitting cardholder data.

Persistent Disk (PD)   Google's high-performance, durable block storage service that provides solid-state drive (SSD) and hard disk drive (HDD) storage that can be attached to GCE or GKE instances.

persistent disks   Hard drives that offer reliable, high-performance block storage for virtual machines.

physical controls   Physical mechanisms used to secure an environment.

Platform as a Service (PaaS)   A cloud operating model that offers customers a simple, cost-effective solution to developing and deploying applications on a scalable and highly available platform.

Pod   A group of one or more container applications such as Docker, Containerd, or rkt.

predefined roles   Roles that offer finer-grained access control than primitive roles and are curated by GCP to accomplish a certain function.

preemptible virtual machine (PVM)   A highly cost-effective instance that is designed for non-fault-tolerant workloads that can withstand possible stance preemptions.

Premium network service tier   The default setting for GCP customers that offers users access to high-performance networking using Google's entire global network.

preventative controls   Security controls designed to stop unauthorized activity from materializing.

primitive roles   Roles that are historically available in the Cloud Console. These include roles such as Owner, Editor, and Viewer.

principle of least privilege   A concept that an individual user or a system account should be provisioned with the least amount of privileges needed to perform their job functions. It is intended to minimize the threat surface.

private cloud   A cloud that has been developed in-house specific to the organization. In an on-premises, private cloud, all servers, storage, and networks are dedicated to the organization and hosted in a dedicated data center.

Private Google Access   A configuration that enables instances without external IP addresses to access resources outside of their network.

Private Services Access   A configuration that enables you to connect to Google and third-party services that are located on other VPC networks owned by Google or third parties.

privilege creep   When users accumulate privileges over time as a result of promotions, transitions to new roles, or requesting one-time access and not removing it, privilege creep results. This violates the principle of least privilege.

project lien   A function that will protect projects against project deletion.

projects   The first grouping mechanism in the GCP resource hierarchy.

public cloud   A cloud that offers services to the public, such as Google Cloud, Amazon Web Services, Microsoft Azure, and Alibaba Cloud.

public images   Images that are provided and maintained by Google, the open source community, or third-party vendors that are available upon image selection or in the GCP Marketplace.

publish/subscribe (pub/sub) messaging   A global messaging and event ingestion solution that provides a simple and reliable staging location for event-based data before it gets processed, stored, and analyzed.

refactoring   The concept of "move and improve," which involves converting any existing applications and workloads to run on modern form factors without modifying code. For example, you can use Migrate for Anthos to convert applications that run on VMs into container-based applications on GKE.

region   A specific geographical location where you can host resources within a number of zones.

rehosting   The concept of "lift and shift," migrating any of your existing applications into GCP without making changes to the platform or applications. For example, you can use GCP VMware Engine to run your existing VMware workloads on GCP without having to make any changes.

replatforming   The concept of "lift and optimize," which involves migrating applications and workloads without rewriting them, but running them on a GCP cloud-native platform. For example, you can use Migrate for Compute Engine to move VM-based workloads to GCE.

resource quotas   Usage-based restrictions to prevent abuse and accidental usage of resources. Everyone gets a default quota.

resource   The lowest-level component that makes up all of GCP services.

return on investment (ROI)   Tangible or intangible gain from an investment.

RFC 1918 IP address range   A private network that uses both IPv4 and IPv6 specifications to define the usable private IP addresses in a network.

risk impact   The effects and consequences of a risk event.

risk mitigation   A mechanism to reduce the probability or likelihood of a risk materializing.

role-based access control (RBAC) model   A model used to define roles for organizations and users, whether they are individuals, groups, or service accounts. Within these roles, the least amount of necessary permissions are granted to enable them to do their job.

role binding   The process by which a list of members is granted access permission as defined in a role.

rolling deployment   A software release strategy that staggers development and releases across several phases. You can, for example, maintain one production environment consisting of many servers and a load balancer. When you deploy the application, you can determine how to stagger the deployment across servers so that some servers run the new application and others continue to host the old one.

routes   Defined paths for egress traffic.

Security Assertion Markup Language (SAML)   An open standard for exchanging authentication and authorization data between parties, commonly between an identity provider (Cloud Identity) and a service provider (third-party application).

Security Command Center (SCC)   A single, centralized dashboard that provides visibility into various security elements of an organization.

Security Health Analytics (SHA)   A tool within the SCC that is focused on vulnerabilities within Google Cloud Platform.

separation of duties   The idea that the duties needed to perform critical business functions should be divided across multiple users so that if one user is compromised, a whole system or process does not get compromised.

service accounts   In GCP, the programmatic accounts that can be granted roles and privileges to perform certain actions on behalf of an application.

service level agreement (SLA)   A contractual agreement created to describe the availability, objective, and other legal language with regard to providing a product and/or service.

service level indicator (SLI)   A quantitative measure of a chosen characteristic of the level of service that is provided from a product or service.

service level objective (SLO)   A target metric that is the objective to achieve for a given service level.

shared VPC   A VPC that enables an organization to connect resources from multiple projects to a common VPC, so that organizations can communicate securely on the same RFC 1918 IP space while having freedom and ownership over their projects.

shared-core machine types   Optimized for cost, these machine types share a physical core and are often used for running very small, non-resource-intensive applications.

Shielded VM   A security feature designed to offer a verifiable integrity of your VM instances so that you can be sure that they are not compromised by boot- or kernel-level malware or rootkits.

Site Reliability Engineering (SRE)   A philosophy, similar to DevOps and oftentimes referred to as a subset or sibling of DevOps, whose sole focus is to leverage aspects of software engineering and apply them to infrastructure and operations problems.

Software as a Service (SaaS) A cloud operating model in which a customer pays to use an application and all management of the application is performed by the vendor.

Standard network service tier A cost-effective, lower-performance network in which the customer loses some access to certain features of cloud networking (such as the ability to use a global load balancer) to save money.

subnet A subnetwork, or a logical subdivision of your organization's RFC 1918 IP space.

subnet route A route that is created for each of the IP ranges associated with a subnet, in which each subnet has at least one subnet route for its primary IP range.

sustained use discounts (SUDs) Discounts that are applied to customers based on certain resource usage thresholds.

system event audit logs Audit logs that contain administrative activities that modify resource configurations and any system-based activity generated by Google systems rather than users.

technical controls Logical mechanisms implemented to protect an organization's assets.

threat Any action, whether intentional or unintentional, that can exploit a vulnerability to obtain, damage, or destroy an asset.

Titan Security Key A FIDO-U2F–compliant hardware token built with a secure element known as the titan chip that verifies the integrity of the keys at the hardware level.

tokenization The process of substituting nonsensitive data, referred to as a token, for sensitive data.

total cost of ownership (TCO) The sum of all the direct and indirect technology costs.

unit tests Tests that ensure that the smallest testable aspect of your code works as expected, even when in isolation; tests are run against individual units of code without the full environment.

unmanaged instance groups A grouping of instances that enables you to load balance and manage a fleet of VMs.

Virtual Private Cloud (VPC) A virtual version of a physical network built on Google's software-defined network stack, Andromeda.

VPC firewall rules Rules that enable you to allow or deny connections to or from your VMs based on a configuration that you specify.

VPC flow logs Logs that provide visibility into VPC traffic and capture TCP and UDP traffic to and from internal traffic, network attachments, servers to Internet endpoints, and servers to Google APIs.

VPC Service Controls   Controls that enable security administrators to define a security perimeter around managed services, such as GCS and BigQuery, to mitigate data exfiltration risks and keep data private inside of a VPC.

VPN peering   A process that enables two separately managed VPCs to communicate with each other.

vulnerabilities   Weaknesses or gaps in a system that can be exploited, intentionally or unintentionally, by a threat to gain unauthorized access to an asset.

web application firewall (WAF)   A layer 7 (application layer) firewall focused on protecting web applications by filtering and monitoring HTTP traffic between a web app and the Internet.

Web Security Scanner (WSS)   A tool within the Security Command Center that is focused on scanning public GCP endpoints for web-based vulnerabilities.

white-box monitoring   A process of monitoring all aspects of your service with full underlying knowledge of the internal infrastructure.

zone   An isolated location within a region.

INDEX